T3-BOH-033

ARISTOTLE'S MAN

ARISTOTLE'S MAN

Speculations upon
Aristotelian Anthropology

STEPHEN R. L. CLARK

Lecturer in Moral Philosophy,
University of Glasgow

CLARENDON PRESS · OXFORD

Oxford University Press, Walton Street, Oxford OX2 6DP

London Glasgow New York Toronto
Delhi Bombay Calcutta Madras Karachi
Kuala Lumpur Singapore Hong Kong Tokyo
Nairobi Dar es Salaam Cape Town
Melbourne Auckland
and associated companies
Beirut Berlin Ibadan Mexico City Nicosia

Oxford is a trade mark of Oxford University Press

Published in the United States
by Oxford University Press, New York

© Oxford University Press 1975

British Library Cataloguing in Publication Data
Clark, Stephen R. L.
Aristotle's man.
1. Aristotle   2. Philosophical anthropology
I. Title
128   BD450
ISBN 0-19-824715-X

Library of Congress Cataloging in Publication Data
Clark, Stephen R. L.
Aristotle's man.
Bibliography: p.
Includes index.
1. Aristotle—Anthropology.
2. Philosophical anthropology—History.   I. Title.
[B491.M27C55   1983]   128'.092'4   83-6568
ISBN 0-19-824715-X (pbk.)

First published 1975
Reprinted 1983

Printed in Hong Kong

Preface

WHEN this commentary on the doctrines of the Master of them that know first took shape I was a very junior Fellow of All Souls. If I had not had that period of relative liberty, as well as a year's absence in the University of Chicago, I should doubtless have been constrained to write a less idiosyncratic survey of the Master. But though I now see many faults of content and execution here, I do not think that the whole would necessarily have been improved by a harsher editorial hand. At any rate, a philosopher in his late thirties has no business unravelling and rewriting what his mid-twenties self composed! Time, in Aristotle's words, 'is a good discoverer or partner in the task' of completing and filling in the details of what has once been well begun (*N.E.* I, 1098^{a}20f.). There has not yet been time enough for me or for my readers to follow up the implications of this vision of Aristotle.

If I were to rewrite this study, of course, I should have many things to take account of. When I wrote it Aristotle was widely regarded as an 'Oxford philosopher', unequalled in his ability to sort through the multiple meanings of ambiguous expressions, though unfortunately ignorant of later advances and inclined to make obvious logical errors. There was little effort to see Aristotle whole, or to consider whether his ethical and metaphysical views might be genuinely relevant to our own concerns. It was against that background that I set myself to see the more outrageous possibilities in the text. Since then there have been many scholarly efforts to 'see Aristotle whole'. John Ackrill, Jonathan Barnes, Martha Nussbaum, Richard Sorabji, Sally Waterlow and others have advanced our understanding. Aristotle's political theory has been reconsidered—and it is perhaps of significance that it has been political and social philosophers who have been kindest in their comments on my discussion. I refer them also to my study of *The Nature of the Beast* (Oxford University Press 1982), and to a paper revising many of my conclusions about the place of women in the Aristotelian universe ('Aristotle's Woman': *History of Political Thought* 3, 1983). The vision of God and the World which I reckon central to an understanding of Aristotle has been challenged by those who hold to a more naturalistic account of the world, and of Aristotle. I remain unrepentant, and make a further attempt to expound the doctrine in a set of Gifford lectures, *From Athens to Jerusalem* (forthcoming from the Clarendon Press).

As I have neither the wish nor the time to rewrite this volume I cannot answer the many kindly and not so kindly comments from reviewers and readers in detail. Some of my answers and my disclaimers may be found in my later published work. Some day I may feel able to attempt another volume on the Master. One point I should perhaps make clear: my chapter on the *Ergon* argument, an earlier version of which appeared in *Ethics* 82, 1972 (and the material re-used by permission of the University of Chicago Press) was indeed designed to show that Aristotle did *not* commit any 'naturalistic fallacy'. That there is such a fallacy I agree (see my 'Absence of a gap between Fact and Value' in *PASS* 54, 1980), but Aristotle did not commit it, did not contend that it was a logical axiom that we should seek to act and choose aright. It is an ethical truism, and anyone concerned about what he or she should do must concede at least this much, that he or she should act well. From this first insight, and from an understanding of what sorts of character and capacity we need to have if we are to have much chance of acting well in the world in which we find ourselves, flow all the maxims of Aristotelian ethics. We need friends and a 'free society', and we need virtues, and we need above all the capacity to acknowledge and wonder at the world in which we live and die. That wonderment, as I now believe, will lead to a more humane approach to those creatures with whom we share the world, who do not have to choose in order to live well (see *The Moral Status of Animals*, Clarendon Press 1977).

As I wrote nearly ten years ago: I am indebted to my teachers, friends and pupils for inspiration, criticism and their ready incomprehension of my more obscure remarks. John Ackrill, Donald Allan, George Devereux, Alan Donagan, Anthony Kenny, Anthony Lloyd, Derek Parfit, Arthur Prior, John Thomas, Hilary Torrance, and Robin Zaehner, as well as my colleagues in Glasgow, have all tried, with varying success, to make me talk, or see, sense. Gillian Clark has saved me from many errors of taste and judgement, and to her my debt and gratitude are greatest. If I have failed to profit by their endeavours I can only plead that it would be a sad day when philosophers said nothing that was not 'sensible'. 'What is now prov'd was once only imagined', as Blake declared: what is now clearly imagined was once only a sense of something missing.

University of Glasgow
26 February 1983

Contents

Summary

I. Words have determinable sense only within a complex of unstated assumptions, and all interpretation must therefore go beyond the given material. Understanding of another's philosophy is an aspect of the interpreter's own philosophical growth, and the result should not be, because it cannot be, assessed as matching or missing an unknowable and possibly non-existent 'original version', but as an intelligible and (hopefully) plausible way of seeing the world that is developed by meditation on the chosen traditum.

II. What is man's place in the Aristotelian world? (1) Man's *ergon*, his defining character, lies in his capacity for choice and action, so that his nature is not wholly determinate. To live well, being human, we must do our own living. The subject of ethical discourse is the free man, and we are thus free because we can be social. We are human because there is a divinity within us. To create and maintain ourselves in being we should live in accord with the god. (2) Man is the most natural of living things. This claim, and certain other oddities in the biological works (particularly the apparently scholastic explanations of structure), can be explained on the assumption that Aristotle was a believer in devolutionary transformism, either in the full sense—that Man is the First Ancestor of all life—or in the modified sense, that the universe is itself, in a way, human. In either case man, particularly the perfect man, is the *telos* of the world. (3) The world is best understood in terms of a complex of wholes that are more than the aggregates of their parts and are to be picked out in terms of their ends. Aristotle's talk of Nature, of Being, of Prime Matter can be explained by reference to the universal Whole, which men can mirror. Teleological analysis is a condition of our seeing the world of common sense at all, and the Whole makes sense in terms of the Aristotelian saint's awareness of it.

III. What are man's abilities and prospects in managing his life? (1) In what are probably his last works, the biological, Aristotle provides animal life with the heart as its central organ. Our sense-awareness is centred in this, and is such that there is some physical correlate for any seeming perception, though not always the one which we first expected. Sensing is a psychic activity, not merely a physical event, and is based on our being at a mean with respect to the different ranges of sensa. The primary sense, our waking consciousness of which the individual senses are aspects, grasps the world under various categories and, being educable, is the origin in us of art and science. (2) Moral awareness also involves the concept of a mean: the form of virtue is elicited from a discussion of the virtues, commonly so called, in the light of biological and metaphysical theses about wholes. Virtue is revealed as a form of balance: the most reliable judge in moral as in other matters is he who is least one-sided, who sums up our various human potentials and so sees straight. (3) The reconciliation of our individuality and our gregariousness, in particular, is to be found in the discovery that we create our identities, so that 'self-interest' is wholly ambiguous. The best self for us to make is one that can love and be loved. Master-slave relationships are to be abandoned in favour of equal friendship, so that we act in accord with the principles of the best society and therefore of the divine in each and all of us.

IV.   How far does Aristotle's treatment of time and history license the sort of dynamic interpretation of his doctrines that I have been giving? (1) He gives an operationalist account of time, such that change is an unanalysable datum. The world cannot be reduced to the static form common in dimensionalist theories of time. The temporal metric is no more than an abstraction from our experience of changefulness. This view is related to various other cosmological doctrines, particularly the indeterminacy of the future. Only such a theory can accommodate organic entities that can fail of their completion. (2) The study of history can never be fully scientific, for it can never be rid of the accidental. The course of history runs in cycles, but not exactly repeating ones, nor can it be fully predicted. Political history involves the development and decay of organic wholes, in which economic relationships are to be understood as properly embedded in the life of the community. The historian must be a man of experience, for history cannot be wholly reduced to rule, and only *nous* stands above the flux. Historical study is important, but there are better things to contemplate than man.

V.   What then shall we do? (1) The good life is one of properly ordered activities, culminating in the absolute value of *theoria*. The logic of wholeness explicates the nature of the structure involved.

The *daimon* of *eudaimonia*, for Aristotle as explicitly for Plato, is *nous*, but a complete realization of this paramount good (which heals the specious breach between inclusive and dominant *eudaimonia*) is only momentary. Civil and theoretic good meet in this, that both are a service of the divine in man. (2) We make our lives, but death may intrude. This problem is an aspect of the metaphysical, that death is at once unnatural (formally) and natural (materially). We can die because there is a world larger than ourselves in which we can have ceased to be. Plato's arguments for immortality lead to Aristotle's belief only in the immortality of *nous*. We can endure death because we turn to the world and seek its perfection by living according to the unaging best in us, energetically rather than kinetically. (3) This *nous* is at once the Prime cosmological mover and that whose presence in us we occasionally realize. It is a thinking of itself, for it thinks and is the principles of being. Our intuition of the world as a unitary whole reveals to us the nature of things and gives us our only deathlessness. In this Aristotle is at one with the doctrines of Ch'an Buddhism. *Theoria, theo-ria*, is the practice of enlightenment.

VI. The ontological model which explains much of Aristotle's conclusions and methods is one of life-worlds, in which the material universe of scientific myth is no more than an abstraction from lived reality, not its transcendent ground. Our escape from egocentricity is via variously social views of the world to an appreciation of the god's view. The body-soul unity posited by Aristotle is not an uneasy yoking of material and mental, but an acceptance of the lived world, from which the object body of science is also an abstraction. To see straight we must see with the god, not just with scale and ruler. The primeval giant from whom the world is made here joins with the Supreme that moves without action, and which is our highest good and ontological ground.

A. The concept of *pneuma* is an attempt to unite the sensory, respiratory, digestive, and generative aspects of animal life, using notions derived from archaic shamanistic practice and culminating in modern theories of the conservation of energy.

B. Aristotle's account of sexual difference, though partly deformed by a Platonizing view of women as inferior men, draws attention to intersexual love and the making of loving couples as the groundwork for a decent society in which virtues are accorded their proper status.

C. My comparison of Aristotle and certain Chinese thinkers is confirmed by noting the misunderstanding of Aristotle shown by Orientalists in urging differences between Aristotle and 'Zen in Confucian guise', the Sung Neo-Confucianism.

D. Krämer's suggestion that the objects of the Prime's thought are the secondary movers can be partly accepted without thereby splitting the Prime off from the *kosmos*. Astronomy and ethics alike involve a hierarchy of ends.

Abbreviations

(Abbreviations used for journals in the bibliography are listed in the bibliography.)

I have marked with an asterisk * those works in the Corpus that seem to me fairly certainly not from Aristotle himself. That the other works are all and exactly what he wrote seems to me somewhat doubtful, but short of a divine revelation I see no way of distilling the true and only Aristotle from those works (see Chapter I *passim*). Fragments are mostly given Ross's numbering. Where Ross does not include them, they are numbered according to Rose's 1886 edition. Titles of lost works are given in the Greek version.

Cat.	*Categories*
De An.	*De Anima*
De Div.	*De Divinatione per somnia (P.N.)*
De Gen. An.	*De Generatione Animalium*
De Gen. Corr.	*De Generatione et Corruptione*
De Inc.	*De Incessu Animalium*
De Ins.	*De Insomniis (P.N.)*
De Int.	*De Interpretatione*
De Juv.	*De Juventute (P.N.)*
De Long. Vit.	*De Longitudine Vitae (P.N.)*
De Mem.	*De Memoria (P.N.)*
De Motu	*De Motu Animalium*
De Part. An.	*De Partibus Animalium*
De Resp.	*De Respiratione (P.N.)*
De Soph. El.	*De Sophisticis Elenchis*
De Vita	*De Vita et Morte (P.N.)*
E.E.	*Eudemian Ethics*
Hist. An.	*Historia Animalium (?*)*
*M.M.**	*Magna Moralia**
Met.	*Metaphysics*

Meteor.	*Meteorologica*
N.E.	*Nicomachean Ethics*
P.N.	*Parva Naturalia*
Peri Phil.	*Peri Philosophias* fr.
Phys.	*Physics*
Poet.	*Poetics*
Pol.	*Politics*
Post. An.	*Posterior Analytics*
Prior An.	*Prior Analytics*
Probl.*	*Problemata**
Protr.	*Protrepticos* fr.
Rhet.	*Rhetoric*
Top.	*Topics*

Introduction:
Methods and Interpretation

1. Philosophers are inclined, perhaps for the sake of simplicity and usually against their better judgement, to speak as if the 'meaning' of a given form of words were some metaphysical object connected by fiat with the words concerned. It takes a singularly naïve intelligence to suppose that a computer can be programmed to translate from English to Russian merely by feeding it an English–Russian dictionary, but few of us entirely avoid a similar folly. Scholars declare urgently 'But that is not what the text *says*', and may of course be right, in some sense, but strictly the text says nothing at all. Students of philosophy must take particular care to remember this, truism though it is: no words mean anything in isolation. Indeed no sounds are even words in isolation. The process of understanding even a simple series of vocables involves prior assumptions, usually but not always automatic ones, about the language of the vocalizer, his beliefs about the world, the context of his utterance, his position and that of the person (if any) currently addressed. There is no one, presumably metaphysical, thing that 'he's coming down on Thursday' means (consider: 'down'—from Oxford, the North Pole, or a tower; 'Thursday'—a date or a pet donkey . . .)—a fact that explains the fascinatingly unresolved character of half-heard conversations, and that decrees that interpretation can never be as simple as we would like to think.[1] It is people who mean, and people whom we must try and understand. The nightmare library of Babel envisaged by J. L. BORGES (1) may contain all possible combinations of the alphabetical signs, punctuation marks, and spaces, and therefore all possible books in all possible languages, but these books are utterly unmeaning until someone comes to interpret them. They provide the material for languages and for meaningful thought, but they are themselves as empty as the patterns made upon the sands by random winds. When we speak of the *De Anima* or *Parva Naturalia* as asserting such and such we are speaking loosely.

[1] This topic, as related to machine translation, is discussed by H. Dreyfus in GRENE (5).

2. The same vocables may convey many different words: consider the multilingual puns of *Finnegans Wake*. The same words may convey many different meanings. 'Gold dissolves in aqua regia' may represent a newly discovered empirical truth, or a definition contingent only in that 'gold' might have meant something else. Conversely knowledge of the same fact may be conveyed variously: 'the cat is on the mat' and 'Georgina's in her favourite place' may be used to convey precisely the same picture of the world. I do not say that they mean the same thing, precisely because neither of them means anything. What we derive from a series of sentences depends upon a collection of largely unexamined assumptions and the sort of guesswork at which we are variously adept. When one Aristotelian scholar, speaking for many, declares that 'a commentator, to my mind, should be concerned with the texts in hand instead of engaging in guesslike inferences' (N. Lobkowicz: MCMULLIN p. 99), he is therefore saying more than he should. Our understanding of the texts in hand cannot so be distinguished from guesslike inferences: our knowledge of and feeling for the Greek language is dependent upon our reasonable guesses exercised over a wide range of Greek texts. Our ability to follow an argument depends upon an ability to catch hold of those reasonable generalizations, common definitions, and the like which can be made totally explicit only at the price of unbearable tedium—if then. Yet if we permit these guesses, these feelings, these beliefs about what is reasonable and what is not to remain wholly unexamined, convincing ourselves that we are operating in true scholarly fashion and keeping to 'what the text says', we are in danger of missing any point with which we are not already familiar. The choice is not between scholarship and guesswork, but between two varieties of guessing. Scholarly guesswork is a function of that same *anchinoia* (*Post. An.* 89^{b}10f.; *N.E.* VI, 1142^{b}5f.) which can intuit the appropriate middle term in a scientific syllogism: its results must be checked wherever possible, but we cannot outlaw it at the beginning.

3. The attempt to check our results is made more difficult precisely by our too-ready acceptance of certain doctrines as reasonable. The WHORF hypothesis that our language unavoidably conditions the thoughts we have about the world may well refute itself by claiming that we cannot understand alien tongues while simultaneously proving the point by translating them into the appropriate English

form, but some less extreme claim is plausible. If we are to avoid the absurdity of that apocryphal French thinker who remarked that it was a peculiarity of the French language that the words are uttered in the same order as the thoughts they represent, we must remember that our languages, as also our institutions, at least partly condition what we think reasonable. If we set ourselves to make sense of some alien locution it may end up only as what *we* think sense, as what our languages tempt us to consider obvious. I shall suggest later (IV.1.12n) that our use of expressions such as '*X* is past/present/ future', our apparent attribution of certain temporal properties to existing individuals, may lead to a temporal model which is at once misleading and likely to obscure our understanding of Aristotle. Similarly the Greek system of referring to abstract concepts by the neuter form of the relevant adjective, and the lack of any distinction in ordinary discourse between 'man' and 'a man', are not unconnected with the Platonic theory of forms. Neither we nor the Greeks are necessarily bound by such failings but as long as we ignore their existence we are very likely to go astray. Just as mathematical problems that are simple to us are soluble only with great difficulty by the speaker of an inadequate number-language, doctrines that are almost self-evident in one language are almost incomprehensible in another. The conventions we employ in understanding linguistic symbols tend to be those which we assume to be most reasonable, those which we ourselves are disposed to count on in our own communications. We should always remember that there are other possibilities.

4. For the self-ignorance involved in our forgetfulness of these difficulties has led some investigators to employ an argument form perhaps best labelled the semantic sneer. Convinced that their own language maps the world in the only possible way they translate other doctrines into their own terms and then hold the results up to derision. This process may of course serve the useful purpose of clarifying one's own theories by contrast with what they make of other men's, but it is usually employed for explicitly polemic ends. Thus: travel into the past is held to be incoherent because the same event might thereby be both before and after a given other event (AYER p. 158); life after death is impossible because an air-crash in which everyone is killed can be described as leaving no survivors (FLEW p. 4); the time-reversed electron posited for theoretical

purposes by some physicists is absurd because it involves a particle's being in up to three places at the same time (MUNDLE); no one can truly suppose himself to be dreaming because no one can suppose anything while asleep (MALCOLM p. 109); Berkeleianism denies the existence of the external world; miracles do not happen because they are precisely things that do not happen; Aristotelianism implies that men are tools. All these arguments, and others like them, depend upon a refusal to learn one's victim's language: let him say *Ax* and *Bx*, the would-be philosophical physician promptly equates *B* and not-*A* and infers *Ax* and not-*Ax*, 'which is a very pretty way of arguing, and a short cut to infallibility' (Locke: *Essay* I.3.20). If it is intended only to depict the victim's system as it appears from a given angle, well and good; it should not be used in conjunction with such phrases as 'what he really means is . . .' Such a reductivist technique can only protect us from any doctrine that we do not already accept, and a debate run on such principles resembles nothing more than the perpetually oblique pseudo-conversation of two confirmed monologists.

5.   Ideally, and where these difficulties are avoided, a dialogue tends toward the mean: the participants learn to translate between each other's systems, to contemplate the world of which each system is a partial map, to find common ground upon which to build (cf. *E.E.* 1239^{b}30f.). That there must always be some such common ground may be taken either as a matter of faith or as a truism; for, if there is none, how are they conversing, indeed how are they even aware of each other in the first place? The techniques involved in this mutual enlargement are various, and one must certainly be the discovery of common emotional interests, common assumptions about what is important, but we should not anticipate this discovery. Nor should we postpone it overlong: the sight of some value judgement or such in an alien setting frequently blinds scholars to its familiarity—witness the pompous nonsense that has been written about the Greeks' 'strange admiration' for such competitive virtues as are shown in athletics. In all this what is required is an openness, an empathy, a concern that seeks windows rather than mirrors, and these qualities are not infrequently found. The difficulty which appears where one party to the dialogue (as it were) is unavoidably silent requires more complex solutions.

6.   'I have read and deeply pondered upon all the main systems,

never being satisfied until I was able to think about them as their own advocates thought' (PEIRCE I, § 3). Such an ideal must indeed, in some sense, be the limit to which we should aspire, but it is hardly one that we are likely to obtain. In the hands of less able thinkers indeed it may well be a short cut to a patronizing complacency that has truly grasped no more than the superficies of the system. For in ordinary discussion the investigator demonstrates his increasing grasp of his subject's intentions by being able to draw conclusions, make correlations, and suggest experiments with which his subject concurs. It is not necessary to listen to everything the subject has to say before understanding him, for a pattern may be formed quite quickly; it is necessary not to be too attached to the pattern one thinks one sees, otherwise communication will be very quickly blocked. Normally the subject will be able to reject any undesired interpretation of what he says, though even his word is not necessarily conclusive: authors do not always make the best critics, though criticism itself may be a kind of authorship. Nor, since the subject *is* alive, is he immune to modification: conversation is modification, so that even here we are not confronted by a static and unambiguous reality. Where he is dead or silent, and one is dealing only with those fragments of his mental life that have been solidified in book-form the case is rather different. A book cannot be interrogated, it is only an image (Pl. *Phaedrus* 274 b f.; Ch'eng Yi: CHAN (1) XI, §14), a cast-off skin which may reveal something of the living creature but is not itself identical with it. We can only attempt to imagine what creature could have left such a skin, but in attempting this task, in trying as far as possible to imagine, even to become such a creature, we must not gaze too long at the skin. We shall not have succeeded when we can wear this tattered remnant but when we can cast a similar skin of our own. We have only understood a theorem when we can elaborate it beyond what we were given, only understood a companion when we know more than he has told us. Yet even if we do amazingly succeed in this enterprise we have not necessarily achieved an authentic, a true interpretation. On the one hand we must go beyond the text to understand it, for reasons I have already mentioned; but on the other there are non-denumerably many possible creatures which could have cast such a skin, and we have no direct way of knowing which one actually did. Our self-transformation may therefore be into something hardly even resembling the lost original. Once we step beyond the text we are in no-man's land, yet step we must.

7. Plainly we have some help in our enterprise; for we can find living animals or at least better-known (?) animals (see App. C) which cast similar skins. We can employ general rules about what can be most probably expected. We can look, hopefully, for further examples of our subject's industry. Yet none of these aids is at all conclusive. Other animals may be subtly different from each other and from our subject. Our general rules about what is 'reasonable' may be hopelessly parochial. No amount of further evidence is likely to resolve our problem completely. For it is not even clear that the subject must always have meant the same things: perhaps there was always a certain distinctive tone to his disputations, but that tone is now indistinguishable and not now to be reproduced by men differently conditioned and probably less able. Nor could we know that we had reproduced his tone even if we had. Nor is it certain that there was ever any sort of consistent system at all: he may have employed concepts and techniques which gave a *de facto* unity to his thought but which he never made explicit, even to himself. There is after all a limit to what can practically be made explicit. In short, no interpretation of a past philosopher can possibly hope for authenticity, and no reading of even a minor text can possibly do without interpretation. All readings are therefore more or less inauthentic, and if we wish to retain the term 'authentic' as a meaningful compliment in this field we must provide some other criteria for its use than a specious agreement with an imaginary past reality.

8. For let us remember an axiom of deontic logic: $CLpOp$, if p is necessary it is obligatory. An ideal that is impossible in principle may function as a beacon, but we cannot reasonably be dissatisfied if we do not reach it. We must be satisfied with 'lesser' things. We can wish for the patently impossible; we cannot reasonably plan for it (*N.E.* III, 1111^b22, 1112^a18f.).

9. Interpretation is always re-creation, whether good or bad, and this need not surprise us. The performance of a Bach fugue is not improved by being notionally authentic, and therefore almost certainly offensive to our modern ears: instruments, styles, musical notations, and the expectations of the audience have changed over the years and we can no more recapture the first innocence than we can hear the songs of Homer as they were first heard by drunken

nobles in the courts of Ionia. A character invented by BORGES (1), Pierre Menard, determined to write *Don Quixote*—not to transcribe it, but to write for himself a work which would coincide with Cervantes's in every detail. Borges feigns that he succeeded at least in producing a few fragments, and adds that 'Cervantes's text and Menard's are verbally identical, but the second is almost infinitely richer'. *Don Quixote* as written by Cervantes and as rewritten by Menard (or as read by any modern reader) are not at all the same thing, nor should we want them to be. Any great work has been co-authored by the generations (cf. *N.E.* I, 1098ᵃ23): some momentary accretions are rejected by those who come after, but it still grows under the hands of readers, critics, and other writers who cause us to see new virtues in the old work. Every writer creates his own predecessors, and so does every philosopher. Those aspects of a philosophy which we can look back and see as the seeds of some more recent movement were most probably unnoticed until that movement: we should not therefore now pretend not to see them.[2]

10. A good interpretation of Bach is accounted good for aesthetic reasons, not historical. An interpretation of Aristotle must be assessed upon other grounds. That it should be orderly, elegant and the like may indeed be required, but it must also pretend at least to some degree of truth, and especially practical truth. If the thoughts suggested to us in our reading of Aristotle have no practical consequences for us to enact then our reading is clearly 'inauthentic' far more truly than in some trivial anachronism. It is also barren. Philosophy is the pursuit of practical truth and it is within the context of this pursuit that interpretations must be judged. It must also be judged upon historical grounds, though not in the ordinary sense: it must, I suggest, contain or reflect other interpretations of Aristotle. If it is to be anything like a worthy member of the Aristotelian line it must in some measure sum up earlier members, as well as providing sidelights on the genealogies of other systems. A good interpretation, in short, is a rich and fruitful one, and as such of considerably more value than one aiming at a specious authenticity. I have no confidence that the thoughts I have to offer are such a good interpretation: rather they are to be regarded as fragmentary

---

[2] This is (obviously) not to say that we can impute any meaning we like to the text: there are some things which the author could not *possibly* have meant and which add nothing to our understanding of the implications of his system (see I.4).

intimations of such a re-creation from which the audience in turn can build their own approximations.

11. Thus: I do not consider authenticity, particularly where it is to be obtained by a studied literalism, an appropriate ideal. We cannot achieve such an authentic vision; it is far from clear that there was ever any one determinate version of the system (?) being studied; we could not know that we were being authentic, even if *per impossibile* we were; nor would such a version be worth having, save as an intellectual stimulus to exactly the pursuit we should have been engaged in from the start. An obsession with ill-understood and usually ill-grounded generalizations about the feelings, customs, and beliefs of the subject's day is often a hindrance in interpretation; to counteract it, to liberate Aristotle from the curse of being blindingly obvious (*Met.* II*, 993ᵇ8f.),[3] we should perhaps occasionally allow ourselves to think of Aristotle as a Zen Buddhist, a Neo-Confucian, an existentialist, or a disciple of Pindar. Not that he was, actually or exclusively, any of these things, so far as we know, but neither was he an anti-Platonist, a Neo-Platonist, a Church Father, a linguistic philosopher, or a middle-class fourth-century rationalist. Aristotle, like any other man, was himself, and we do him no service by claiming him as the author of a complete and unambiguous system. Neither do we serve ourselves.

12. But if our Aristotle can only be what we make him why should we trouble ourselves with the given material at all? Will the result not simply be a more or less distorted reflection of our own face? What have we to learn from that? Even if, however, that is all we can expect, it is unclear to me that there would be nothing to be gained from such a reflection; at the least we shall have clarified some of our own ideas, shall have been compelled to reassess our standard judgements in order to provide a sense for what the texts 'say'. Rather as an addict of the Book of Changes or the Tarot can learn or clarify his psychological state by contemplating random patterns, so the interpretative philosopher creates not only his own Aristotle but himself. Furthermore, as my analogy is intended to suggest, what we have of Aristotle is not entirely random, and not entirely uninformative. The flexible system which is slowly formed in an interpreter's mind as the groundwork of his interpretation is

---

[3] * signifies that this is not to be taken as Aristotle's own work.

not, or should not be, imposed from outside: it develops from the 'guesslike inferences' and interpretations of individual passages as they are increasingly seen in relation to each other.

13.   This process, a mixture of the intuitive and the deductive, is an attempt to escape from partial, conditioned views of reality, which is to say from partial and conditioned personalities, into something that will in some sense mirror the world. 'We must attempt to gain conviction about all these things through *logoi*, using the testimony and example of experience' (*E.E.* 1216^{b}26). The position from which we begin this odyssey does not greatly matter: it is in a way as random a choice as that involved in tossing yarrow sticks or shuffling cards. 'Everyone has something of his own to contribute to the truth' (*E.E.* 1216^{b}31; cf. *Met.* II*, 993^{b}12f.). 'Everything possible to be believed is an image of the truth' (BLAKE p. 151). Nor does the process have any determinable end: there is unlikely ever to be a complete account of the universe, and it is partly for that reason that we should avoid solidifying a philosophical tradition.

14.   My reasons for this conclusion are partly empirical, partly formal. Those nineteenth-century scientists who thought that everything was known have been proved wrong so conclusively that only the most sanguine of thinkers could ever make the same claim without hearing the distant titter of a cyclotron. Furthermore, while it may be possible to count the number of electrons in the universe, on the basis of some complex field theory, it is plainly not possible to count the number of things, still less their relationships or the events in their histories. 'I cannot exhaust all there is to see in my visual field' (EVANS p. 51), for the more I look the more I can discern. Where there are non-denumerably many, and possibly infinitely many ways of dissecting the unimaginable complexity of pure event the hope of a conclusive dissection, a perfect language seems specious (cf. Bambrough: BAMBROUGH pp. 166–7; BORGES (2) p. 108). Do we in any case wish to have read or to remember such a celestial directory where every thing has its individual address, its own true name (which surely itself contains a complete picture of the universe as seen from that point of view)? Is this the truth that will make us free? Plainly not, and to suppose that it might be is to commit much the same error to which I alluded before, that of forgetting that a linguistic world is primarily a personal world. As is implicit in my principal formal objection: the body of truth can only be complete

when there is nothing left to know, but this condition implies that there can be no one to know that body of truth, and it is therefore a purely notional concept. So long as we exist to know the truth we modify and expand it simply by knowing it. If the universe is deterministic, we could perhaps suggest that the body of truth will be complete when there is nothing that can surprise us: but even if it is deterministic, it is not subjectively so, and our own knowledge of and actual reaction to the body of known truth cannot be included in that body (cf. PRIOR (1) ch. 4). This conclusion is at one with that of Gödel's theorem, and also with the metaphysical intuition that reality is what exceeds our grasp.

15. The expansion and modification of a living philosophy to the point of truth cannot therefore be described as the pursuit of some perfect system which will then be the object of our thought. Rather should we remember that the expansion of a philosophy is equivalent to the philosophical growth of a living person. And in this growth we seek not a certain possession, but to be such and such. We do not seek 'the truth', but to be truthful. That we clearly seek to know the truth of any given matter does not make this alternative mode of speech valueless: it is a reminder that we should be concerned with self-reformation rather than possession. Our scientific, scholarly, or philosophical pursuit must always be a moral one: moral, because concerned with purging ourselves of bias and dishonesty to achieve that lucid condition of which we catch elusive sight from afar. Someone who has not heard, half-heard the call of that distant divinity may find the chase inane, and for him all that follows can at best only be an example for sociological research, if he should bother.

16. It is a commonplace among students of Chinese philosophy (e.g. CHANG pp. 253f.) that the Chinese differ from the West in their insistence on mind-control and character-reform rather than the use of exterior techniques of investigation. There may be some truth in this, though I am unimpressed by the facility with which such generalizations can be made, but Aristotle at least must surely then be accounted Chinese. The ideal of ch'eng, variously translated though the term is (Legge: sincerity; Needham: integrity; Hughes: realness), is one to which my Aristotle at least has considerable affinity. 'He who is sincere is one who hits upon what is right without effort and apprehends without thinking. He is naturally and easily

in harmony with the Way' (*Doctrine of the Mean* § 20: CHAN (2) p. 107). 'Sincerity means the completion of the self, and the Way is self-directing' (*Doctrine of the Mean* § 25). To hear such words while reading Aristotle is to grow in understanding of both, however many other routes there may be. Before we can know we must be knowledgeable. 'Knowledge in its fulness is not vouchsafed except where it is first deserved' (MARCEL p. 207). 'In ordinary beings there is the constant effort to attain stability, to overcome inner contradiction, and so to become more organized and more coherent. The Tathagata is not disturbed by the succession of things. He is not caught in the parts of the mechanism. For he discovers the nature of the mechanism and identifies himself with it' (J. H. WOODS p. 137). 'The wise one is he who knows a lot by nature: those chatterboxes who have had to learn it all gabble their empty dreams, like crows against the godly bird of Zeus' (Pindar *Olymp.* II.86f.). Somewhere in this cross-cultural mandala lies the Aristotle who is, inevitably, the self-image of my own philosophical enterprise: not a system, but a man.

17. To understand a philosophy is not to chant the unmeaning words on cue, but to understand a man. To understand a man is not to have him neatly tabulated, written down and dead, but to enter into him and feel with him. And that is never to remain wholly separate from him, and in the case of historical interpretation it is not to be confronted by any sort of distinguishable object, but rather to inform, reform oneself. In this procedure one's disposition and the world of one's awareness are two sides of the same coin. Our philosophies, which are our dispositions ordered and emended, create the worlds we see. Just as a madman finds a terrible significance in a closed oak door, or as a lover finds a more welcome meaning in his beloved's body, so in our fashion do we all (cf. BEVAN, VAN DEN BERG). Our emotions as human beings are conceptual (*Rhet.* 1378^{a}19f.; *Top.* 127^{b}30f.; Pl. *Philebus* 40 d, 42 a; FORTENBAUGH (1)): the terror and the significance come together, though in such disordered cases the predictive value of the experience is small—for there is no 'real' danger to be expected from behind the door. Plainly we wish that the conceptual aspect of our responses should be valid: we want a philosophy, a disposition which enables us to see things straight, not necessarily dispassionately. There is no possibility of 'doing without a disposition', of 'just being reasonable', any more than there is any way of doing

without assumptions and guesses: if we refuse to remake ourselves we shall simply continue to employ mistaken, because unexamined, assumptions, attitudes, and the like. The conviction that all 'savages' are tyrannized by sorcerers and ghouls was a product of the anthropologists' own deistic or naturalistic myths (see DOUGLAS (1)). A similar situation obtains with regard to the fabulous Trobrianders' alleged ignorance of physical paternity (LEACH pp. 85f.). None of us dare claim to be free of such astigmatisms: all of us must desire to be rid of them, yet it seems impossible to be rid of the fact of perspectivity without being rid of awareness in general, impossible to be rid of emotional flavourings without also being rid of our humanity. The effort to resolve this difficulty, to become someone whose response is always appropriate and who can see all things as they are, was that upon which Aristotle as I see it was engaged. The philosophical disposition of the Aristotelian saint must therefore form a unity with 'the true nature' of nature: the feeling-tone of the saint's world must always be appropriate. It will not necessarily be the cold dispassion that is the subjective counterpart of a universe of dead matter: that, after all, is a disposition as much as any other, and as conditioned by its time. To attempt this 'sanctity' is to move within the experienced world examined by phenomenological philosophers. As I shall suggest below (VI.7f.) the absolute need not be considered, as it is in this age, a mindless object-world of quantifiable matter: the Absolute is the perfect Mind.

18. 'The thorough understanding of Aristotle is the highest achievement to which man can attain, with the sole exception of the understanding of the prophets,' said Maimonides. Doubtless he exaggerated. To worship Aristotle is an error precisely on Aristotelian terms: 'one should not give a man more honour than the truth' (Pl. *Rpb.* 595 c 2). 'Where both are friends true piety is to prefer the truth' (*N.E.* I, 1096[a]16). *Aletheia* is primarily truthfulness: one pursues to exemplify rather than to have it. *Eudaimonia* is not something to be possessed as an object (*N.E.* IX, 1169[b]28). A philosophical investigation, in so far as it 'seeks the truth', is self-reformation or clarification, and this fact as much as any other is a symptom of the philosophical disposition I am concerned to isolate. This is the rationale for Aristotle's own dealings with previous philosophers, as in the *Metaphysics* or *Physics*, that he aims to make the best sense he can of their remains (see IV.2.21). For this

introduction does not purport to be a summary of arbitrary or subject-neutral techniques: it is a summary, sometimes elliptical, of the Aristotelian disposition itself. The method is the man. All that follows is expansion or explanation of this first insight, that philosophy is essentially a way of life, and hears the voice of the god. How the experience of vocation can be described, explained, acted on, made coherent with our various duties and beliefs is Aristotle's central theme. And also, or identically, mine.

II.1. The *Ergon* Argument

1. In finding my way through the labyrinth of the Aristotelian texts I shall be concerned primarily with questions, speculations, and occasionally answers related to the nature of man, or less abstractly of men. It may therefore be as well to remind ourselves from the start that such an emphasis is in the end unaristotelian, 'It would be absurd to reckon the art of politics or practical wisdom the most worthwhile, unless man were the best thing in the world' (*N.E.* VI, 1141ª20; see *E.E.* 1217ª22). It is for this reason, amongst others, that Aristotle regrets Socrates' exclusive concern with ethical questions (*Met.* I, 987ᵇ2). He would presumably have agreed with that doubtfully historical Indian mentioned by Aristoxenus of Tarentum, who laughed at Socrates, declaring that one could not understand the human if one knew nothing of the divine (Eusebius: *Preparatio Evangelica* XI.3.28; see CHROUST (1), (2) I ch. 16). Even where he momentarily urges the study of psychology in general (and as equivalent to biology (*De An.* 402ª1f.)) or in particular (for the use of statesmen (*N.E.* I, 1102ª23f.)), it is as a means to the study of more important matters. The charming naïveté of one author of a work on self-analysis who announces that he can imagine nothing more entrancing than a voyage of discovery through oneself, is very far from Aristotle's concerns. None the less it is always appropriate to advance from the more familiar to the less (*Phys.* I, 184ª16f. *et al.*), even though it will be through those less familiar principles that we shall in the end understand those more readily accessible to us. Man is the most familiar animal in the world, indeed the most familiar thing in the world, and is therefore an appropriate beginning (*Hist. An.* 491ª19f.). He is also and for obvious reasons one at least of the more immediately interesting things in the world: 'what shall I do to be saved?' is a question that all of us ask at some time, even if we do not put it like that and even if we conceal its import behind a host of lesser questions—'what shall I have for dinner, how can I impress that blonde, how much longer can I endure this paper?' We must start from where we are, and at the moment we are hopefully attempting to understand Aristotle and ourselves.

2. 'What shall I do to be saved?' Or to put it another way which

may seem more Aristotelian: 'what is the nature of the good life for man?' In the first book of the *Nicomachean Ethics*, after discussing various popular and philosophical answers to this question, Aristotle concludes that we can at least agree on what name such a life should have, namely *eudaimonia*, commonly translated 'happiness'. But although this fact may involve some substantial information on its probable nature (see below on Eudaimonia), it is not very informative as it stands, for the point is certainly not that we all seek or should seek to be *happy*, in the sense of felt contentment. Rather we wish to live well, and to that living we give the name *eudaimonia*. Aristotle therefore suggests that it may be appropriate to consider first the nature of man's *ergon*.

3. 'Are there acts and *erga* of builder and cobbler, but not of man? Is man born to be inactive? Or rather, just as eye and hand and foot and in general every part clearly has an *ergon*, should we not suppose that man has an *ergon* on top of all these?' (*N.E.* I, 1097ᵇ28f.; see *De. Part. An.* 645ᵇ14f.).

4. HARDIE, accepting the usual translation of '*ergon*' as 'function', makes a standard response (p. 23): 'The obvious answer is that one may not, unless one is prepared to say that a man is an instrument designed for some use . . . Only the fact that a cobbler is an abstraction makes it possible to think of him as a means. It is only the fact that the eye and hand are parts of the body that makes it possible to think of them as tools.' In short, and if we disregard the verbal infelicity that suggests that the red-headed man round the corner who mends my shoes is an abstraction, Hardie suggests that a thing can only have a function in a system, that to have a function is to serve some external end. Only tools have functions, though bodily organs may be said to have them by analogy. Hardie deals similarly with Plato, suggesting that according to *Republic* 353ᵃ10 'if it is true of something that it could be used to produce certain desirable results, and if anything else would produce them, if at all, less effectively, then the thing is probably a tool and producing these results is probably its function'. He might have added that even if man was designed as a tool we do not therefore have an automatic obligation to acquiesce in this condition.

5. But although the Republican Socrates does introduce the concept of an *ergon* through the examples of pruning-hooks and the like, Hardie's paraphrase does not seem to me a satisfactory rendering of

Plato's argument, still less of Aristotle's. 'When a word seems to imply a contradiction (or any particularly absurd argument) one ought to consider how many things it could mean in the context' (*Poet.* 1461ª31f.).

6.   In the *ergon* argument itself sight is named as the *ergon* of the eye, implicitly (*N.E.* I, 1097ᵇ24f.) or explicitly (*E.E.* 1219ª16). But the relationship is also described in other terms. If the eye were a living animal, 'sight would be its soul' (*De An.* 412ᵇ18). Similarly the *erga* of the vegetable soul are 'to reproduce and feed' (*De An.* 415ª25; cf. *N.E.* I, 1098ª1f. *et al.*): alternatively the vegetable soul is 'the life of feeding and increasing'. 'Life', 'soul', and '*ergon*' can all refer to the same features. So also can '*telos*', for sight is also the *telos* of the eye (*De Gen. An.* 778ª33f.). 'Each thing's *ergon* is its *telos*' (*E.E.* 1219ª8). 'For the *ergon* is the end, and the activity the *ergon*' (*Met.* IX, 1050ª22) (see CLARK).

7.   Final analysis is a topic to which I shall return (see II.3.9f.). For the moment I wish to make two points. Firstly, the *ergon* of a variety of living creature, tool, or organ is the particular form of life, of activity which 'makes sense' of its structure. A part of an animal which seems to us to be superfluous, odd, deformed is suddenly explained when we see how it is generally, normally, characteristically used. This is of course perfectly compatible with its original production by random mutation. The whole structure of an animal also makes sense in terms of its form of life. That is not to say that it makes sense in terms of just any individual's actual form of life: perhaps that individual is injured, lazy, bloody-minded, or asleep. Once we have 'understood' a living structure in this manner we are in a position to assess its health, suggest profitable modes of behaviour. My second point is that we are in no position even to identify the creature in question until we have seen what its *ergon*, its *telos*, its form is. In order to identify our subject-matter we must employ final analysis. 'To say then that shape and colour constitute the animal is an inadequate statement, and is much the same as if a wood-carver were to insist that the hand he had cut out was really a hand' (*De Part. An.* 641ª5f.). Such analysis does not imply that the analysandum is a means: rather the reverse. Life is activity, and we are here concerned with what the entity does, not what is done to it (this is true even in the case of admitted tools: see below). A race of space-travelling anthropophages might think men uniquely suited

to the broiler rather than the casserole, rather as Chrysippus seems to have thought of pigs as locomotive meals, with a soul instead of salt. But to think thus is not to be aware of men or animals as entities rather than as so much stuff. And so to be ignorant.

8. Emphasizing the second point for the moment, I suggest therefore that the *ergon* argument is a way of defining our subject-matter: what are these 'men' we are talking about? When Socrates inquired what the *ergon* of a good citizen might be, he was merely asking what it was that a good citizen distinctively did (Xenophon *Mem.* IV.6.13f.), what it was that a good citizen *was*. Or to make the same point in a slightly different way: we require to know how to live well, being men, but 'to live' is not unambiguously definable for all 'living' creatures, 'nor does life seem to be predicated in one sense alone, but is different for animals and plants' (*Top.* 148ª29; cf. *De An.* 413ª22f.). Before we can answer the question 'what is the good life for man?' we must know what it is we are asking. An object is not a good book for being a superb doorstop; a person no better a cobbler for making lots of money; before we can know what makes the good life for man, what makes a good man, we must know what men are.

9. But does not this too commit some form of the 'naturalistic fallacy'? If Aristotle chooses to define humanity in such a way that my preferred life-style falls outside the pale, what is that to me? If I am to be a good cobbler I must fulfil certain criteria: I am not obliged to be a cobbler. What is it to me if most or all men commonly so called do such and such things? Man is one of the few animals to be permanently in rut (*Hist. An.* 542ª26), and probably the only one ever to make a life's work of it: only the horse is more salacious (*Hist. An.* 575ᵇ31). It is not therefore immediately obvious, least of all to Aristotle, that Don Juan was right. Why must we assume that there is any one thing that all men commonly so called have in common? Man is the most versatile of animals (*De Part. An.* 687ª23f.), more various than any other with respect to eye-colour (*Hist. An.* 492ª5; *De Gen. An.* 779ª34), and to what is found pleasurable (*N.E.* X, 1176ª3f.). The class of men is taxonomically parallel to that of birds, not that of ostriches (*De Part. An.* 644ª12f.), seemingly because Man is more various within his kind than any other animal. In a specifically biological context the old belief that

the true nature of a species can be seen in some archetypical individual has largely been replaced by a polytypic account of species (BECKNER (1) p. 64; HULL; cf. GRENE (1) after Schindewolf).

10.   Thus: why should there be anything that all men do? Why should it matter to me in my ethical inquiry that there is (or is not) any such thing? Why should I not go against the norm, if there is one?

11.   But though these objections may seem apposite, I think they miss the point. It may be that the notion of 'the good life for man' is strictly a figment, that there is no general account of what Jemima, Tom, and Vladimir all do in 'living well'—short of the vacuous 'living well' itself. Maybe the conclusions I reach about what I ought to do will have no relevance at all to what anyone else should do. Maybe, though I am surely not as original a monster as all that, but the only way to find out that something does not exist is to make every effort to find it. Let us first see whether there is something we can agree on before deciding that we are all far too unique and individual to have anything to say to each other. It may be that given John's nimbleness, head for heights, discriminating aesthetic judgement, and so forth, he would do better to be a cat-burglar than anything else, be a better cat-burglar than anything else he might be (it is not unreasonable, though it is also not obligatory to take as your purpose in life that at which you are better than anything else). It may be that he would say, like one of Plato's honest citizens 'that he had a job to do [an *ergon*] and life was not worth living if he could not do it' (Pl. *Rpb.* 407 a 1). His job is his life, what makes him a single and a happy person rather than a muddled and disheartened one. I shall be returning to this point (see III.3.4f.); it is not unconnected with my first point about final analysis (II.1.7), but it is not one that need affect the *ergon* argument. What behaviour the all-important 'well' licenses may well vary from case to case, and the behaviour appropriate to a middle-aged woman is not necessarily appropriate to a young man (*Pol.* III, 1277^{b}20f. *et al.*): we are not therefore reduced to writing individual prospectuses any more than in the case of medicine: the mean is relative to the individual case (*N.E.* II, 1106^{a}26f.), but men commonly so called are sufficiently alike to permit more compendious advice. Why should the case be different in the ethical sphere?

12. But why should I concern myself with what men do? Certainly my neighbours may provide me with useful information, but I am at liberty to refuse whatever game it is they are playing. Certainly, though it may be foolish to ignore the accumulated experience of mankind. I am not obliged to ape my fellows. But if men are generally sexual beings it would be very foolish to make no mention of sexuality in a general discussion of the way men should live. It may be that the proper place of sexuality in human life is at the top of our priorities, or at the bottom: there is no point in refusing to discuss it if we are aiming at producing something that will be of interest to more than a few unusually monastic types. Aristotle is not committing 'the naturalistic fallacy' merely because he thinks it appropriate to consider what men's interests and habits are before discussing what to do about those interests and habits.

13. But why is the discussion of the good life for men supposed to be relevant to me? It may be not merely characteristic but definitive of men that they like honey: it may be, if that is how you wish to use the term, and if I am thereby shown to be non-human I am not therefore compelled to acquire a taste for honey. 'Homo non vult esse nisi homo', said Nicholas of Cusa, after Aristotle. 'No one chooses to have everything at the price of becoming what he is not' (in this case a god) (*N.E.* IX, 1166ª19). To choose not to be a man is to choose not to be the one man one was, and therefore to choose death. Such a choice is obviously possible, but suicide notoriously removes the entity concerned from the sphere of ethical or judicio-moral intimidation: if the good life for man is anything but a figment it plainly does not consist in suicide. But why is ceasing to be human death, while ceasing to have hair, live in England, or play croquet is plainly not? Certainly it is a case of substantial change, but that is to state the problem, not to solve it.

14. In fact, if living in England or playing croquet has been taken as his chief purpose in life by some person, then not to do these things any more will be emotionally equivalent, at least, to death. Physical death may actually be preferred to physical safety at the cost of ontological suicide. Does this help with the ethical problem, if not with the metaphysical?

15. Consider the sort of objection that a Sartrean might make. As an ego, an awareness, I am more than just a human being. In so far

as I am aware of my human nature, however defined, I stand above it. I can will my death and ruin as a man, can deliberately go against all values of survival and thereby ensure my identity as a free, undetermined, permanently transcendent ego. Neither I nor anyone else can ever put a label on me. Wherever I turn to look at myself my true self always turns behind me: I can never know what I am, though I can be aware of what I was and shake it off in the act of knowledge. In becoming an object to myself I cease to be the subject-self.

16. This position does have a certain attraction to it, and it derives it from several sources. Firstly, it is the latest avatar of that splendidly poetic vision preserved us in the Eddas, of men fighting without hope against a chaos that must at last be triumphant. If atheism did not exist we should have to invent it. Secondly, to argue that Romeo must feel the socially approved hatred that 'all his family' feel for Juliet's is to assume that Romeo's being is exhausted by his family connections. Such an assumption that the victim is not an individual, indefinitely determinable, and personally responsible being but a cardboard type is the ultimate insult (cf. IV.2.7). The Sartrean generalizes this and concludes that all formulae are similarly insulting. He confirms himself in this by noting the paradox of awareness, that one can never quite catch oneself being aware, simply because this is to turn from contemplating the former object to contemplating oneself (see V.3.10f.).

17. The Sartrean's problem, however, is that in thus describing human identity he has himself defined it, and pinpointed that aspect of our being to abandon which does indeed seem suicidal. 'Man is condemned to be free': I am something that must choose. To abandon one's policy in living may seem worse than death: the general form of this is the abandoning of one's self-determination. There is no reason not so to abandon one's freedom which will convince one weary of living, or utterly without confidence in his own capacities. But such a person is precisely not engaged in our present effort to discern the nature of the good life (though it may be that in some circumstances we should all accept slavery as the best available option). There is no point entering a discussion with one ignorant of the basic principles of the discipline concerned: 'one ought not to discuss geometry with those ignorant of it' (*Post. An.* 77^{b}12: *Phys.* I, 184^{b}25f., 193^{a}5f.; cf. *Top.* 105^{a}3f.; *E.E.* 1214^{b}28f.).

There may be some hereditary men—indeed there are—who are not free, or do not wish to be, but anyone engaged in Aristotle's inquiry cannot pretend not to be a man in the relevant sense. One who intends, or hopes, to run his life well is bound to admit that the good life for men, for us, is precisely running our lives well.

18. And is this Aristotle's judgement? Certainly: for human life as he defines it is 'practical activity of what has *logos*' (*N.E.* I, 1098ᵃ3f.). Siegler's response (WALSH/SHAPIRO pp. 30f.), that wicked men can act on reasons as well as good men, is of course quite irrelevant, for the good life for man is not 'practical activity etc.' but 'good practical activity etc.' 'The *ergon* must be one and the same for the soul and its excellence, and the *ergon* of the excellence will be a good life' (*E.E.* 1219ᵃ25f.), to be sure. Living and living well are, in a way, the same, for not to live well is to draw that much closer to not living at all (see below on the Mean). But this is to say that wicked men draw close to the wholly irrational, for their reasons are bad ones. Another objection, that men have many more aspects than the practical—for man's nature includes animal and vegetable—and that human life should also embody these aspects, is no more difficult a criticism. As men, we also digest our food, perceive our prey, move to reach it, and struggle to procreate our kind, but success in these activities is not a debatable issue. It is in that variety of living which is peculiar to man, which constitutes men as unitary organisms (see II.1.7, and II.3.5), that we find our chief problems. Man's nature is complex: his *human ergon* is what is crucial. As we shall see (V.1) his variety of living may itself require further analysis into what is more or less important (see *Protrepticus* fr. 6 Ross).

19. What is this variety? Practical men get things done, but how does that differ from ordinarily doing things? 'It is clear from beasts' having sensation but no share in *praxis*' (*N.E.* VI, 1139ᵃ20). This is because they have no share in *proairesis* (*N.E.* III, 1111ᵇ12, *E.E.* 1225ᵇ27), nor therefore in *eudaimonia* or good fortune (*Phys.* II, 197ᵇ4f., *N.E.* I, 1099ᵇ32f.), for *proairesis* is the source of *praxis* (*N.E.* VI, 1139ᵃ31). Slaves too have no *proairesis* (*Pol.* III, 1280ᵃ32f.), and therefore no share either in *eudaimonia* or even in *bios* (*N.E.* X, 1177ᵃ8), for *bios*, human life, is *praxis* and not *poiesis*, doing and not making (*Pol.* I, 1254ᵃ7f.). To live as a tool, an instrument, is not really to live oneself. 'One who is a man not by his own nature but

by another's is naturally a slave' (*Pol.* I, 1254ᵃ15):[1] a slave is in a
way a part of his master (*Pol.* I, 1255ᵇ11f.; cf. *N.E.* V, 1134ᵇ9f.).
This must surely remove any last traces of a belief that Aristotle
thought or ought to have thought, given his form of argument, that
men were tools: one who is a man by his own nature cannot be a
tool. It is the free man who shows what it is to be human, and a man
is free if and only if he is 'for himself' (*Met.* I, 982ᵇ25). 'The
superior man is not a tool' (Confucius's *Analects* 2.12: CHAN (2)).

20. I have said (II.1.8) that final analysis is a method of identifying
one's subject-matter: so also here. In isolating practical activity as
the defining character of humanity Aristotle is identifying the free
man as the subject of ethical discourse. It is the free man who asks
the question 'what shall I do?' and the free man who must decide
(even if he decides to abandon his will in the matter). Whatever
lesser good natural slaves, or beasts, can obtain is not directly
relevant to what we, as free men, should do with our lives. Ethical
categories are wholly irrelevant to beasts, and only derivatively
appropriate for slaves.

21. But why are slaves human by another's nature? *Proairesis* is
deliberative desire (*N.E.* VI, 1139ᵃ23). Man is the only one of the
animals that deliberates (*Hist. An.* 488ᵇ24). Neither children nor
beasts (alike in many ways: *Hist. An.* 588ᵃ33f.) can 'act', only one
who has reflected (*E.E.* 1224ᵃ28). They lack *proairesis* because they
lack the ability to deliberate and 'the concept of "why"' (*E.E.*
1226ᵇ23f.). Conventional slaves presumably usually can deliberate
in some sense, though maybe to no purpose: natural slaves 'cannot
make their minds up'. What is it that men have which enables them
to deliberate, therefore to plan, therefore to act?

22. Some beasts have only sensation, others have memory and can
therefore learn, but man alone has experience (*Met.* I, 980ᵇ26f.):
'numerous memories of the same thing induce the effect of a single
experience'. Experience is the rule-of-thumb origin of art and
science and is not inferior to its children for practical purposes
(*Met.* I, 981ᵃ13f.). Men, that is, can discern the general in the
repeated particular and locate it by a word. Of those animals that

---

[1] ὁ γὰρ μὴ αὐτοῦ φύσει, ἀλλ' ἄλλου ἄνθρωπος ὤν, οὗτος φύσει δοῦλός ἐστιν: I see
no need to translate this in terms of 'naturally belonging to someone', a concept which
I find opaque, but if this translation is preferred it must still be unpacked as I suggest.

retain their perceptions in memory 'some get a *logos* out of their perceptions' stay, others do not' (*Post. An.*, 99ᵇ36f.). 'The human soul is so constituted as to be thus impressionable' (*Post. An.* 100ᵃ13f.: note slightly different context). Because of this ability only men can reminisce, can think of things in their absence (*Hist. An.* 488ᵇ26), for this reminiscence is a form of reasoning (*De Mem.* 453ᵃ3f.). Beasts, lacking the ability to see those generalizations which reveal causal structure, cannot determine their future actions in terms of a stable concept of the world. An amnesiac woman, interviewed some time after her loss, declared that 'you can't plan for the future if you don't remember your past' (BBC I: 7 Apr. 1970), but she had at least retained her grasp of language and with it a considerable body of general information. Lacking that, men would indeed be lost, particularly as we do not have the stabilized abilities with which lesser animals survive. Only men can live in hope (*De Part. An.* 669ᵃ20).

23. '*Logos*, language, is more characteristic of man than the use of the body' (*Rhet.* 1355ᵇ1). Beasts can make sounds, but not semantic sounds of a distinguishable sort (*De Int.* 16ᵃ26; *Poet.* 1456ᵇ24; *De An.* 420ᵇ27f.). Written language is derivative: it is vocal language, speech, conversation which is primary. Prior indeed even to mental soliloquy, so that the blind from birth are more intelligent than the deaf and dumb (*De Sensu* 437ᵃ15).[2]

24. I stress this conversational aspect of language to introduce a further aspect of humanity. For cattle living-together is no more than pasturing in the same field: for men it is sharing in *logoi* and in thinking (*N.E.* IX, 1170ᵇ10; *E.E.* 1244ᵇ25). Man alone possesses speech and can therefore be aware of the useful, the right, and the just, 'sharing in which makes household and city' (*Pol.* I, 1253ᵃ18). Without such ordered societies speech would be superfluous, and therefore swiftly abandoned by a nature that does nothing to no purpose. Such societies are prior to the individual man, for without the possibility of communication the individual is no man, and if he ceases to desire it he must be either a beast or a god (*Pol.* I, 1253ᵃ19f.). Beasts cannot be practical because lacking a language they can have

---

[2] This is not an attack on the possibility of a solitary intelligence, but confirmation of the thesis that human intelligence depends for its growth on the exchange of information and ideas: in practice we are not solitary thinkers, nor wish to be, but co-thinkers (see III.3.8f.).

no sense of obligation, community, policy (except so far as related to immediate pleasure and pain): they are not practical because they are not political. Neither, of course, are gods: 'anyone examining practical concerns one by one would see that they [practical concerns] are trifling and unworthy of the gods' (*N.E.* X, 1178^{b}17f.).

25.   Science and community have their single source in the *logos* which we share. It is that which makes us men. 'Planning to live together [*proairesis*] is friendship' (*Pol.* III, 1280^{b}39), and it is only between human beings that friendship properly so called can arise, for only they have *proairesis* (*E.E.* 1236^{b}5; see III.3.8f.). That man is a 'political' (*Pol.* I, 1253^{a}2) and a 'rational' animal come to the same thing. So also that he is an upright animal (see II.2.3).^{3}

26.   'Esse homini est coesse' (CROSSON p. 172). Human life, defined by the ability to sense and to think (*N.E.* IX, 1170^{a}16), our life, is practical because it is political. This is our problem, to reconcile our freedom, our self-determining individuality, and our sociality— bearing in mind that it is because we are, and wish to be, social that we have the equipment to be individual. A *polis* that was totally at one would no longer be composed of individuals, and therefore no longer be a *polis* (*Pol.* II, 1261^{a}16f.). A man that was totally and willingly eremitic is hardly imaginable, and if *per incredibile* he existed his mental powers would surely soon atrophy. Suicide is always open to us.

27.   This analysis of human sociality is partly justified by the fact that we should obviously know what human interests are before deciding what to do about them. Secondly, it is an expansion in general terms of what Aristotle and any other being likely to be engaged in this pursuit finds as his identity.^{4} 'No one would choose to have all good things but by himself, for man is social and born to living-together' (*N.E.* IX, 1169^{b}17): no one, or at least no one of us. Thirdly, it is intended to suggest one of the directions we should look for criteria to assess the success of our 'practical activity'. If we

---

^{3} Compare Herder: 'The upright gait of man . . . is the organisation for every performance of his species and his distinguishing character' (STRAUS p. 164).

^{4} 'Finding as one's identity' refers to the same phenomenon as that discussed in II.1.14f.: one finds *x* as one's identity if *x* is what one chiefly feels bound to do. In general, I take 'identifying something', saying 'what it is', to be equivalent to finding its purpose in being (see II.3.10f. for a discussion of the general thesis, and III.3.5 for its application to human life).

so act as to destroy all our hopes of society we must surely be making a mess of our lives. Further, wherever some ability *A* is consequent upon some higher ability *B* or organ *C*, and we wish to exercise *A* in a satisfactory way it is surely advisable to pay some attention to the health of *B* or *C*. If they are in good order, the chances are that *A* will also be (see V.1.19f.).[5]

28. The immediate consequence of this account of man is an intensification of the point made in II.1.17, that it is paradeigmatically those discussing the nature of the good life for man who are men. Anything with which we can converse is a human being. That man is an unfeathered biped is only contingently true (*Met.* VIII, 1043^{b}11), and it is *possible* that men could be found in other materials and shapes (*Met.* VII, 1036^{b}3f.).[6] Animal species are not delimited merely morphologically (how then could we tell that duck and drake were a single species?), but as interbreeding, as it were 'consensual' groupings (MAYR). UEXKUELL (pp. 236f.) draws the possibly exaggerated conclusion that a species is itself a sort of self-maintaining organism, but even without going so far we must admit that a species is not an arbitrary collection of more or less phenotypically similar individuals. Much more could we say (though hereby saying more than Aristotle ever does) that *x* is a dog if and only if it is recognized as such by the dog 'community'. Beasts evince their recognition sexually, affectionately, ritualistically, and the like: men recognize their kin by these methods too but the stress is far more upon the community of mind. Hydrocarbon arachnoids from Jupiter are men as well as we, if they can converse with us and we with them. So perhaps are the salamanders of the moon (*De Gen. An.* 761^{b}17f.; *De Motu* 699^{b}19; cf. *De Gen. An.* 737^{a}1, *Hist. An.* 552^{b}10).

29. HERRIGEL (p. 100) makes an Aristotelian point in declaring that 'no other beings outside or below man live: they are lived' ('*bios*', not '*zoe*'). If we hope to live well as men we must attend to

---

[5] Compare Aristotle's treatment of the heart: 'The other parts depend on the heart, and when this source itself is ailing, there is no place for them to get help' (*De Part. An.* 667^{a}34). On the whole–part hierarchy see also WOODGER (1).

[6] Though certainly human life could not be embodied in just *any* shape (see II.2.17), for there are conditions to be met on the physical level (as hands, and upright posture): what is crucial is the form of life, not the material conditions for that form's embodiment —man's shape, even if it be a necessary shape, is no part of man's definition (his posture, the way he moves and stands, may be).

those capacities which make us able so to attend. If we hope to run our lives well we must get on with it. It is this recognition, that 'living well' is something we must *do*, not merely something to enjoy, which provides a reasonable basis for further discussion. It may be that we shall eventually decide to do our best to live like Sardanapallus, but such a conclusion will still be our decision and we shall still have to seek ways to implement it. To reject the easy declaration that 'living well' just means 'enjoying oneself' is to realize that, the world being what it is, we have no fairy godmothers on call, and whatever sort of life we choose to live it is we that must live it. Even if we choose to live from one decision to the next, trusting in our impulses and counting on good fortune, we cannot pretend not to be responsible for our chosen life-style (see V.1.9).

30.   Aristotle, at least as I shall expound him in the chapters that follow, would think that a man who made no effort to make a unity of his life, being free, was very foolish (*E.E.* 1214^{b}7f.). For the possible rewards are very great. Although he tells us that no man can wish to be a god, for such is suicide, he urges us to follow Plato's advice (Pl. *Tim.* 89 e), not Pindar's: 'one ought not to follow the advice of those who tell us to think mortal thoughts, being mortal, or human thoughts being human, but ought to immortalize ourselves as far as possible' (*N.E.* X, 1177^{b}31f.). This may well seem a contradiction, for we are simultaneously told to immortalize (and thereby divinize) ourselves, and warned that to escape from human temporality, human society, all the weakness that is man ('for human nature is slavish in many respects' (*Met.* I, 982^{b}29)) is to lose ourselves. We are fortunate that immortality is impossible (see *N.E.* III, 1111^{b}22). 'Human things cannot be continuously active' (*N.E.* X, 1175^{a}4). We must live according to the best that is in us (*N.E.* X, 1177^{b}33), according to that element which is responsible for our linguistic, social, deliberative capacities. One needs a share in something divine to be capable of the good life that we seek (*E.E.* 1217^{a}27f.; cf. *N.E.* X, 1178^{b}28, *De An.* 430^{a}14f.). Man's *ergon* is divine, but also human (see V.3.30).

31.   If my interpretation of the *ergon* argument is correct, that *ergon* and *eidos* are here identical, a given individual may clearly be said to actualize its (potential) nature to a greater or a lesser degree, may be said (for example) to be more or less actively human. The real nature of humanity is seen in those who actualize their potential

most clearly. Children are human because they can grow into men: it is the adult, and sane, man who is primary. In the *Categories* Aristotle denies that substance can admit of degrees (*Cat.* 3ᵇ33f.): by the time of *Metaphysics* VI he is prepared to grant that substance as the composite individual does admit of degrees, for potential can be more or less actualized (1044ᵃ11). In the case of men this potential is such that it is we who must actualize it.[7] Portmann (GRENE (2) p. 47) emphasizes upright posture, speech, and rational action as the chief characteristics of man, and that all three must be learnt. 'Man has to become what he is' (STRAUS p. 141): his perfection is not given him but acquired. And it is he who has acquired that perfection, in whom our various capacities and interests are given their proper place, who best shows the nature of man. It is the Aristotelian saint who is most especially human, in that it is his life which gives sense to human structure and society—and also, as I shall argue, to the world.

32.   Beasts grow up, whether they will or no, and so do we at some levels, but it is up to us to grow up fully. If Aristotle is correct we have very far to grow.

---

[7] Though in the end we can do no more than receive the form from outside (V.3.23f.).

II.2.   The Biological Continuum

1.   Men, whatever else they may be, are clearly animals: they differ
from lesser beasts in the ways I have outlined, but there are also
sufficient resemblances and relationships to require some account of
man's standing, as it were, in the world of life. Is he 'a diseased
animal' (UNAMUNO p. 36)? A creature quaintly upright, with flat feet
and slipped discs as the price he pays for his unnatural stance? A
neotenic, 'deformed' ape? To attempt an Aristotelian answer to this
question I shall mention certain oddities in the biological works,
suggest a model which accounts for these, and infer certain metaphysical and ethical theses from this model. In doing so I shall
certainly go beyond anything that 'the text' explicitly says, and it
may be argued that if Aristotle had believed the (devolutionary
transformist) model which I shall impute to him, he would have said
so. I myself see no reason to believe that men habitually reveal their
every belief in what they write; but even if the historical Aristotle did
not make this model explicit even to himself, it may help to reveal
the form of his biological beliefs (see *Met.* I, 989ᵃ3of.: IV.2.21).

2.   For what follows is, in essence, a further expansion of the *ergon*
argument. By seeing more clearly what beasts fail to be or do in
falling short of the human, we may get some hint of how to preserve
and improve our humanity. 'Animals and plants, but especially
animals help(ed) Man to understand *himself*' (SINGER (1) p. 13). How
do they miss the distinctively human?

3.   'Man is the most characteristic, most polar and most living form
of life' (CHARDIN p. 17): the sentiment is Aristotelian. Man has the
most divinity of all the animals, if any others have any at all (*De
Part. An.* 656ᵃ7). He alone has his parts in the natural place (ibid.),
for in him alone are the three polarities (upper, lower; right, left;
front, back) distinguishable from each other and arranged as they
are in the world as a whole (*Hist. An.* 494ᵃ27f.; *De Inc.* 706ᵇ9f.). He
is the most right-sided animal (*De Inc.* 706ᵃ18; *Hist. An.* 493ᵇ17f.,
497ᵇ20), paralleling the laterality of the universe (*De Caelo* 284ᵇ6;
HERTZ; G. E. R. LLOYD (1)). He alone is upright (*De Part. An.* 656ᵃ10,
669ᵇ4 *et al.*; STRAUS pp. 137f.), 'because of his nature and essence

being divine' (*De Part. An.* 686ᵃ28), or because he has a lung (*De Juv.* 468ᵃ5f.; *De Resp.* 477ᵃ19)—which amounts to the same thing (see App. A.6). All other animals are relatively dwarfish (*De Part. An.* 686ᵃ25f.). Indeed in this latter passage Aristotle seems to consider all non-human creatures, down to and including plants, to be degenerate men. Adapting a mythological device of Plato's (*Tim.* 91f.) he suggests that the head and upper parts slowly lurch forward; as the heat of life drains away the resulting quadruped becomes a creeping thing, then a mollusc with his head unnaturally at the bottom and finally a plant. The animal's head and the plant's roots are analogous organs, functionally equivalent (*De An.* 416ᵃ4; *De Inc.* 705ᵇ6). Similarly in the *De Generatione Animalium* Aristotle's biological continuum descends from man, the most perfected of all (*De Gen. An.* 737ᵇ27), through the other vivipara, the two classes of ovipara, to the larvipara (insects) (*De Gen. An.* 733ᵇ1f.). The downward progression is marked by decreasing heat. It is significant in this context that the sexual residue is greatest in humans, for the heat of life has not been diverted into the formation of tusks, hair, and the like (*De Gen. An.* 728ᵇ14f.; *Hist. An.* 521ᵃ25f.). The human male, of course, is the real man: women are, more or less, infertile men: 'the female exists by a sort of incapacity' (*De Gen. An.* 728ᵃ17). The front and upper parts are more developed in the male, the lower and back in the less developed female (*Hist. An.* 538ᵇ1): a fact which once compels Aristotle to admit that the male is more dwarfish than the female (*De Long. Vit.* 467ᵃ33: but see III.2.23). It is a further proof of the degenerate nature of the ovipara and larvipara that the female is larger and longer-lived than the male (*Hist. An.* 538ᵃ22). A female is a maimed male (*De Gen. An.* 737ᵃ28). Even the conception of a female child is an anomaly, a failure of generation almost on a par with actual deformity, though it is a 'necessary anomaly' (*De Gen. An.* 767ᵇ7; cf. 769ᵇ30: 'an anomaly is a sort of deformity'). That Aristotle should allow accident to enter his scheme at such a point despite his rejection of Empedocleanism is itself an anomaly that will eventually require explanation (see App. B). Clearly he wishes to mark the priority of the human male 'which has a nature that has been completed' (*Hist. An.* 608ᵇ7). What really does this priority imply?

4. Everything is deformed relative to man. Some things are deformed relative to lesser types. The seal has no ears 'because it is a

damaged quadruped' (*De Part. An.* 657ᵃ24; *Hist. An.* 498ᵃ32; cf. 487ᵇ23f.). Lobsters are deformed members of their group and use their claws not 'for their natural purpose', but for locomotion (*De Part. An.* 684ᵃ35f.). Cephalopods are like vertebrates bent double (*De Part. An.* 684ᵇ35f.). Flatfish are like one-eyed men: 'their nature is twisted' (*De Inc.* 714ᵃ6f.). All testacea, mussels, and the like are maimed, like seals and bats, and move 'against nature' (*De Inc.* 714ᵇ10f.). Serpents are stretched and legless saurians (*Hist. An.* 508ᵃ8f.). The nature of all amphibia from dolphins to newts seems to have been twisted (*Hist. An.* 589ᵇ29). The nature of tortoises (*De Part. An.* 671ᵃ16) and of fishes (*De Part. An.* 695ᵇ2f.) is stunted; so is the crocodile's tongue (*De Part. An.* 660ᵇ26f.: its jaws are upside down), and so is the mole (*Hist. An.* 533ᵃ1f.; cf. *De An.* 425ᵃ11). How much is Aristotle claiming here?

5.   And how do these passages fit the form of causal explanation which he regularly uses? Man has such and such organs because it is man's *logos* to have them (at least as regards the essential organs) (*De Part. An.* 640ᵃ33). The reason that some creatures have no blood is that this is part of the *logos* that defines their being (*De Part. An.* 678ᵃ32f.). Lobsters have claws because they are members of the group of clawed animals (*De Part. An.* 684ᵃ34). A certain breed of octopus have one row of suckers on their tentacles 'not as the best arrangement, but as one made necessary by their essential formula' (*De Part. An.* 685ᵇ15). The seal, though a viviparous quadruped, has no ears: if it did it would be because it was a viviparous quadruped. There are also more complicated versions. The elephant's mammae are not by its thighs for it is polydactylous and none such have them in that position (*De Part. An.* 688ᵇ6). Birds are bipeds because red-blooded creatures have only four limbs (*De Part. An.* 693ᵇ5). Men could not have wings because they are red-blooded (*De Inc.* 714ᵇ2). The crab's side functions as a back because it has several leading legs (*De Inc.* 713ᵇ12f.). These passages are perhaps not as vacuous as they sound: they still demand explanation. In conjunction with the passages alleging deformity they suggest the complete arbitrariness of generic standards. If the best Aristotle can do in the way of explanation is this sort of scholastic tautology, why should we not extend the system? Seals have no ears because they are earless quadrupeds. This is the antithesis of explanation. There can be no answer to the question 'why is *x*

itself?', for 'that is what *x* is' is itself the ultimate answer (*Met.* VII, 1041ᵃ12f.). We can, of course, ask why there should be anything that fits the definition of *x*, and be nothing to fit the definition of some *y* (such as the goat-stag).

6.   D. M. Balme (MANSION) has drawn attention to the lack of any uniform or unified taxonomy in Aristotle's biology (cf. A. C. LLOYD (1); BALME (1)). He considers that Aristotle may have hoped for such a taxonomy. But there are difficulties. SINGER ((2) pp. 41f.) thought that Aristotle's methods were descriptive rather than strictly classificatory, and that no attempt was therefore to be expected to avoid the same creature's appearing under more than one heading. This may be so, although Aristotle attacks the Platonic system of division on precisely this point (*De Part. An.* 642ᵇ30f.; cf. *Met.* VII, 1037ᵇ28f.). But even if Aristotle is attempting classification he cannot hope for a wholly exact nomenclature. We must examine animals 'according to their kinds' (*De Part. An.* 643ᵇ10f.), but these kinds often cannot be precisely delimited, nor located inarguably in higher groups. 'Nature stretches without a break from lifeless objects to animals through things that are animated but not animals, so that there seems to be very little difference between one thing and the next, they are so close together' (*De Part. An.* 681ᵃ12f.; cf. *Hist. An.* 588ᵇ4f.).[1] The definition of 'continuity' or 'being without a break' (*Phys.* V, 227ᵃ10f.) precisely suggests that all 'adjacent' groups in a continuum share some individuals, and that no continuum therefore can be rigidly divided, once and for all. Sea-squirts come half-way between plant and animal; sea anemones likewise are like plants 'in being incomplete and fastening tightly upon the rocks' (*De Part. An.* 681ᵇ5). Cetacea, seals, bats, and Libyan ostriches are all intermediate between different groups (*De Part. An.* 697ᵃ15f.). Mussels and the like are between plants and animals (*De Gen. An.* 731ᵇ8). Indeed what plants are to earth, shellfish are to water (*De*

---

[1] 'So that there seems to be' represents the Greek ὥστε δοκεῖν: *dokein* differs from *phainesthai* in being a matter of opinion rather than appearance. It is more likely that Aristotle here, and in similar contexts, reports common judgement rather than illusory appearance. It *may* be that he would wish to reject such judgements, or at least to modify them, and I shall point to the existence of discontinuous *gene*. But we cannot assume that where Aristotle uses *dokein* he is expressing doubt about the thesis in question: on the contrary, 'what everyone thinks (ὃ πᾶσι δοκεῖ), we say is true' (N.E. X, 1172ᵇ36f.: see chapter VI). I may sometimes make Aristotle sound less tentative than he was: I do not think this one of the occasions.

Gen. An. 761ᵃ13f.). Pigs are midway between the cloven and the solid-hoofed, both types occurring (*De Gen. An.* 774ᵇ19). Hares are mixed *vis-à-vis* the two types of vivipara, producing both complete and incomplete offspring (*De Gen. An.* 774ᵇ5). The crocodile is both a land and a water animal (*De Part. An.* 690ᵇ22). The selachians are midway between vivipara and ovipara (*De Gen. An.* 733ᵇ1f., 749ᵃ17f.). These intermediaries play less of a part in the less considered *Historia Animalium*, but even here Aristotle reminds us that it is impossible to draw hard divisions, taking testacea as a bridge example (588ᵇ4). He also recognizes that crosses between species can produce fertile offspring that breed more or less true (though with a tendency to grow more like the mother species) (*De Gen. An.* 738ᵇ27f.): only mules are generally sterile (*De Gen. An.* 746ᵇ14f.). He notes especially the wolf–bitch cross, the fox–dog (which produces the Laconian hound) and the Indian dog, one of whose grandparents is allegedly (*Hist. An.* 607ᵃ3f.; corrected to 'a wild dog-like animal' *De Gen. An.* 746ᵃ33: A. PLATT) a tiger. Certain hawks, the rhinobatus, most Libyan animals (*De Gen. An.* 746ᵃ29f.) may also be hybrids; the partridge and the common fowl interbreed as well (*De Gen. An.* 738ᵇ32f.). In discussing the true-bird eagle he notes, unbelievingly but without disdain, the popular belief that this is the only true-bred bird: 'all others have been mixed up and adulterated by each other' (*Hist. An.* 619ᵃ10).

7.   No Aristotelian classification can be other than flexible in the nomenclature employed—a fact also instanced in the psychological divisions which he employs (cf. ANDO pp. 70f.; SKEMP p. 56; SOLMSEN (1)). 'There are in a way infinitely many parts of the soul' (*De An.* 432ᵃ24f.), precisely because any such parts are mere abstractions from the whole life of the organism (*De An.* 411ᵃ26f.). What we call a given feature of the process of living, how we relate it to other features may well vary for our convenience: there is no once and for all psychological analysis: remembering the frequent Aristotelian parallel between biology and psychology we should not be surprised if the biological continuum is similarly fluid. How can there be any generic groups in such a continuum?

8.   How, in particular, can Aristotle accommodate the difference he alleges between analogous and homologous organs? Within phenotypes, morphologically similar groups, variety consists in the homologous parts' being bigger or smaller (*Hist. An.* 486ᵃ15f.; *De*

Part. An. 644^{a}13f.). Variations between such phenotypes are such that structures can only be analogous, functionally rather than morphologically similar, as are hair, feathers, and scales (*De Gen. An.* 782^{a}17f.). In modern terms, the wings of a bird and the arms of a man are homologous; the wings of a bird and those of an insect are analogous (BLUM pp. 181f.). Yet the continuum thesis would seem to suggest that all variation should be upon a single theme. 'We cannot find a single name to give to cuttle-fish shell, fish-bone, and spine, but these too have common properties as if there were some single nature' (*Post. An.* 98^{a}20f.; cf. *Hist. An.* 497^{b}20, *De Part. An.* 652^{a}3f., 653^{b}35f.).

9. To summarize the questions I have raised: (i) what is involved in the priority of human beings, particularly male human beings? (ii) how much is Aristotle claiming when he describes e.g. seals as deformed quadrupeds? (iii) what sense can we give to the apparently vacuous explanations of structures? (iv) how do these explanations cohere with the notion of deformity? (v) what, if anything, is suggested by the continuum thesis, and how can we fit the fact of stable and distinct generic kinds into this thesis?[2] (vi) how in particular are we to handle the difference between analogous and homologous organs? A seventh question, how we are to relate the sort of explanation I have described as 'making sense of' to all this, is not unconnected with the first six, particularly the fifth, but must wait a little longer.

10. The answers to these questions are perhaps not beyond all human conjecture, but they should certainly involve a much lengthier treatment from both Aristotelian scholarship and the philosophy of biology than I can attempt within the limits of my present discourse. It is the mark of a properly cultured man not to demand more accuracy than the subject matter allows (*N.E.* I, 1094^{b}23; *Met.* II*, 994^{b}32f.; the Hippocratic *On Ancient Medicine* ch. 9; PANTIN pp. 20f.) or requires; it is sometimes necessary to demand even less. It is not possible to meet every possible objection within finite time: some things will have to be assumed (cf. *Met.* I, 992^{b}24f.).

---

[2] The question can be phrased more generally: how is it, in a world where there are infinitely many degrees of similarity and dissimilarity, where individuals are various in indefinitely many ways, that there are stable and distinct kinds to be observed? With such variety theoretically available, why are not there so many 'intermediary species' as to make all species boundaries wholly arbitrary? (see II.3.11).

11. I begin from the obvious fact that we live in a world of more or less stable and distinct generic lines, in the sense that entities of a certain type produce offspring of that type rather than any other (cf. *Met.* VII, 1032ᵃ16f.: 'man begets man'). There are differences between things and these differences are to a considerable extent perpetuated. A well-known fragment of Epicrates mocks the Platonic Academy for its concern with the problem of division, and philosophers have generally disregarded or disdained Plato's efforts 'to slice at the natural joints and to try not to snap off any part, like a bad cook' (*Phdr.* 265ᶜ). The introduction and the culmination of *The Sophist* are habitually ignored (though see ACKRILL (1)). Like Aristotle Plato is unable to locate generic kinds unequivocally as subclasses of larger kinds: are birds flying land-creatures (*Pol.* 264) or feathered sea-creatures (*Sph.* 220ᵇ)? Are we to suppose that there is an actual solution to this or similar problems? In a world of totally fixed species, where bats are bats and eels are eels and ever more shall be so, there is surely no solution which is more than a decision on our part to note certain homologies and disregard others. We employ the more informative description: to call a whale a fish is to imply that it has no limbs, lives in the sea etc. To call it a mammal is to remind one's hearers that it breathes air, suckles its young, gives meat rather than fish-flesh etc. We label it according to our current interests and there is no sense in asking for the 'correct' label. Plato seems to have thought otherwise, that it was possible to divide 'according to form', rather than merely according 'to the name itself' (*Rpb.* 454ᵃ), that it was possible to infer the models which the demiurge had used (*Sph.* 265ᶜ, *Tim.*). In supposing this he was saying no more than common sense would suggest. There clearly are larger groupings than those of species level: if it were not so descriptions of animal forms would be immeasurably more tedious. Within the limits of such groups, morphologically isolated, as Birds, Fishes, Cephalopods, Testacea, variation is in terms of more and less (*De Part. An.* 644ᵇ7f.), thereby permitting much more compendious descriptions. A *genos* is a collection of animals whose differences are of excess or defect, whose parts are homologous; specific, formal sameness occurs where the definition of the group permits no such differentiation (*De Part. An.* 645ᵇ23f.). Species, being units (see II.3.3) are indivisible (*De Part. An.* 643ᵃ8f.). It is a mistake to break up 'homogeneous' animals (*De Part. An.* 642ᵇ16), for this is to ignore the obvious unity of the group; nor should

wider kinds (such as Bird-and-Fish) be posited, for animals of different *gene* are only analogously structured. But though these *gene* are not arbitrary, it is the species which are the reality (*De Part. An.* 644ª24). There is, as it were, no consensual community of Birds (cf. II.1.28).

12. It may be that this difference between *genos* and species in point of reality should be connected with the remark in *Categories* (2ᵇ7f.) that 'of the secondary substances the species is more a substance than the *genos*, since it is nearer to the primary substance (the individual)'. Similarly 'being a man is closer to what is peculiar to Coriscus than being an animal is' (*De Gen. An.* 767ᵇ31). But 'animal' is certainly not the name of a *genos* in the biological sense, and *gene* do have an existence, whereas animalkind does not—there simply being lots of creatures all capable of sentience. Is the whole distinction simply one of degree? 'What would be found common to horse and ass, the *genos* nearest them, has not received a name, but would doubtless be both, like a mule' (*Met.* VII, 1033ᵇ34). There is no creature which is just an ordinary horse-ass (apart from the anomalous mule), while there are creatures which are ordinary horses, exemplifying all or most of the characteristics of horses in general. The *genos* is therefore not as real as the species, for there is no one good example of the *genos*, and there is or could be of the species. The *genos* is an inferred grouping. Being an animal is just being animated and sentient: not only is there not, but there could not be supposed to be, a creature that was just an ordinary animal (with one possible exception: II.2.28). I *identify* certain creatures as men; I only *describe* them as animals (cf. Woods: MORAVCSIK).

13. Is there any connection between being homogeneous in the sense defined above and being homogeneous in the more ordinary, genetic sense (*Met.* V, 1024ª29f.)? 'Obviously not, for Aristotelian species are immutable and can be related only descriptively, not historically'. But is this so? Species can interbreed (II.2.6), and there is no obvious reason why the intermediary species should not be supposed the product of such hybridization. Continuity between animals, plants, and the inanimate does not necessarily imply a like continuity between kinds and species: an entity may be certainly a sponge, but only doubtfully an animal—the mere fact that we cannot say for certain whether pigs are solid or cloven-hoofed (for as a species they have characteristics of either) does not mean that we

cannot be certain that an animal is a pig. But the existence of hybrids *does* raise this question, just as the existence of Libyan ostriches raises the question 'is it bird or beast?'. There is no general statement in Aristotle's extant works of continuity between kinds and species: there are particular examples of such continuity. And once the rigid barriers between species have been lowered, can we not imagine that intermediaries are perhaps hybrids, that 'as-it-were deformed' animals are precisely de-formed (II.2.15)? To be sure, animals are said to be 'as-it-were divided plants' (*De Gen. An.* 731ᵃ21), presumably without any realistic implication. But if we suppose a historical relationship between species (if species are not related, seals may as well be deformed fish), we can take Aristotle's comparisons more seriously, and also his explanations.

14. 'But surely I have also cited the evidence that proves the fixity of Aristotelian species?' Man begets man. 'Coming to be follows being' (*De Gen. An.* 778ᵇ2f.). Acorns come only from oaks (not just because it is not an acorn if it does not) and any form of entity comes only from an entity with the same form. The only way to breed cats is to breed from adult cats. These objections are not enough, for they would be admitted by any reasonable transformist theory, but there is a truth hidden in them. Parents do not produce offspring of just any form, but of their own (*De. Gen. An.* 715ᵇ12f.)—otherwise there would be no stability of kinds at all. But to argue against all trans-formist theories on this account is far too general an argument (cf. *De Gen. An.* 748ᵃ8f.). Equally, to argue against them because each species strives for eternal being is too general (cf. IV.2.11): to strive is not always to succeed (II.3.1).

15. Acorns do not always grow into oaks, at least into healthy oaks. Nature, as it were, can err, as in the case of atavisms or (absurdly) women: 'in these cases their nature has somehow strayed out of their kind' (*De Gen. An.* 767ᵇ7). Dwarves and megalocephalic types are marked as not-quite-men by their bad memories (*De Mem.* 453ᵃ31), as also are the young and old: the young because they are dwarfish, the old because they are decayed (see below on Death) (ibid.). A human child is rather like an animal, as an embryo is like a plant, and could certainly stay like that (cf. *Hist. An.* 588ᵇ1f.), if something went wrong with its constitution. The rapid growth of those who live luxuriously is unnatural (*Phys.* V, 230ᵇ1); so is the baldness, conjoined with excess pubic hair, brought on by over-indulgence in

sex (*Hist. An.* 518^{b}24). Physical changes follow upon moral decline as much as upon natural error and in all these ways a potential man may fail of his promise. What is more, deformities may be transmitted, though rarely, to one's children (*Hist. An.* 585^{b}28f.; *De Gen. An.* 721^{b}28f., 724^{a}3f.), and it is surely tempting to suppose that certain of the deformed groups were produced in much this way: others are presumably hybrids (the deformed are often also intermediate).

16. Consider the case of a talking horse. Such a horse would be human, for reasons mentioned in II.1.28. How can we imagine such creatures being produced? A mare–stallion match could not produce such a child. Something cannot come out of nothing; coming-to-be does follow being; there cannot be more in the offspring than in the parents. Wherever *B* has been produced by *A*, by art or generation, the form of *B* must have been in *A* (*De Gen. An.* 734^{a}30f.). Horses have no potential for speech: therefore they could not transmit it. A woman–stallion is equally unhelpful, for it is the male who more exemplifies and alone transmits the specific *eidos* (*De Gen. An.* 766^{a}30f.). The matter provided by the female could not drag itself up into humanity. We are left with a man–mare cross, which is unlikely since the material provided must at least be amenable to the form imposed (*De Gen. An.* 740^{b}18f.), or a very unsuccessful man–woman mating. 'That from which the seed comes has in a sense the same name as the offspring (in a sense, only, for woman is produced by man) unless the offspring be in imperfect form' (*Met.* VII, 1034^{b}1f.). Human life comprises beast life, just as beast life comprises vegetable life, just as the square potentially contains the triangle (*De An.* 414^{b}30) (presumably because we must be able to link three points if we can link four). The condition that the form of the product must have been in the producer can therefore be met in this case. Not that men entirely contain the potential for being horses, but that they contain the potential for being beasts; it is not impossible that human parents should fail to procreate qua humans but succeed qua animals in such a way that the product is technically monstrous (*De Gen. An.* 768^{a}2f.). 'But Aristotle explicitly denies that a human child with a ram's head (or the appearance of a ram's head) could be a ram, for the gestation periods of man, sheep, dog, ox, and so on are entirely different, and none of these animals could possibly be formed save in its proper period (*De Gen. An.* 769^{b}16f.).' Certainly, and this is enough to outlaw the sort of extreme case

which I have been employing as an example, but not enough to outlaw transformism. For Aristotle's point would undoubtedly be accepted by any modern transformist: that sort of instantaneous leap across species boundaries is not to be expected. Transformist change is more gradual than that.

17.   The talking horse must be human not only in soul, but also in ancestry. Could a human soul express itself in such a form (cf. *De An.* 407ᵇ20f.)? A horse larynx and mouth would need considerable modification before they could express any recognizable tongue. Teeth and hooves are no substitute for hands: certainly man has hands because he is intelligent rather than the reverse (*De Part. An.* 687ᵃ7), but a creature unable to manipulate its environment in characteristically human ways would find it very difficult to express its potential. Certainly the talking horse could try, but would most probably have given up in despair long before coming to its notional completion. If it survived it would have to be as a horse, though perhaps a cunning one. And if the monster bred true future generations would not even wish to talk. Only man can wish for the impossible.

18.   By parity of argument man is not a deformed ape. Apes more likely are deformed men (cf. *De Part. An.* 689ᵇ31f.: apes are intermediate between men and quadrupeds). Which is of course what Aristotle effectively says (II.2.3). If he did hold a general transformist theory then the only known candidate for First Ancestor is man. It is not irrelevant in this context, and in view of the point made above, to note that man's extreme variability (II.1.9) is also shown in the number of offspring in a litter and in the length of the gestation period (*De Gen. An.* 772ᵇ6f.). By attributing this doctrine to him we immediately provide a sense for the polarity of man, the deformity of seals, moles, and the rest, and for such judgements as that lobsters have claws because they are members of the *genos* of clawed animals. Nor is man's historical priority utterly unreasonable: it has at least been suggested, perhaps ironically, as an alternative to more orthodox theories by GOLDSTEIN ((1) p. 494: 'the less perfect becomes intelligible as a variation and aberration of the "perfect", but not the opposite'; GRENE (2) p. 237).

19.   Before modifying this account in fairly simple ways to answer my remaining problems, I wish to suggest that neither Aristotelian nor orthodox transformism are to be taken simply as flat, scientific

theories. Whereas it purports to be a purely historical account evolutionary transformism is in great measure a way of marking out the present world, with man triumphant in the centre.

20. The theory of evolutionary transformism, in particular unifocal evolutionary transformism, is frequently presented in this age as a fact quite as certain as that the world is round (cf. WITTGENSTEIN (2) pp. 26–7). Any layman who hears it questioned is almost certain to find himself attributing unworthy motives to the questioner. Nineteenth-century popular Darwinianism, as cultivated by Herbert Spencer, is now generally recognized as scientistic rather than scientific, the expression of that age's *laissez-faire* capitalism (GREEN). Huxley's evolutionary ethics and Chardin's mysticism are also accepted as largely poetic pictures of man in the world. In fact few writers on evolution can resist the temptation to show its 'meaning' for us. Evolutionary theory is scientifically a set of hypotheses, few of which are even open to direct confirmation; emotionally it is as dominant a myth as the notion of 'procession' was in late antiquity and the Middle Ages (BREHIER pp. 43f.). Its force is emotional and not scientific. Considered as a theory it is far from secure—though this is not to excuse the appallingly bad arguments loosed against it by philosophers who ought to know better (cf. HULL), as that 'the survival of the fittest' is a tautology. The original Darwinian position amounts to precisely the combination of random variation and selective death to which Aristotle objects in Empedocleanism (*Phys.* II, 198^{b}29f.). That such variation does occur within a given population is certain (see the famous case of black versus white moths in industrial areas: KETTLEWELL) but largely irrelevant. As SIMPSON ((1) pp. 73f.) observes, if new forms are produced only by isolating existing tendencies the end result would be a dead level of non-varying, enclosed types—quite apart from the absurdity (?) of supposing that the earliest micro-organisms already contained the potential for humanity. We must therefore hopefully appeal to mutation and to the magic of hybridization. Known mutations, resulting from 'damage' to the genetic material, are overwhelmingly harmful, and it is sometimes suggested that beneficent mutations have had insufficient time to accumulate unless some other factor than sheer chance is involved (cf. HARRIS pp. 233f.). In fact the fossil record seems to suggest (though SIMPSON (1) pp. 103f., disputes this) that we can only connect living creatures into genealogies on

the assumption of quantum evolution, 'macro-evolution' (BER-
TALANFFY (1) pp. 85f., 180f.), a form of relatively sudden change 'for
which no laboratory evidence is available, and no satisfactory
explanation yet forthcoming' (MEDAWAR). Consider the famous
'demonstration' that Equus is descended from the much smaller
Eohippus. What of Eohippus itself? 'Eohippus had no direct
ancestors on either continent [*sic*], so far as we know, and its sudden
appearance is part of a dramatic and mysterious episode in the
history of life' (SIMPSON (2) p. 115). The author of this passage later
speaks with complete confidence of Eohippus's descent from the
condylarth. At this point we may well wonder what would, in
practice, be allowed to disprove evolutionary transformism
(BERTALANFFY (1) pp. 89f., see BECKNER pp. 163f., HULL). It appears
to function solely as a very general model into which various facts
can be fitted, and which has neither predictive nor (as yet) ex-
planatory force. The only reason for believing it is as a vague, near-
explanation of structural homology, yet there are parallels which
cannot plausibly be explained by common ancestry: the eyes of the
octopus and of man; men and leeches etc. To concentrate on the
problem of descent is to avert one's eyes from the possibility of
more direct explanations, and leads to such loose claims as that *x*
has such and such organs 'because' its ancestors did. Organisms
'make sense', and to insist on transformism as the basic condition
for scientific investigation at the expense of more immediate explanations is to make nonsense both of the organic world and of the
very concepts, such as 'adaptation', employed in neo-Darwinian
theory. It leads to the telling of fairy-stories hailed as demonstrations which can usually be told in reverse without disturbing any
particular facts (THOMPSON; cf. the case of breathing lung and
hydrostatic bladder, SIMPSON (1) p. 192).

21. My purpose in making these remarks is not to denounce
evolutionary transformism. I am neither qualified nor inclined to do
so. It is to point out that the view I have attributed to Aristotle is no
more mythical in purpose nor much more lacking in unequivocal,
concrete evidence than modern theory. Both evolutionary and
devolutionary transformism are in large part myths (likely enough
stories with a moral or metaphysical purpose), and the Aristotelian
story is almost as likely, even on modern terms, as the other. Aristotle
perhaps makes it too easy for himself by treating plants as rather

primitive animals, and by tentatively accepting the genetic trans-
mission of acquired characteristics (though he qualifies this in such
a way as to suggest that they can be transmitted only if they are part
of, or are implied by the form of the parent, and therefore innate
(*De Gen. An.* 724ª3f.)). If we cannot accept the theory as an account
of our history, we can conflate it with evolutionary transformism:
suppose that all terrestrial life does derive from highly complex
macro-molecules. On Aristotelian terms these would be larvae (*De
Gen. An.* 762ᵇ28f.; cf. Empedocles 31B62D–K) and all evolution
would be the working-out of a pre-set pattern, with man as the *telos*
of terrestrial life (see II.2.20). These larvae, sown by a proto-man,
or (as is more likely) generated by the earth itself, would derive their
form from an earlier possessor: the earth itself, we may suppose,
contained the form of man.

22.   Such a conflation, in fact, is also implied by certain of Aristotle's
claims or admissions. The modification needed to make an essentially
devolutionary view acceptable to us as biologists is also needed to
make the view compatible with Aristotle's recorded words. For
though Aristotle may have been, in part, a devolutionary transformist, he did not have a universal or unifocal theory. The fact that
dissection of one sort of animal can give information about others
(*De Gen. An.* 746ª21f.), the theory of difference by excess and defect
(revived in D'arcy Thompson's Transformations), such claims as
that the crocodile's jaws are upside down (*De Part. An.* 660ᵇ30) all
tend to show a family relationship between living things. But some
creatures are produced not from parents of the same kind, but
spontaneously (*De Gen. An.* 762ª8f.). Not all living creatures can be
forced into a single family tree, for Oceanus and Tethys have not
ceased to procreate. This may well be a concession to apparent facts
against his general theory: he records that testacea appear in the
same area as their congeners (*Hist. An.* 546ᵇ31f.), and his logic
should require him to outlaw these events. In this context SHERRING-
TON's remark (p. 98) that 'Aristotle had no expectation of the fact
that every individual is always a bud from a previous one' is
peculiarly wrong-headed: coming-to-be follows being (cf. BALME
(2)). Faced by the apparent lack of parented eggs in certain cases
Aristotle is unwilling to disregard the phenomena in the name of
theory (cf. *De Gen. An.* 748ª11, 760ᵇ30f.). None the less testacea and
certain insects are enough to cast universal transformism into doubt.

The phenomenon of *gene*, mentioned at II.2.11f., also provides a difficulty.

23.   In the meantime the causal explanations cited at II.2.5 have to be incorporated into my account. That lobsters have claws because they are members of a particular *genos* is obviously explicable. The lobster's claws are not used for the same ends as those of its *homogenoi*, but for locomotion: we identify them as claws, and hence lobsters as crustaceans, by their structure, which is not best suited to the end for which they are actually employed. On the basis of a belief that organisms make sense or have made sense, we conclude that claws are part of the lobster's material inheritance. The lobster is a viably deformed crustacean. Every animal-type is given material with which to work, and to use it for one end is to do without it for another (see App. A.7). Thus certain creatures have to have a single row of teeth and a third stomach because they have horns (*Post. An.* 98ᵃ16f.; *De Part. An.* 663ᵇ31f., 674ᵃ22f.): they have no material for upper front teeth and must therefore have additional digestive apparatus if they are to survive. Nature does the best it can with the material provided by genetic degeneration (cf. *De Gen. An.* 744ᵇ16, *De Inc.* 708ᵃ9f.): this is, of course, consistent with its being the result of selection. Non-viable deformities precisely do not survive (*De Gen. An.* 771ᵃ11f.): those that do, make sense. The crab's side functions as a back because it has several leading legs (*De Inc.* 713ᵇ31f.). That is, the crab's side functions as a back because the crab moves obliquely; it moves obliquely because otherwise (there being several leading legs, which bend obliquely because the crab is a hole-dweller) the legs would get entangled. Given the crab's crustacean heritage it can only survive as a hole-dweller if certain morphological and functional adaptations take place. Its present structure and habits can be understood in terms of its end (see II.3.14f.). The connection between the having of blood and the having of four limbs (including fins or flippers), which is at the root of some of the passages cited (II.2.5), may be similarly explicable, though Aristotle does not and perhaps cannot provide any such account. He remains convinced that the constant coincidence of two or more characteristics cannot be just coincidence 'as always throwing a six at dice would be' (*E.E.* 1247ᵇ17). Some adaptations are positive, whether in the exaggeration of an existing organ or in the acquiring of new habits, and others negative: the seal 'lost its ears'

because they would be a hindrance in the water—a connection revealed by the cetaceans' lack of ears (*De Gen. An.* 781^{b}23). Other adaptations are merely material consequences of the essential: we need not assume that everything is for the best, and in this respect Aristotelianism is much less teleological than some of the early Darwinians. Yet other characters are not even derivatively necessary —a fact revealed by their variability within the species (cf. *De Gen. An.* 778^{a}30f.).

24. Creatures take up different habits where there are different food supplies (*Pol.* I, 1256^{a}21f., cf. *Hist. An.* 605^{b}22f.). Subsequent generations may acquire organs suited to these ways, by normal processes of more and less variation. Having pipes is posterior to learning to play pipes, for pipes are superfluous without the capacity (*De Gen. An.* 742^{a}25f.). Structural change is dependent, in the broadest sense, on ethical. As is known in folklore: the true-bird eagle was once a man, transformed in punishment for his in-hospitality (*Hist. An.* 619^{a}18). But we are not confronted merely by men 'making beasts of themselves' (or of their descendants): glandular change is also relevant. 'In the case of all amphibia their nature seems as if it has been warped, as it were, just as some males get to resemble the female, and vice versa. The fact is that some animals, if subjected to a modification in minute organs are liable to immense modifications in their general configuration. As in the case of gelded animals: only a minute organ is mutilated, and the creature passes from the male to the female form [! cf. *De Gen. An.* 716^{b}5f.]. We may infer then that if in the primary conformation of the embryo an infinitesimally small but essential organ sustains a change of magnitude one way or the other, the animal will in one case turn to male and in the other to female . . . And so by the occurrence of modification in minute organs it happens that one animal is terres-trial and another aquatic (and others both)' (*Hist. An.* 589^{b}29f.). Large effects issue from a small change at the centre (*De Motu* 701^{b}24f.).

25. In such a world of genetic devolution stable kinds are possible because nature does in general abhor the indefinite (*De Gen. An.* 715^{b}12f.): form is usually conserved across the generative process (see App. A). This stability is perhaps enough to ensure that the biological continuum is not wholly continuous—there are *gene* that form distinct groupings, not a single *genos* (animal-kind or life),

because animal types intermediate between the *gene* are not themselves stable enough to survive in intermediate form. Alternatively we may suppose that these *gene* are originally distinct, such as to have no common ancestor except the very first. This question is a problem in modern taxonomy (GOUDGE) as much as in Aristotelian: are phyla merely preferred groupings in the theoretical continuum of populations or historically prior kin-groups within which classes, families, and species have subsequently been differentiated? The second alternative should, I think, be associated with the larval theory mentioned above; the seeds in the beginning were modified into the various groups. The former goes with the straightforward devolutionary account. It is not necessary for me to suppose that Aristotle had made any choice between these positions. In either case the difference between homology and analogy is preserved: that lung and hydrostatic bladder are homologous but disanalogous is a consequence of the use of old material in a new way (see II.2.23). In the absence of evidence it is to his credit that he concerned himself with making sense of existing animals, not imaginary ones.

26. What happens in devolution (even if the larval version is preferred the other makes what is happening much clearer)? The male principle is what imparts motion to the material provided by the female (*De Gen. An.* 716^{a}4f., 766^{a}30f. *et al.*). It follows that the male enshrines the power of nature to a greater degree, a power evinced in a greater supply of heat. Descent down the hierarchy is accompanied by a gradual loss of heat and of differentiation. The *Problemata** suggest indeed that there are more female births in damp climates where there is less heat available (*Prob.** XIV, 909^{a}32). Male and female are one species, however (*Met.* X, 1058^{a}29f., *De Gen. An.* 730^{b}35), and degeneration does not get into its stride until later. Top, front, and side are progressively confused (*De Inc.* 706^{b}f.) until the plants bury their heads in the earth. So also are male and female (*De Gen. An.* 763^{b}20f.). This confusion is on the one hand reminiscent of the Platonic indictment of organic beings whose parts meddle in each others' affairs, and on the other of the Darwinian standard of evolutionary progress in terms of the differentiation of parts (DARWIN ch. 4, after Von Baer). Health requires distinctness and balance of parts. In 'the most perfectly finished animals' liver and spleen (*De Part. An.* 666^{a}28), heart and brain are distinct and equal. As heat (cf. *De Resp.* 477^{a}32: against

Empedocles), distinctions, and balance decline so also does unity. It is the heart, the centre of the heat (*De Juv.* 469^{b}9f.; *De Part. An.* 665^{a}10f., 670^{a}23f., 678^{b}2f.; *De Somno* 456^{a}4f.; *De Resp.* 474^{b}7f.), the 'heat of life' (*De Gen. An.* 762^{a}20) which makes semen fertile (*De Gen. An.* 736^{b}35f.), that is the basic standard of organic unity (*De Gen. An.* 773^{a}8f.). Aristotle's selection of the heart as against Alcmaeon's brain (*Met* V, 1013^{a}5f.) may have had many motives (see VI.13): one was the principle that whatever is the cause of perception in the organism must itself be especially perceptive (cf. *Met.* II*, 993^{b}24f.; *Post. An.* 72^{a}29f.) and the brain is manifestly not (*De Part. An.* 656^{a}23f.); another was the phenomena of embryology. Whereas Alcmaeon had believed that the brain was the first organ to form, Aristotle's experiments led him to conclude, incorrectly, that the heart came first (*De Juv.* 468^{b}28; *Hist. An.* 561^{a}4f.; *De Gen. An.* 734^{a}16f.). Embryological research at least confirmed him in his opinion of the process of differentiation (*De Gen. An.* 741^{b}25f.; E. S. RUSSELL (1) pp. 22f.): embryos are not formed by composition, but by differentiation of an existing whole. Taking the heart as the source of organic unity he concludes that all properly (i.e. red-) blooded animals are single (*De Inc.* 707^{a}24): polypodal creatures are as it were made up of several animals (cf. *De Juv.* 468^b: the nutritive soul is potentially plural). Insects can live long when divided into parts (*Hist. An.* 531^{b}30; *De Long. Vit.* 467^{a}18; *De Juv.* 468^{a}27; *De Resp.* 479^{a}1f.; *De Inc.* 707^{a}24; *De An.* 409^{a}8); plants for even longer (cf. II.2.13), can indeed reproduce by fission (*De Long. Vit.* 467^{a}18 *et al.*). Even in men both heart and genitals function 'like animals' (*De Motu* 703^{b}20f.), and the soul though one is potentially plural (*De An.* 413^{b}16f.). Human unity is built upon the ordering and control of an internal plurality, and 'in general there is the greatest diversity of parts in animals capable of living well' (*De Part. An.* 656^{a}3f.).

27. The unity of the organism is the singleness of the soul in the diversity of balanced parts. Lapses from this ideal are of the form of de-generation; health, physical and ethical, is to be found in what maintains the organism as itself. 'Each thing's good is what preserves it' (*Pol.* II, 1261^{b}9). Aristotle's account of degeneration, that is, reveals certain important aspects of human health: balance (see III.2.4f.), the preservation of unity (see III.3.6 and V.1.9f.), and perhaps the need to preserve the internal heat (see App. A). Dis-

order is schizophrenic: 'the impulses of the acratic man go in opposite directions' (*N.E.* I, 1102^{b}21). In losing their human unity, becoming imbalanced, creatures must consolidate their lesser powers as best they can. In doing so they are deprived of the power to make long-term plans for living well, and act only to achieve present satisfactions. Beasts are committed solely to seeking some lesser end (e.g. the building of nests) whose pursuit makes sense in terms of a higher-order pursuit of which they are unaware (e.g. the procreation of the species: cf. AGAR pp. 29f.). It is therefore in terms of our knowledge, of human activity, that we can make sense of the procedures of living organisms. Life's meaning, if such there be, is to be found in terms of human activities. We use everything as if it were for us (*Phys.* II, 194^{a}34), and so, in a sense, it is (see *Pol.* I, 1256^{b}15).

28. I have suggested (II.2.12) that there are creatures which are ordinary horses, which are at a mean in terms of their congeners; that there has been or might be something which was an ordinary horse-ass, similarly at a mean in respect of horses and asses; and that there neither was nor could be something which was just an ordinary animal, with perhaps one exception. The exception, of course, is man: 'the fineness of the blend in man is shown by his intelligence' (*De Gen. An.* 744^{a}30). Man, the most naked and least earthy of organisms (*De Gen. An.* 745^{b}15f.), is himself the mean of animal life. For men are built to the same specifications as the universe (*Hist. An.* 494^{a}26f., cf. II.2.3)—a doctrine also espoused, along with the claim that animals and birds are men sunk to the horizontal and that plants have stuck their heads into the earth, by the Neo-Confucian Chu Hsi (cited by CHANG pp. 265f.). And by Chinese thinkers before him. 'As we look at man's body, how much superior is it to that of other creatures and how similar to Heaven! . . . Man alone stands erect, looks straight ahead and assumes a correct posture . . . Heaven and Man are one' (Tung Chung-shu *c.* 179–104 B.C.: CHAN (2) pp. 281–2). The folk background of this and of Aristotle is the tale of the primeval giant from whom the world was made and of whom we are the unworthy descendants (see VI.2f.). What it says, in Aristotelian terms, is that the Human Form, the human way of living, is the one original form from which all other lives and forms are degenerate. The story of that decline gives us clues to what we need to stay human; that it is a decline from the

form of the world gives us another. Whether the world is human or superhuman, it is reasonable to suppose that what makes it *one* will also be what makes a man. If men are 'human' in that they mirror the world's form, let us seek if we may mirror it well.

II.3   Wholes and Ends

1.   Aristotle differs from Chardin and other moderns in that he does not suppose that the world had a beginning (*Phys.* VIII, 250ᵇ11f. *et al.*; see IV.1.13f., IV.2.10f.). There have always been men descended from earlier men, so that the generations of men are infinite (*Phys.* III, 206ᵃ26). And since men could not exist without beasts and plants and the total terrestrial environment (see *Pol.* I, 1256ᵇ15), these too have always existed, though no particular species need have. This fact does not conflict with the devolutionary thesis: even if there had always been e.g. cats, it does not follow that any particular cat's parents were just cats. There is, as it were, a continual spin-off of deformity from the central (human) line—a· deformity as necessary as that which produces women. Every species seeks to maintain itself in imitation of the celestial wheel (cf. IV.2.12): it does not follow that every species always succeeds, although the whole terrestrial economy of beasts, plants, and men is perhaps more successful. This introduces the concept of a self-maintaining biosphere, a sort of whole with man as its heart, the centre of its heat (cf. II.2.26). It is the nature of this whole with which I am now concerned.

2.   I shall argue that certain of Aristotle's remarks about *ousia*, being, can be explicated with the help of the concept of a teleologically identified whole. I shall defend 'final causation', so called, both in the case of admittedly living creatures and in that of the universe itself. Nature's 'purposiveness' is of the same order as the functioning of a living entity, the dynamic wholeness of independent organisms. I shall suggest that we only see 'what there is' in the world if we are aware of such dynamic wholes, and that it is in our awareness of the chief whole, the universe itself, that we find the being of being. This last point will recur in chapter V.3, 'finalistic identification' in III.3, the impossibility of non-dynamic entity in IV.1, and my defence of the phenomenological approach in VI.

3.   Aristotle was notoriously an exponent of the value and ontological priority of individual entities. He insisted that 'being' had as many senses as there were categories (*Met.* V, 1017ᵃ7f.; *N.E.* I,

1096ᵃ23f.) and that it was the individual entities which were primary. Even these did not 'exist' univocally, for each did so in the manner appropriate to what it was. The being of a stone is not the same as the being of a tree, simply because a stone is not a tree. Any entity exists in the mode proper to its kind—a fact which is presumably related to Aristotle's alternative suggestion that it is species which are *ousiai*, entities, not or not merely the individuals within them (*De Part. An.* 644ᵃ23f.). The unit in counting horses is one horse; in counting men, horses, and gods 'perhaps one animal' (*Met.* XIV, 1088ᵃ8f.). To count in such increasingly generalized units, culminating in the dummy expression 'thing', is to leave out more and more of the characteristics of the entities being counted. It is very easy to assume that the abstract *ousia*, *entitas*, is just what everything has in common with everything else, mere generalized existence—which is as devoid of content as generalized goodness (*N.E.* I, 1096ᵃ11f.; *E.E.* 1217ᵇ33f.). It is very difficult to believe that such a vacuity could occupy the peak of Aristotle's metaphysics. What is an *ousia*? What is *ousia*?

4. Plants and animals are not alive in the same sense (II.1.8): Mencius had made the same point (*Book of Mencius* 4.8: CHANG p. 34). If a wind-egg be examined for signs of completeness, 'it is complete qua vegetable embryo, but not qua animal's' (*De Gen. An.* 757ᵇ18f.). It is senseless to ask whether a thing is alive when one does not know what sort of life is in question. If a corpse's hair continues to grow we are not therefore confronted by a living man. 'For living things to exist is to be alive' (*De An.* 415ᵇ13). A dead man is not a man (*De Int.* 21ᵃ22f.; see V.2.3). But if this be so, how are we to deal with Aristotle's talk of nature? To say that nature does this or that, makes use of secretions generated by material necessity and so forth, can only be to say that certain organisms are involved in certain processes always or for the most part. That nature did *x* is only to say that *x* happened 'by nature', 'naturally'. There is no one nature, nor therefore a *telos* of the All (cf. ALLAN (1)). There are only natural objects, and the final causation so dear to Aristotle is only 'with reference to the essential nature in each [individual] case' (*Phys.* II, 198ᵇ8f.). The sense organs, for example, are arranged to suit the peculiar nature of each animal type (*De Part. An.* 657ᵃ11f.). Indeed there could not be one Nature, 'for in the case of things in which the distinction of prior and posterior is present that which is

predicable of them all cannot be something apart from them' (*Met.*
III, 999ª6f.; cf. *N.E.* I, 1096ª17), and living things do stand in such a
hierarchy (cf.II.2.16). Is this all that can be said about 'nature'?

5. The paradeigmatic *ousiai*, entities, are those with an obvious
principle of unity—animals, plants, natural bodies, stars (*Met.* VII,
1028ᵇ8f.; *De An.* 412ª11). Natural bodies in their totality, that is:
any particular bit of earth, fire, water is only derivatively so. Stuffs
such as earth, air, water, flesh are (apart from such theoretical
constructs as 'all the earth' or 'all the air') only potentially entities:
'it is only a heap until it is concocted and some one thing come to be
from them' (*Met.* VII, 1040ᵇ9f.). Earth is an element and identifiably
earthy in all its parts because it tends towards the centre of the
universe (*De Caelo* 268ᵇ13f.). It is completed, achieves its *telos* at
one point. Its movement, though—in a way it *is* a movement—is
simply the sum of the movements of the bits of earth. If there were a
smallest particle of earth this might be a true entity, but magnitude
is infinitely divisible (*Phys.* III, 207ᵇ15 *et al.*). What is one *x* is
indivisible qua *x* (*Phys.* III, 207ᵇ5f., cf. II.2.27). And what has or is
one entity is single (*Met.* III, 999ᵇ21). Earth and its cognates are not
the best examples of entities. The latter are necessarily anomoeomerous: they have structures, and their activity cannot in reason be
reduced to the chance agreement of their parts. 'In natural science
it is the composite and the entity which most concerns us, not the
materials, which are not found apart from the entity' (*De Part. An.*
645ª34f.). 'The living thing is an organization of different substances' (BERTALANFFY (2) pp. 100f.; cf. *De Part. An.* 646ª12f.). A
city is not a chance aggregate (*Pol.* V, 1303ª26), nor is any substantial
whole. A corpse is only derivatively one being, for it used to be the
corporeal aspect of a living thing (cf. *Met.* VII, 1035ᵇ24f.; *Meteor.*
389ᵇ31f.; *Pol.* I, 1253ª21f.; WOODGER (1) p. 89).

6. This analysis is confirmed by Aristotle's discussion of 'whole'
and 'all' (*Met.* V, 1023ᵇ26f.; cf. Pl. *Tht.* 204 b f.). A whole is something complete, perfect without addition and dependent for that
perfection upon its arrangement (cf. R. Levins on 'Complex
Systems': WADDINGTON III.73f.). Whatever is unaffected by re-
arrangement may have 'all' or '*pan*' attached to it, but not 'whole',
'*holon*'. We speak of 'all the water', not 'the whole water' (though we
may speak derivatively of 'the whole lake' and so on). A man, a horse,
a god, being unities, are also wholes. A molecule of water could of

course be called 'a water'—we should then speak of 'many waters' rather than of 'a lot of water' (*Met* X, 1056ᵇ16). We can speak of a mountain or a rock as if it were an entity, but half a rock would still be a rock, a bit of rock. For this very reason there is no way of saying precisely where a given mountain begins, nor of counting how many mountains there are. Admittedly we can count pebbles. Half a man is not a man, nor can a man sanely be called a bit of man (cf. II.1.7). An amoeba can form two amoebas, but it does not do so by simple fission: a new organization is involved—Driesch employed a parallel fact to refute mechanicism. It would make no difference to the rock's being a rock if we swapped parts of it around. Entities are organized and therefore wholes. 'In the case of aggregation and crystallization, the arrangement continually remains incomplete. At any time a new contribution of matter is possible from outside. In other words, in the star or crystal there is no inherent unity, confined within itself. All there is is simply the emergence of an accidentally rounded-off system' (CHARDIN p. 20; cf. BERTALANFFY (2) pp. 100f.; *De Gen. Corr.* 321ᵇ25.: it is surely arguable that stars do have a structure and unity—they are not just gobs of fire—and Aristotle would class them as living (*De Caelo* 292ᵃ19f.)). Matter can be introduced into a living entity as well, but the entity maintains its structure, and assimilates the matter in a way that 'non-entities' do not, and that was one of the earliest problems of philosophy. Life is self-maintaining, though not uniquely so—certain meteorological phenomena also are (cf. PANTIN pp. 37f.). These distinctions, though not always precise, are surely aspects of a real distinction in the world. There is a difference between entities and stuffs (cf. Strawson: LOUX pp. 67f.), a difference whose denial is associated with a model of time at once false and unaristotelian,[1] and the main examples of entities are living creatures and certain artificial wholes (houses, statues, tools).

7. Such artificial wholes are secondary (*Met.* V, 1023ᵇ35), for their forms are contained in their makers' lives (*Met.* VII, 1032ᵃ32). Consider two varieties of crustacean: one grows its shell, the other

---

[1] If all entities really are what e.g. rivers apparently are, namely groupings of ostensively selected entity-stages (river-stages), then we might reasonably replace the concept of an entity as against a stuff by the concept of a 'bit': a man would then indeed be a bit of J. Smith, and by extension, a bit of man. Quine's claim that e.g. Japanese actually has such a locution (as pidgin-English: 'five piecee ships' = 'five ships') seems to be mistaken.

makes it out of bits of stone and twig. If the former's is not an independent whole, but only a part, why should the latter's be anything but a part? A chair is only a chair because there are people to sit in it: apart from this functional aspect there is only an oddly formed piece of wood, steel, or plastic. A tool is a sort of inanimate slave (*E.E.* 1241ᵇ24f.), and I have already noted that slaves are, as it were, parts of their masters (cf. *N.E.* VIII, 1161ᵃ32f.). To live as a channel for another's life is not truly to live: to be only a part is to be derivative. An eye is not a real whole, for it can only be an eye if it is part of an organic and living body. 'There is no [mechanical] difference between what is attached by growth and what is not so attached; for the stick becomes a kind of detached member' (*De Motu* 702ᵇ4f.). Reasonably: for the hand is itself a tool (*De Part. An.* 687ᵃ18f.). Artificial wholes have the source of their unity in living wholes.

8. These reflections give rise to a further distinction, between the closed and the dynamic. Consider a lump of stone: it is merely a lump, having no unity or organization. It is incomplete, as Chardin would say, or more accurately it is non-complete. Simply as a lump there is no way of completing it. It is also closed: it does not speak to us of anything beyond itself, it has nowhere to go, it has no meaning, it is simply what it is. UEXKUELL cites (p. 106) the case of a Negro boy who could see a ladder as nothing but an arrangement of planks and holes until its use was demonstrated. A geologist of course might find significance in the stuff itself or even in certain features of the rock, but not in its being exactly this sort of lump: it does not have a sort, a species at all. This is so even if it is ruby, not yet *a* ruby, or even if it is clear evidence of some past material event. But you are now informed that it is a stone axe: and it at once becomes open, significant, meaningful. Even its shape is more readily discernable when we know that it has a specific shape, not an indifferent one: we can even label its accidental features, its failures, now that it is no longer only what it materially is. It is dynamic but its dynamism is derived from the men who made and used it. A similar story is of course true of the artificial products of non-human organisms, from the structured ant-hill to the stone worn down to a comfortable seat by generations of baboons. The point here is not that we can infer a cause for the shape of the object being studied, as a geologist also may: for if the said cause had happened

to produce a slightly different object no *failure* could possibly be involved. 'Disorder', at a material level, is logically impossible: all motions have *some* order. Nor that intentions are what is being inferred, for not all beasts can be said to have intentions, though they may leave products of an artificial sort (see below). Consider finally the case where the lump of stone turns out to be a fossil trilobite. You are made aware that it is the relic of a dynamic entity, a living being, in a more immediate sense than before. In either case it has a unity, a meaning which reaches beyond the given. It carries with it intimations of a world of experience, an environment that is more than an envelope, a world of action (see VI.3). We can say that the fossil has been damaged or is incomplete or is of a diseased specimen: a lump can be none of these things. 'In so far as it is regarded in itself it is only an object of contemplation or a presentation; but when considered as relative to something else . . . it is also a mnemonic token' (*De Mem.* 450ᵇ25f.). When that something else is a living thing the object is seen to have an essence, an *ousia*, against which its accidents can be plotted.

9. This sudden 'seeing in a new light', this glow as the object becomes more solid, more readily to be grasped by the mind, as what were once random features to be learnt (if at all) by rote become easily discernable patterns, is the intuitive aspect of that technique which a biologist or psychologist must employ more laboriously, that variety of explanation which is 'making sense of' the explicandum. The notion of teleological explanation has received considerable attention from philosophers of science (e.g. CANFIELD; BECKNER (1) (2)), particularly with a view to reducing such apparently causal explanation to some more material or efficient form. NAGEL's suggestion, for example, is that x is the function or point of y if y is the necessary condition of x. Beckner rightly observes that this is to substitute a greater claim: that the function of chlorophyll is to enable plants to perform photosynthesis does not imply that this is the only possible way in which photosynthesis could be performed ((1) pp. 129f.). Nor is it obvious, as Nagel's formula would make it, that the function of water's achieving maximum density at 4°C above freezing-point is the production of life (HENDERSON; BLUM p. 63)—though the latter is undoubtedly *a* function of the former. Nagel is confusing 'a function' and 'the function': with this proviso, and adding that his y is necessary in that there is no other way of

producing *x* within the material limits of the organism, his formula may stand. But not as a very illuminating one.

10.   None the less, 'an eye *is* made for seeing, and this is no accident even though no one or no One planned it in advance' (SIMPSON (1) pp. 181f.). Seeing is not only a function of the eye, an activity impossible to perform without that organ or some analogous and unavailable structure: seeing is the function of the eye. An eye is something that enables the organism to see, and the material object in question is not correctly identified except as such an eye. It is not a bit of flesh merely, but an organ, and organs are identified as such not by their material nature, nor by what produced them, but as functioning parts in an organic whole which would not have the structure they do, nor be perpetuated in the genetic line, had they no such point. So also, *mutatis mutandis*, the organic whole itself. This is how we identify our subjects, by grasping them under functional categories (cf. II.1.8).

11.   How do we set about so grasping them? How are we to justify taking one characteristic of a given individual as more essential than another—one 'Nagelian' function as *the* function? A given thing, commonly called a fan, may be used as a fan, as a cake-dish, as a missile, as a veil. If we try to name it once and for all as a fan, are we not disregarding its sheer individuality (see IV.2.6)? Yet how else can we deal with the world? Are all essences merely nominal, so that we may with equal right speak of a towble (a brown table (Copi: MORAVCSIK)) or of a cloak (a white man: cf. *De Int.* 18ᵃ18, *Met.* VII, 1031ᵃ19f.) (ACKRILL (2) pp. 130f.)) as of a table or a man as a substantial concept?

12.   Locke's claim that 'the boundaries of species are as men, and not as nature, makes them' (*Essay* III 6.30) is in fact true only on a prescientific level (cf. II.2.11f.). 'There is epistemic knowledge of a thing only when we know its essence (τὸ τί ἦν εἶναι)' (*Met.* VII, 1031ᵇ6f.).[2] It is conceivable that any two individuals resemble each other in some respect, but this does not warrant our *identifying* them under that respect, particularly if disjunctive properties (being either a horse or a man) are admitted. The usually 'accidental'

---

[2] The expression, τὸ τί ἦν εἶναι, I take to mean 'what it was to be': the concept is exactly that which I have introduced as dynamic identity (II.1.27n). That of a kitten is 'to be a cat': men are unusual in that they must choose their completion and may be mistaken in taking something as their purpose in being.

nature of such resemblance would be shown in our inability to infer other shared characteristics from the first and by the impossibility of assigning any one cause to e.g. my aunt's and your cat's both having the name Esmeralda, or both having blue hair. To identify two pieces of flesh as both being hearts, on the other hand, does permit various inferences to the likely properties of the rest of the organism, leads to the possibility of the cure of ills, and enables us to talk about a common cause. Similarly in identifying two creatures as walruses.[3]

13. In seeking to find what a given object *is* we cannot concern ourselves only with what *it* does, for it does non-denumerably many things and stands in non-denumerably many relations (see IV.2.7). We must also consider what those objects relevantly like it do, and it is obvious that this process may be circular, and must be self-reinforcing. We select the class of fleshy objects homologous with e.g. Callicles' heart and detect the relationships and habits of most or all such objects. It may be that some apparent hearts are thus revealed as nothing of the sort; it may be that the essence of hearts turns out to be something quite other than we had thought. It can hardly be doubted that the end of this investigation, revealing that Callicles' heart is essentially a blood-pump rather than a sensory ganglion (cf. II.2.26) or (this with the aid of imaginary rather than real cases: cf. *Met.* VII 1040ª29f. on the sun) a noise-maker, adds to our knowledge of reality. This is how Aristotle rebuts the identification of lungs as cushions for the heart (*De Part. An* 669ª18f.).[4] As before, however, it is living organisms themselves which provide the most obvious subjects for such analysis. Tools and organs alike are, at least at first, classified according to our impression of them: organisms classify themselves (cf. II.1.28). That this is an epistemological rather than an ontological difference does not remove its significance.

[3] Definitions which do not lead to the discovery of derived properties are futile (*De An.* I, 402ᵇ25f.), but even non-futile definitions may be more or less valuable, uncover more or fewer attendant properties. Similarly with the discovery of causes: it may be that there *is* some one cause for blue hair, but no one cause for the operation of that cause. Does being blue-haired matter to the organisms in the same way?

[4] Plato, whose account this was, might reply that lungs not employed for the human purpose were as deformed as lobsters' claws (II.2.23). If lungs were obviously cushions in man, the reply would be apt—we should not ignore the obvious merely because other creatures have homologous organs more or less adapted to disanalogous functions. But the identification is not obvious, and we should not assume deformity without reason. That such investigations are not rigorous does not make them valueless.

14. 'Of one thing we can be certain: that such a complicated and regular phenomenon must have some definite purpose' (MARAIS p. 178) 'It is so commonly true that degenerating structures are highly variable that this may be advanced as an empirical evolutionary generalisation' (SIMPSON (1) p. 75). Where there is no point to a structure, and therefore no evolutionary or conservative pressure on it, it tends to vary and to vanish (though a new organ materially equivalent may appear in its place). Existing structures are therefore reasonably to be identified functionally.

15. The final cause in terms of which a structure thus becomes intelligible is not an efficient cause. It is not itself an agent, nor is there any coherent sense in which the future acts upon the past in the case of final causation—the term 'causation' may indeed be misleading: functional and teleological analyses (which for my purposes are identical) may suggest causal explanations, but they are not themselves such. In the case of animal movement it is not the actual end-state (maybe never actualized at all) but the animal's desire that moves it efficiently. In the case of growth it is also not the final, adult form that somehow beckons to its past self: rather the embryonic entity has a structure that characteristically develops in certain ways, and whose potential is inherited from others who had actualized such a potential. The ways in which an embryo may develop, or an animal move to its goal, are very various as it makes use of the available material (BERTALANFFY (1) p. 57) but it is the present organism which so moves: 'at every cross-section of the spatio-temporal "event" which is development the organism is a complete and co-ordinated whole' (E. S. RUSSELL (1) p. 6). In the case of living entities, the paradeigmatic *ousiai*, formal and final cause are much the same (*Met.* VIII, 1044ª36).

16. This position is at once an acceptance of the view that the primary subjects of discourse are qualified particulars (Long: LOUX) and an insistence that the relevant qualities are, at least in the case of true entities and possibly in the case of stuffs, finalistic. The first point is a rejection of the argument from the convenience of the dummy expression 'thing' or '*x*' to the reality of something which is just a thing, just *x*: that some of the entities in the world are men does not prove that man is a human thing, a thing with the quality of humanity as an extra. Rather there are men, tables, trees, and stars. The identifying features of such entities define the sort of

unity they have, in respect of which we do not merely experience bits of flesh or matter, but entities. Identification is identification as something, and that something is in the clearest cases and perhaps in all a finalistic concept. Classification and functional analysis come to the same thing (cf. II.2.9).

17. Entities take time. There is neither motion nor rest at an instant (*Phys.* VI, 234ª24f.).[5] The human mind, or that of composite individuals, is in a certain period of time (*Met.* XII, 1075ª8), and similarly a certain amount of time is needed for a man to have achieved *eudaimonia* (*N.E.* I, 1098ª18). If a given process is completed in time *t* it will not therefore be half-finished in *t*/2 (*Phys.* VIII, 253ᵇ14f.; cf. VII, 250ª10f.). Thus at a mathematical instant there is no such thing even as an electron; for at an instant there is no particular energy-value, just as there is no particular velocity at a definite point in space. This by virtue of Heisenberg's formula in its stricter interpretation: 'if the instantaneous cut of the temporal flow according to Heisenberg's formula leaves energy completely undetermined, does not this prove that the universe needs a certain time to take on precise forms?' (Zawirski: quoted by CAPEK p. 239). Different structures need different periods for their existence: some occur so swiftly that we do not see them (cf. *Poet.* 1450ᵇ38f.); others too slowly for us to see, as certain cosmic changes (*Meteor.* 351ᵇ8f.). 'The organization of the protoplasm is not static but dynamic' (BERTALANFFY (1) p. 34): so also is any organism.

18. 'What each thing is when fully developed we call its nature, whether we are speaking of a man, a horse or a family' (*Pol.* I, 1252ᵇ32f.; see IV.2.16), though a given individual may of course fail of its promise. WOODGER ((2) pp. 131f.) objects with some justice that to say that a puppy is a dog is not just to say that it is going to be a dog. Its dogginess is shown as much in its present state as it will be later. But there are many routes along which an organism can grow to completion, and it is not inconceivable that some routes to being a grown dog should be indistinguishable from some routes to being a cat: its nature may not be fully clear till it has all its parts complete—a puppy that never grows to be an adult dog is at least

---

[5] It is of course true that, by virtue of the differential calculus, we can calculate the 'instantaneous speed' of more ordinary entities to any desired accuracy; but this 'speed' is only a theoretical limit of the average speeds over progressively smaller periods. It does not imagine motion at an instant.

not the best place to see what dogs are. Organisms are completable (II.3.8): 'all being is time' (Dogen: DUMOULIN p. 169), and where there is no sufficient time there is no being.

19. Thus, the paradeigmatic *ousiai* are wholes; the paradeigmatic wholes are living entities; living entities exist dynamically in such a way that they are wholes at any point in their existence (so that their parts exist by differentiation rather than the whole by combination: cf. II.2.26) but that their growth and nature is completed over a period of time. We can only pick such entities out, can only say what they are, by referring to their *ergon*, and to fail so to identify them is not merely to find no subject-matter for biology, it is not to live in the world of common sense at all—the reality from which we all begin is one of entities such as dogs and people, not of congeries of atoms or pieces of stuff (see II.1.7). If a purely material account of the world does not accommodate final 'causation' (as indeed it does not), so much the worse for that account (see VI.6f.).

20. 'A living organism is a hierarchical order of open systems which maintains itself in the exchange of components by virtue of its system conditions' (BERTALANFFY (1) p. 129; cf. HARRIS pp. 180f.). Not all 'systems of systems' are commonly thought to be living (e.g. certain meteorological phenomena), though it is not easy to say exactly why not.[6] Nor is the totality of things obviously an open system (though it is arguably not a closed one either (see TOULMIN pp. 23f.), but on Aristotle's view, and possibly correctly, it does maintain itself in the exchange of components. In a sense, it lives. 'We say that nature is the source of the elements' movements' (*De Caelo* 268^{b}16; cf. *Phys.* VIII, 250^{b}13f.). This clearly says more than that certain processes happen naturally, because of the structures of those things involved in the processes. The natural movements of earth and fire are towards their natural places, those parts of the world where there is no further pressure on them (*Phys.* IV, 212^{b}29f.). They move, and change into each other, as part of the natural process of the world. That they do change into each other has long been a problem for interpreters: it cannot be in the nature of earth to become fire (see V.2.3), nor can it be in the nature of primary matter to alternate between earthiness and fire, for primary

---

[6] Some questions are plainly relevant: does the system *store* energy? Does it take up energy from elsewhere if one source dries up?

matter has no nature and is not an entity at all (*Met.* XI, 1060ᵃ20f.; *De An.* 412ᵃ9; *De Gen. Corr.* 329ᵃ8f.; MCMULLIN, CHARLTON; cf. II.3.16). Matter is what makes it possible for an entity to be other than it is, and primary matter is simply the matter of the Whole. As Owens (MORAVCSIK) rightly says, it is a concept of natural philosophy, not of primitive physics. Although it is introduced by analogy with a carpenter's material we should rather reassess what we are ourselves to mean by 'material' than pretend that primary matter is anything like an independently discernable stuff, still less one with no discernable features. Such a pretence leads to the unanswerable questions (i) how can something without determinate nature be made into anything (it is because bronze has certain determinate properties that it can be turned into a statue)? (ii) if it can become anything at all why not just anything (against *Met.* XII, 1069ᵇ27f.)?[7] Rather is it the nature of the world to pulsate (cf. II.3.5). It is the world that changes, as Aristotle hints at *Phys.* IV, 214ᵃ26f.

21. 'The god and nature do nothing superfluously' (*De Caelo* 271ᵃ33). The god in question here is not the absolute deity outside space and time (*De Caelo* 279ᵃ12f.; see V.3.9, 15), but the world considered as a unitary and animated whole, divine nature (cf. *De Div.* 463ᵇ14; the Hippocratic *On the Sacred Disease*). I grant that it is the heavens which are here explicitly said to be alive (*De Caelo* 285ᵃ29), but in so far as they delimit and define the world, it is the world that lives: the heavens are the world's heart (see V.3.6). MERLAN (1) 3.75 observes that '*ouranos*' and '*kosmos*' are used interchangeably in *De Caelo* I.8 (and see REICHE pp. 111f.). This world is ceaselessly active: 'a god's activity is deathlessness' (*De Caelo* 286ᵃ8). 'From this all other things derive their being and their life, some more directly and others more obscurely' (*De Caelo* 279ᵃ28f.). Apart from the stability provided by the heavens, there is also the variety in unity generated by the motion of the sun (*De Gen. Corr.* 336ᵃ32f.), which plays its part in sexual reproduction (*Met.*

---

[7] Attempts to eliminate Prime Matter entirely from Aristotle's system (by KING or CHARLTON) seem doomed as long as the Elements are offered as the ultimate material of the universe. I am inclined to think that a better candidate is the pair of polarities, 'hot' or 'cold' and 'wet' or 'dry' (as *De Part. An.* 646ᵃ17f.). Prime Matter certainly does not exist separately from these (*De Gen. Corr.* 329ᵃ24f.), and it is by virtue of their formal properties that elemental change is possible. For my present purposes, however, it is enough that 'Prime Matter' is not a stuff, but pure potentiality.

XI, 1071^{a}15; *Phys.* II, 194^{b}13; see below on Pneuma). The world is a whole, an organism, not an haphazard aggregate (*Met.* XII, 1069^{a}18f.: see 1076^{a}1f.; *De Part. An.* 641^{b}15f.). 'The world is a visible living creature, it contains all creatures that are visible and is itself an image of the intelligible and it has thus become a visible god, supreme in greatness and excellence, beauty, and perfection, a single, uniquely created heaven' (Pl. *Tim.* 92). Aristotle only once, in the extant works, likens the universe to an animal, and that in an *aporia* (*Phys.* VIII, 252^{b}24; and see *Peri Philosophias* frs. 18, 22 Ross), but it is not the parallel to which he objects in his solution, and it does not seem likely that he could consistently have done so (see IV.2.13; and *Peri Phil.* fr. 18, where Aristotle is said to have mocked those who thought the universe was a *made* thing: REICHE pp. 122f.).

22. 'In the works of nature the reason why and the beautiful are more present than in the works of craft' (*De Part. An.* 639^{b}19f.; cf. 645^{a}23f.; *Met.* XI, 1065^{b}2). The order and beauty of the heavens hailed at *De Part. An.* 641^{b}15ff. could perhaps be described as the mere consequence of the earth's rotation, and no mark of objective order, but it is perhaps also worth remembering that stars are not scattered randomly through space, and do follow laws of development and coexistence, even though they are not the ones we first expect. The world may still be an organic whole (at all levels it is a world of wholes—atoms, molecules, cells, stars, galaxies, and so forth: why should we not expect a total whole?). To show how Aristotle deals with these concepts, and remembering that not all events are teleologically explicable (*De Part. An.* 677^{a}15f.; *De Gen. An.* 778^{a}30f.; cf. *Phys.* II, 198^{b}17f.), I wish to consider a sequence of arguments, mostly against Empedocles, at *Physics* II, 198^{b}33f.

23. The first runs from 198^{b}33 to 199^{a}8: everything that happens *phusei*, 'by nature', happens always or for the most part, but nothing that happens *apo tuches*, 'by chance', or *apo tautomatou*, 'just of itself', happens thus frequently. Therefore no natural events are thus purely accidental, and therefore all natural events are non-accidental. But all non-accidental events are *heneka tou*, 'serve some purpose', are given sense by their ends. The apparent equivocation on 'accidental', to which most commentators object, need not, I think, entirely wreck this argument. It is important to remember that Aristotle is not here denying the possibility of something's happening

by necessity, as the unpurposed product of natural events, whether it happens often or only very occasionally. He is speaking of the persistence of certain types of event or organism. It does not rain to make the crops grow nor to make them spoil, but we cannot understand the persistence of this meteorological phenomenon simply by seeing how one particular rainstorm is produced. The fact that rain is always being produced makes it impossible to doubt that there is an organic system here, and such systems are 'finalistically' identified. To answer the question 'what is it?' we must reply in terms of its natural line of development. Events that are not themselves required consequences of a given system's working, but rather the occasional product of systems' interaction, are not generally repeated. It is impossible that everything should happen thus incidentally: there are systems at work of a self-maintaining sort such that their processes may be completed, deflected, and the like. These systems are grasped under functional categories—for there is no other way to grasp them. Sequences that are merely necessary under some system's operations cannot themselves account for or identify the system, for material causation is simply inadequate to defining a system as against an aggregate. It is ridiculous to suggest that the spine is (always) accidentally broken into vertebrae in the womb (*De Part. An.* 640ᵃ13f.: Empedocles 31ᴮ97ᴰ⁻ᴷ); *genesis*, the process of coming-to-be, is what it is because *ousia* is what it is (cf. II.3.15), and not vice versa—to suppose otherwise is not to have noticed the *ousia*. The world of nature can only be described finalistically.

24. The second argument runs from 199ᵃ31, and deals specifically with living things. In the production of craft the earlier stages provide the basis for the later, they are produced in due order. So are natural products. 'The egg is not merely a cell dividing as best it may, under the stress of simple and obviously mechanical conditions. It is "a builder which lays one stone here, another there, each of which is placed with reference to future development"' (E. B. Wilson 'The Cell in Development and Heredity' p. 1005: E. S. RUSSELL (2) p. 94). If the productions of craft are in some sense goal-directed, so are those of nature. Consider a house that is perfectly adequate for the general ends of houses: you are now informed by the proud owner that he did not commission architects and builders but secreted it himself. Why should you suddenly reverse your previous acceptance

of its goal-directedness? 'If the ship-building art were in the wood, it would produce ships in just the same way by nature' (*Phys.* II, 199^{b}28). Why should grown shells differ so radically from collected ones (II.3.7)? 'No hard and fast line can be drawn between behaviouristic activities . . . and physiological and morphogenic processes' (W. M. Wheeler, 'Foibles of Insects and Men'; E. S. RUSSELL (2) p. 102; cf. II.2.24). In the case of constructed houses the form exists apart from the individual house in the house-building art of the builder (*Met.* XII, 1070^{a}14, ^{b}33; cf. *Met.* VII, 1034^{a}24: 'the art is the form'). In natural products it exists directly in the product or in the whole of which the product is unambiguously a part. 'Craft is a source in another, nature in the self' (*Met.* XII, 1070^{a}7; *De Gen. An.* 735^{a}2f.). The distinction in the case of derivative 'entities' is unclear. Someone may urge that craftsmen have conscious purposes, whereas other creatures do not, nor (perhaps) even desire what we see to be the end of their 'actions'. But neither need craftsmen have explicit purposes, or blueprints—the more skilled the craftsmen the more like 'second nature' is his activity and the less he need think about it (see *Phys.* II, 199^{b}28; *N.E.* III, 1112^{b}1f.). We cannot conclude from the goal-directedness of natural entities that they are all aware of what they are doing, or that Nature is, but neither can we conclude from their (possible) insentience that they are not goal-directed (see *E.E.* 1224^{a}15f.). Spiders, stickle-backs, mice, and swallows are not the fortunate recipients of blind luck—they do not throw twigs or whatever about and find they have a 'nest': they build nests. How such a world of end-directed entities came about, or if it was thus from the beginning, may be disputed: that it is so now is indisputable. To ignore the end, the completion of an entity's life or action, is to remain ignorant of the ecologic of the situation. We cannot even delimit the class of nests except functionally: there is no generally valid material description of 'nests' or their methods of construction. 'Being a nest' is a teleological concept, and if we exclude such concepts we shall be unable to pick out those entities like nests and nest-builders which go to make up the world.

25. My point about shells introduces a consideration which will recur in III.3.5. Houses are not 'dead matter' but natural secretions of mankind. 'In a sense the handiwork is he that made it, in his activity' (*N.E.* IX, 1168^{a}7; *De Part. An.* 652^{b}13f. does not contradict this). The limits of an entity are not the limits of its immediate body:

further material may be incorporated into the entity (see Scott: GRENE (5) p. 124). The agent is responsible for his tools. This understanding of human and other constructs also makes the machine an inadequate model for interpreting living beings: machines are parts of living beings.

26. The third argument, 199ª33 to 199ᵇ13, is directed specifically against Empedoclean monstrosities. In discussing it we may note that neo-Empedocleanism, that amino-acids etc. exist prior to their organization and form cells by random combination, is not utterly without opponents at the present day. At every level of development we appear to be confronted by an organic whole and not a microcentaur. That monstrous births do occur is not a good argument against the 'prolepticity' of nature (a term introduced by PANTIN p. 58): there are, after all, similar effects in the operation of human craft. Monsters are precisely miscarriages, incidental to some main line of development, and if there were such creatures in the beginning they were the products of some corrupted principle. Particularly as seed precedes adult, as Empedocles admitted (cf. II.2.21): 'whole-natured forms rose first from the earth' (31B62). The second stage of the argument is *ad hominem*, a mocking reference to man-faced oxen and olive-bearing vines. That any organism is an arbitrary combination of parts is an absurdity. Our parts would not be what they are if they were not parts of us (cf. *De Gen. An.* 722ᵇ17f.). Neither this nor the previous point is the verbal one that creatures cannot be called monsters save in respect of some standard, nor parts without a whole to belong to. Rather it is imaginable but unbelievable that there could be things like independent hands or creatures whose parts are at odds with one another, except as corruptions of whole organisms (see II.2.23; though cf. III.3.15). 'The whole is the system that makes the parts the parts they are, even though the parts are the conditions (in traditional language, the material causes) for the existence of the whole' (GRENE (4) p. 196; see *Met.* V, 1019ª10). 'In all organisms the various organs do not become adjusted to each other by mutual wearing away . . . but from the very outset they are quite perfectly congruous with one another' (UEXKUELL p. 321). There is no such thing either as a bone or a blood-vessel in isolation: there is a skeleton, and a vascular system (*De Part. An.* 654ª32f.). Or rather, there is an animal. Development, both embryonically and (if such there be) genetically, is a matter of

increasing differentiation of an original whole, not of contingent and extraneous additions (cf. II.2.26).

27. 'Nothing can be the cause of its own generation' (*De Motu* 700^{b}1), nor can any entity come to be simply because it is of a sort to come to be (PRIOR (1) ch. 7): until it has come to be there is no such sort. Coming-to-be is therefore a matter of actualizing the potential of some currently existing entity. If (as seems likely) we are right to posit a temporal beginning of terrestrial life, that beginning was the realization of a pre-existing potency. The accidental is what is not required under a given description of an act or entity (*Met*. V, 1025^{a}14f.): it is incidental (as at *Phys*. II, 199^{b}20f.), not giving the clue to an organic and goal-directed system which may be expected to produce such events (as always throwing a six at dice strongly suggests a loaded die). The origin of life might have been such an accident—a possible result of material processes then occurring (an accidental meeting, as it were, rather than a rendezvous) which gives no clue to the real nature of those processes. But if that is the case we must still suppose that the pre-animate universe was one of systems, for it is only in such a context that accidents can happen. The notion of an unsystematic universe, a period when everything happened arbitrarily, is absurd: that is not how things are now, and even 'accidental' events require a more organized background. Purely Empedoclean, stochastic accounts of the origin of life are therefore outlawed.

28. The possibility remains that although the pre-animate universe was organic and although the production of life was always a possibility, the possibility was only κατὰ τὴν ὕλην (see V.2.6): the universe perhaps *can* produce life, but only in the sense that a living being *can* decay or wine go sour. Wine's being, its τὸ τί ἦν εἶναι, is not vinegar; a kitten's being is not a corpse. Life perhaps is a disease of matter: the universe best to be understood as a sidereal system, without reference to its incidental decay into the animate. The heart is a blood-pump which incidentally makes noises: the universe perhaps is a system of sidereal systems which incidentally makes creatures who seek to understand that system. There would still be hearts even if they were silent, but not if they could not pump blood. There would still be a sidereal universe even if there were no star-gazers, nor ever to be such.

29. The dilemma is not easily to be solved, if at all. Modern orthodoxy has a tendency to accept that the world's being is quite other than living, but it is unclear that orthodoxy has any sound grounds for this opinion. It is admittedly counter-intuitive to suppose that one can produce a living creature merely by combining a few elementary, unliving parts ('on the one hand, if they had no soul or life they could not endure; on the other, if they were as-it-were separate animals, they could not grow together to form one animal' (*De Gen. An.* 722^{b}22; cf. *Met.* V, 1014^{b}23f.))—the customary analogy with machines is, as we have seen, inadequate (II.3.25). That life is really incidental to the world's being is a conclusion so odd as to need much more defence than it normally receives: decay is, characteristically, a lessening of complexity, not its increase. The orthodox are also purveyors of paradox in that, in the act of identifying the universe in terms of the non-living, they are explaining it in terms of a vision of the universe which only exists as the vision of living beings: to say that we must make sense of the universe solely in physical terms is to accept a particular variety of life, a living vision of things as they are in themselves as the form and final cause of being. Aristotle was less confused in making sense of things in terms of a sort of life, a sort that we can share (see V.3.27, VI.14). Orthodoxy, in fact, is not obviously a triumph for reason, but rather a superstition. Consider: suppose a lump of clay sprouted locomotive organs and began to walk and talk. Suppose that this lump was unduly impressed by a modern philosopher and announced in ringing tones that the world was an unthinking mechanism, and clay a sort of sludge . . . If we were not completely mesmerized by the lump's mentor, it might occur to us that the lump was talking nonsense, merely because it was talking. If the universe can speak it is obviously not dumb.[8] Yet when a lump of carbon proceeds to bite its mental throat by denying intelligence to things it is acclaimed for the profundity of its pessimism and elected to the Royal Society. The notion that life is alien to the world is but the superstitious relic of Manichaean or Gnostic thought: superstitious because long-deprived of the metaphysical system that gave it sense. If the two-worlds thesis

---

[8] 'As well say that a chair is living, simply because there is a cat in it.' Certainly any life the chair has derives from the cat (and others; see II.3.7f.). But the universe and the cat are a living system as chair and cat are not. It is not in the end very convincing to claim that the universe derives its claim to life solely from its parts' life. But the final proof of the nature of the Whole's being must wait upon enlightenment (see V.3).

be denied it is absurd to suppose that we are not part of this one. The world is alive, for we are part of it (cf. A. R. Peacocke: RAMSEY pp. 35f.; BERTALANFFY (1) pp. 102f.): there are laws which govern our relation to our environment, there are processes in which our contributions cannot be clearly distinguished from the 'natural'. Nor do we miraculously disobey the second law of thermodynamics in order to display our independence (BLUM pp. 94f.; BERTALANFFY (3) pp. 73f.). 'The animal and plant communities (biocoenoses) in a certain area, such as a lake or a forest, are not mere aggregates of many organisms, but units ruled by definite laws. A biocoenosis is defined as a 'population system, maintaining itself in dynamic equilibrium' (Reswoy)' (BERTALANFFY (1) p. 51). A biocoenosis is not itself wholly an organism, though extreme cases can be imagined, but it is surely plausible to maintain that the universe is much more such a biocoenosis than a mere aggregate, and perhaps a whole in the strict sense. Certainly many parts of the world are unliving in themselves—but so are many parts of my body, and sheer weight and volume are not normally paramount. If there is such a thing as the world at all in a substantial sense, as there is not such a *thing* as a muddle (though things may be 'in a muddle'), then that world is an organism, and very probably a living one.

30.   The nature to which Aristotle refers need not be taken as an untypical appeal to some abstract principle but rather first to the nature of the Whole, and derivatively to the various distinct natures of those organisms and stuffs which are components and constituents of that Whole. The world is not merely everything that is the case, but rather everything subsumed in a unitary whole. We grow out of the world: plants have the earth as their stomach, and animals carry an earth about with them (*De Part. An.* 650ᵃ20f.). Like children from their parents (*N.E.* VIII, 1161ᵇ27) we are split off from the world. We take and return nourishment (cf. *Pol.* I, 1258ᵃ35), we are formed out of the environment and impose our form on it. Selachians (and, allegedly, cetacea) have their mouths underneath partly to permit their victims' occasional escape (*Hist. An.* 591ᵇ25f.: *De Part. An.* 696ᵇ26f.), partly to prevent their own gluttony's destroying them, and partly as a consequence of their given material (*De Part. An.* 696ᵇ26f.). Similarly the cells of our bodies live their own lives in a fashion not wholly unlike that of their independent cousins, but also serve to maintain the wider unity that is the human being. All living

entities are at once entities, and active (cf. II.1.7), and also material, and passive (at least in the sublunary world). The cells of our bodies must in some sense 'be aware' of their place in the body (as is clear from embryology, and regeneration), containing the form of the whole. Similarly all lesser entities maybe mirror the form of the Whole: 'all things naturally have something of the divine' (*N.E.* VII, 1153^b32: N.B. slightly different context). Men, in particular, who are the most perfect and complete of sublunary things, do so (see II.2.28, V.3).

31. 'I-ch'uan expressed it very well when he said that principle is but one but its manifestations are many. When heaven, earth and the myriad things are spoken of together, there is only one principle. As applied to man, there is in each individual a particular principle . . . The Great Ultimate is nothing other than Principle . . . The Great Ultimate is simply the principle of the highest good. Each and every person has in him the Great Ultimate and each and every thing has in it the Great Ultimate. What Master Chou calls the Great Ultimate is a name to express all the virtues and the highest good in Heaven, and Earth, man and things' (Chu Hsi: CHAN (2) pp. 635, 638, 640).

32. The god and nature do nothing superfluously, but they are not invariably successful. There are miscarriages, and there are incidental results which may or may not be fruitful. Matter was potentially living from the beginning (if there was a beginning), and finds its fulfilment in receiving form (see *Phys.* I, 192^a17). The ultimate form it 'hopes' to receive, as I have already hinted, is the divine life of the Prime (see below on Nous), and it is in so far as we too receive that form that we can understand the world. Soul and body, form and thing are made one by the moving principle (*Met.* XII, 1075^b37; cf. VIII 1045^b18; *De An.* 412^b6). Reality is that substantial world poised between form and matter, understood in so far as it is seen as expressing the intelligible form of Nous but not itself purely identical with that form. The fundamental *ousia* is neither notional bare matter nor the abstract quality of being: it is the world—it is This, Tathata, the So-it-is of Buddhism. Nothing else after all would fit: 'no common predicate indicates a "this" but rather a "such"' (*Met.* VII, 1039^a1f.), and the more general a concept the less substantial it is. The Being with which we should be concerned is no common property but the Whole. In this conclusion Aristotle is one with many 'mystical' philosophers: he differs at least from the

less sophisticated mystic in admitting the possibility of failure (at least at the sublunary level). Precisely because the Whole is a living and perennially unfolding whole (II.3.17) there is a real indeterminacy in event (see IV.1.11). The being and the intelligibility of the Whole lies in its perennial effort to reflect, to become Nous: the being of man is in the end the same.

III.1. Perception

1. I wish now to examine certain details of our existence and of the theories I have been expounding. I have been taking for granted that the human entity is an organic unity, at least potentially, and that this is an opinion which can be fairly attributed to Aristotle. I have also assumed that we can trust our perceptions of the world—that reality is what it appears to be. Finally, I have assumed that Aristotle's biological works may fairly be combed for helpful addenda to his ethics and metaphysics. The topic of organic unity will pervade the next three chapters, firstly in terms of man's (educable) awareness, secondly with reference to the moral good sense which is dependent upon the self-cultivation of a balanced disposition (the making of an organic entity), and finally with reference to the making of one's self in a social context. That reality is what it appears to be I shall affirm in this and, more metaphysically, in my concluding chapter. That his biological works must be taken seriously as considered expressions of his philosophical attitude, I shall affirm in this chapter.

2. It is convenient to study his account of sensory perception first through the eyes of Irving Block. In doing so, I shall discuss particularly the relation between the 'primary' and the 'special' senses, and the concept of the senses as self-aware which is used in the earlier biological works. I shall then consider the concepts of corrigibility and accuracy, and finally the doctrine of sense or the senses as means. The last point will lead on to the ethical mean; self-awareness and accuracy to my discussion of *nous*.

3. Where Aristotle sets himself to discuss some problem, such as those provided by the concept of sensory perception, which more modern investigators have solved or radically transformed, it becomes difficult to read him with due care. He avoids the Empedoclean complexities of visual rays issuing from the eye as from a lantern (*De An.* 435ª5f., *De Sensu* 437ᵇ9f.; cf. Pl. *Tim.* 45 c, *Tht.* 156 d f.) and so scores a point, but he also rejects other Empedoclean doctrines, that colours are emanations from the objects (*De Sensu* 440ª15f.; cf. III.1.19) and that light travels (*De An.* 418ᵇ20f.; *De*

Sensu 446ᵃ26f.), thereby straying irrevocably from the path of modern truth (though he does once show himself prepared to think of light's being propagated as a stream of particles (*Post. An.* 94ᵇ30)). Nor does he merely miss the way: he hardly seems to wish for the same destination. The questions which have oppressed later philosophers, of realism and idealism, physiology and psychology, seem not to trouble him. He employs bafflingly bad arguments to inane conclusions (as that there are no more than five senses (*De An.* 424ᵇ22)), unilluminating locutions (as that the sense-organ is potentially what the sense-object is actually (*De An.* 418ᵃ3f. *et al.*)) and illiberal value judgements (as that those with hard skins are ill-endowed with intelligence, those with soft well-endowed (*De An.* 421ᵃ23f.: see III.1.17). We may still learn from him.

4. The view of Ross and Nuyens, that the essays known as the *Parva Naturalia* represent an early, Platonizing phase superseded by the *De Anima*, seems to me to have been thoroughly refuted by BLOCK (1) (see also HARDIE p. 73). KAHN has taken Block's argument to its obvious conclusion with his rejection of Block's theory that the *De Anima* is actually superseded rather than elaborated in the *Parva Naturalia*: primary sense-awareness plays no great part in the earlier work, but there is no necessary contradiction with the later. *De Anima, Parva Naturalia, De Partibus* and *De Generatione Animalium* clearly form a compact series in their present form, and mark the late elaboration and discussion of things which had concerned Aristotle for most of his life.

5. Block bases his claim that Aristotle progressed beyond the doctrines of the *De Anima* on three observations: (i) that the concept of a primary sense and sense-organ is absent from the *De Anima*; (ii) the sense-organs are held to operate independently; (iii) the individual senses are self-aware—we see that we see, and so forth (*De An.* 425ᵇ12f.). It is clear that these points, in a modified form, demonstrate the priority of the *De Anima*; it is not clear to me that they demonstrate any radical inconsistency with the later accounts.

6. Certainly the common sensibles introduced at *De Anima* 418ᵃ16f., motion and rest, number, shape, and size, are not viewed as the special objects of some one sense defined (like the special senses: SORABJI) by its objects. Indeed Aristotle expressly denies that they could be so viewed (*De An.* 425ᵃ13f.): 'in that case all other senses would perceive them incidentally as sight perceives sweetness'

(as KAHN has pointed out, the clause at 425ᵃ14, ὧν ἑκάστῃ . . ., is part of the rejected hypothesis, not a description of the way each sense does in fact perceive the common sensibles: the contradiction between 425ᵃ15 and 425ᵃ27 imagined by HAMLYN (1) does not exist). 'Of the common sensibles we have a common awareness, not an incidental one: so there is no special sense for them' (*De An.* 425ᵃ27). The argument obviously makes no sense at all if 'common sense' refers to some special sense: rather we are aware of the common sensibles in every sensory dimension, or at any rate in those of sight and touch (*De An.* 418ᵃ19f., *De Sensu* 442ᵇ4f.). So far Block is correct, but his very accuracy reveals the presence of a unitary principle in perception. The fact that we know felt motion and seen motion to involve one and the same attribute shows that there is an over-all awareness. This judging faculty must also be invoked (as at *De An.* 426ᵇ10f.) to explain how we distinguish white and sweet (rather, colour, and taste) or compare bright and loud. If vision, taste, and the rest were really without any point of contact no such judgement would be possible.

7. Ross and Block are agreed that the *De Anima* places no especial stress, as being prior, on any part of the body, such as the heart (though Ross considers this a more, and Block (correctly) a less sophisticated position than that of the other biological works). Nor does it, but neither is there any rejection of such a stress. That the heart is the physiological base of emotion, notably anger and fear, is thrice remarked (*De An.* 403ᵃ30f., 408ᵇ5f., 432ᵇ31f.) though some other part is involved in the case of pleasure (*De An.* 433ᵃ1). Further Aristotle comments that the region round the heart is especially in need of the external, cooling air brought in by respiration (cf. II 2.26: the heart is the centre of the heat.) Further, although he does not name the heart or any other organ as the organ of touch, he does insist that the flesh is only the medium of touch (*De An.* 422ᵇ35f.) and 'the primary sense-organ is something else, inside' (*De An.* 422ᵇ22f.). Any such organ has an excellent claim to be the criterion of the animal's unity, for touch is the sense that makes a given creature an animal, and excess in the tangible is the only perceptual excess that destroys the animal (*De An.* 435ᵇ3f.). Finally: 'the air makes the pupil such and such, and this another, and hearing likewise: the last thing affected is one, a single mean, though plural in definition' (*De An.* 431ᵃ17f.). As Block says, this remark is unclear,

but it is explicit enough for us to be sure that Aristotle intended the senses to meet at the centre, though he had perhaps not yet settled the brain versus heart dispute to his satisfaction.

8. Block's second point, that the senses operate independently in the *De Anima*, is difficult to answer because difficult to understand. 'If the eye were an animal sight would be its soul' (*De An.* 412ᵇ18). It does not follow that an eye could be an animated individual just as it is, and it is absurdly literal-minded to conclude that Aristotle thought either that it could or that the ability to see was a function solely of a small piece of transparent flesh. Obviously it is a function of the eye properly so called, the ensouled eye, the eye that is part of the individual. It is the individual that perceives, remembers, and the like (*De An.* 408ᵇ13f.), though we may occasionally speak loosely as if 'the eye' saw (cf. Pl. *Tht.* 184d). There would be no sense-faculties at all were they not precisely 'of a sentient being' (*Met.* VII 1035ᵇ24f. *et al.*), and though Aristotle may have come to emphasize the wholeness of organisms more clearly (e.g. *De Part. An.* 645ᵃ30f., 645ᵇ14f.: see II.3.26) it is implausible to suggest that he could seriously have been ignorant of it before.

9. Thirdly, Block stresses the theme that the senses are self-aware (*De An.* 425ᵇ12f.): we are aware that we see by sight, and so throughout (which is admittedly denied at *De Somno* 455ᵃ17f.). This still does not involve any 'autonomy' of the senses, nor is it even clear that Aristotle is convinced of this account. He argues that if it is by some other sense that we are aware of seeing then (i) this other sense must perceive both the seeing and the object of the seeing (they being indistinguishable) and will therefore include the concept of sight—will be sight; and (ii) another sense is then needed whereby we can perceive our perception of our seeing. It is more economical, and more reasonable, to posit that we *see* that we see. But what is it to see that we see? If it is to be disposed to say 'I am seeing . . .' or 'Seeing is what I am doing', then we surely require some degree of philosophy, or at the least a habit of introspection: it is not obvious that we are thus aware of what it is we are doing by sight. And we certainly do not *see* our seeing eye (*De An.* 417ᵃ2f.). At *De Sensu* 437ᵃ27 Aristotle takes it as obvious that 'it is not possible not to be aware that one is seeing something that is being seen'. If one is seeing something, then one is aware of seeing something: not to be so aware is not to see. 'So people are not aware of what is impinging

on their eyes if they happen to be thinking hard, or are afraid or hearing a loud noise' (*De Sensu* 447ª15f.). Sensing something, in short, is not just a physical event, not at least a case of being subjected to certain sensory pressures (cf. *De An.* 424ª32f. on plants): it involves being aware of being so subject. As it is therefore impossible even in thought to distinguish sensing and awareness of sensing we must do both in their various kinds by one and the same sense. I see my seeing, for seeing is precisely a type of awareness (cf. V.3.11). This is not, of course, to deny that I may sometimes recall what had impinged on my eyes and say either 'I didn't see it at the time' or 'I must have seen it—I just didn't notice.' So long as one knows which sense of 'see' is intended no difficulty is posed. In short the very passage which Block picks out as typically opposed to the later account leads to a theory of perception which he asserts (with reference to *De Sensu* 447ª15f.) to be opposed to the whole tenor of the *De Anima*. I conclude that Kahn is right to dismiss this part of Block's thesis.

10. The self-awareness of the senses perhaps also accounts for their incorrigibility on HAMLYN's (2) interpretation. 'Each sense makes judgements about its own proper objects, and is never deceived in judging that here is a colour or here a sound' (*De An.* 418ª14f.). We cannot be unaware that we are seeing a colour if we are seeing a colour at all. To see is knowingly to see colour (or luminescence). This logical incorrigibility seems to be different from the near-infallibility attributed to the senses at *De Anima* 428ᵇ18: 'the perception that here is something white tells no lies'. It is not part of the concept of seeing that we should knowingly see white, black, or a blend: we are merely very unlikely to be mistaken. On the other hand, whereas to see we must be knowingly seeing some colour, we can quite well be seeing the son of Diares without knowing it: the proper and incidental objects of sense are to be distinguished (*De An.* 418ª20f.).

11. But do we knowingly see coloured patches or coloured things? If Aristotle is speaking, in effect, of sense-data, why is there any chance at all of error with regard to the claim 'here is white'? If it seems to me that there is a white seeming-to-me then there is. But if he is speaking of public objects may there not be error with regard to 'here is colour'? There is a continuous echoing in our ears if we can hear at all, but 'a noise is external not private property' (*De An.*

420^{a}17). In dreams we seem to see certain things, but as they are not there we are not really seeing (*De Ins.* 458^{b}3f.). We may have fantasies with our eyes shut, so that fantasizing is not seeing (*De An.* 428^{a}15). To see is to see something, but to fantasize is equally to fantasize something, and we may be mistaken as to which we are doing.

12.   Aristotle appears to have two responses to this. Firstly, he suggests that perceptions are always true, and fantasies mostly false (*De An.* 428^{a}11f.). Sight makes no errors in considering its proper objects, or only very rarely. We may erroneously consider that we are seeing (*De Ins.* 461^{b}29f.). Secondly, he suggests that in cases of delusory 'seeing' we are not mistaken in thinking 'here is colour' but rather in our judgement as to what is coloured. A sick man finds everything bitter, but it is not the food he eats that is thus actualized qua taste: rather his mouth is full of bitter moisture (*De An.* 422^{b}8f.). He tastes something but is mistaken as to what it is (*De An.* 418^{a}16). The sense-organ may retain the colour, taste, or whatever of a past object so that we continue to experience the appearance (*De An.* 425^{b}24f.). Thus we are truly seeing, but not seeing what we might suppose. Similarly spots before the eyes may turn out to be debris in the eyes.

13.   In either case the objects of our perception are external. Something's making a noise and someone's hearing a noise are the same event, though differently described (*De An.* 425^{b}30f.): there is only one sound, not a real sound and an echo in our minds. But there can be an unheard potential for sound. Things can be potentially noisy both in the sense that they can in general make sounds (e.g. bronze (*De An.* 419^{b}5f.)) and in the sense that they could now be heard if one were there to hear. 'We must think that the same nature which is coloured on the surface also exists within the object' (*De Sensu* 439^{a}33f.). We cannot identify colours apart from our perception of them, but we remain convinced that colours are part of the world (see VI.7f.). Taking the objects of perception as intentional (ANSCOMBE), they can obviously be given different descriptions. If I claim to see a giraffe, and there is none, then I am fantasizing and not perceiving. If I claim to see white, and there is no public white, I am truly seeing something white (though I may *possibly* be seeing something that is really grey, if we could but examine my eyes) and I am inarguably seeing something coloured. Aristotle is not, I think, prepared to believe in a seeming perception without *any* public

correlate. 'Sight is the sight of something, not of that of which it is the sight (though this is true) but relative to colour (or luminescence)' (*Met.* V, 1021ª33f.): 'the perceptible is prior to perception' (*Cat.* 7ᵇ36). Things may be coloured or tasty in potential (*De An.* 426ª15f.) though there can be no colours in a blind man's world (*Phys.* II, 193ª7f.). Our seeing is contingent on there being things that are visible (*De An.* 417ᵇ24).

14. The extent to which I commit myself to the claims made by my perceptions with regard to their proper, or defining, objects and to their incidentals is a matter to determine in each individual case. 'As a rule the governing sense affirms the report of each sense, unless some more authoritative sense contradicts' (*De Ins.* 461ᵇ3). We and the world are adapted to each other, so it is hardly surprising that we should usually make the correct decision.

15. BLOCK's (2) attempt to make this concept, of adaptation, explain why we are generally correct in our perceptual judgements is more successful than his use of the same fact to explain our errors in regard to the common sensibles (3) (*De An.* 428 ᵇ18f.): that is, that they are not the proper objects of any sense specially adapted to them. That they are not the proper objects of any one sense may indeed be relevant: there is the possibility, as there is not in the case of colour, of two senses issuing contradictory reports. But it very rarely matters whether we recognize *x* as a colour, or even as a particular colour. Our recognition of extension and movement are plainly more important and biologically more primitive: the frog sees movement, not static things—as do the outer regions of our visual fields. Furthermore 'it is impossible to see white and not quantity' (*De Sensu* 445ᵇ10). Colour and seen extension go together and we can separate them only in thought. We cannot then be mistaken in thinking that here is a case of extension (whether it be public or only in our eyes). Aristotle apparently thinks it easier to err in answering 'how large?' than in answering 'what colour?' but this surely cannot be because sight is ill adapted to this question. Nor is it simply because we may have conflicting testimony from our different senses.

16. For what would our adaptation to the common sensibles be like? For Aristotle, and presumably most of the Greeks, the sun seemed about a foot across (*De An.* 428ᵇ3); to Blake, and I suspect to most of us, it seems for the mundane eye about the size of a guinea (BLAKE p. 617). Note that I say 'it seems' and not 'it seems to

be', which it plainly does not. This discrepancy is resolved by supposing that we and the Greeks are comparing the sun's disk to some object held at a certain distance: apparently, as might be expected in a more open-air scroll-reading society, the Greeks had a rather greater optimum visual distance than we. Our opinion of the size of the moon's disk as it sinks to the horizon is also dictated by subconscious assessments of its distance. Similarly if I imagine a monster, the question 'how large does it look?' can only be answered when I have included some notion of its distance in my imaginings: similarly if I see something sufficiently unusual, as E. A. Poe's insect on the windowpane (cf. *De Mem.* 452^{a}14f. on images in mind's eye; ANSCOMBE). Our assessment of speed is also dependent on our assessment of distance. Shape and number too, though less obviously, require judgements about the object's three-dimensional aspect. In short, as soon as the third dimension has been introduced, it becomes impossible to have detailed certainty: for our assessment of distance is itself a matter of framework rather than content (how far away are your feet? what if you are three miles tall—imagine it?). So long as I am healthy and the situation is normal I can expect almost complete accuracy in my special sense-judgements: to get such accuracy in the case of the common sensibles I need additional information, and I cannot even say what the world looks like in these respects until I have selected my assumptions. HAMLYN (2) is possibly right in connecting this chance of error with Platonic worries about relational properies (as at Pl. *Rpb.* 479 b) but it is not a parochial point. Block is right in talking of our adaptations in that we are precisely adapted to dealing with our immediate localities—we lack the broad contexts which would assign correct values to the sun's disk, or prevent our seeing it as rising, but it does not seem likely that our senses could conceivably be perfectly adapted to such questions. They are not asked of our senses but (in the modern sense) of our common sense.

17. Before advancing to a consideration of the material and critical aspects of perception, I wish to consider the concept of accuracy in the special senses. It is because the human sense of touch is more discriminating than that of other beasts that men are the most intelligent of animals (*De An.* 421^{a}23f.).[1] The thinnest skin is best

---

[1] It may be that our sense of touch is a proof of our wisdom rather than an explanation of it (see *Post. An.* 78^{a}22f.): structure is normally explained in terms of function and not vice versa (cf. II.2.24).

for discerning differences (*De Gen. An.* 781^{b}17f.), which explains Aristotle's prejudice against the thick-skinned (cf. III.1.2). We may presumably connect it with the versatility of the human hand (*De Part. An.* 687^{b}2f.)—for it is with our hands above all that we feel and 'manipulate' the world. Our sense of smell on the other hand is inferior to that of many animals, 'and is not aware of any smell without pain or pleasure, as the sense-organ is not accurate' (*De An.* 421^{a}10f.). Accurate perception does not operate only in terms of one's desires, nor parcel the world into two divided camps on such an immediate basis. On the other hand 'What has perception also has desire' (*De An.* 414^{b}1) and awareness of pleasure and pain (*De An.* 413^{b}23). We therefore have the peculiar result that to perceive is to operate in pleasure/pain terms, and to perceive well is to escape from these terms. Inevitably: 'the deerhunter doesn't see mountains, the miser doesn't see men' (MIURA/SASAKI p. 101). To generalize: to survive as a good human being it is necessary to be interested in other things than one's own survival (see V.2.15). The importance of 'accuracy' comes out most strongly in the case of sight, for this is the sense *par excellence* (*De An.* 429^{a}2f.). 'All men by nature desire to know. A sign of this is the delight we take in our senses; for even apart from their usefulness they are loved for themselves; and above all others the sense of sight. For not only with a view to action, but even when we are not going to do anything, we prefer seeing (one might say) to everything else. The reason is that this, most of all the senses, makes us know and brings to light many differences between things' (*Met.* I, 980^{a}22f.; *Protr.* fr. 7 Ross; *Poet.* 1448^{b}12). Although our sense of touch is less involved in pleasure than that of beasts, it cannot be wholly non-involved and the danger is always present. It is the pleasures of touch that the *sophron* must avoid, 'as the other animals share them, so that they seem slavish and beastly' (*N.E.* III, 1118^{a}23f.). The pleasures of vision are not so distracting (*N.E.* III, 1118^{a}3; Pl. *Phil.* 51 b). Sight is a distance sense. It is also the sense that most grasps a simultaneous whole—the objects of hearing are temporally rather than spatially ordered, and 'the palpable is never simultaneously apprehended in all its parts' (UEXKUELL p. 5). Although we do perhaps have a sort of *gestalt* awareness of our bodies and their immediate environment on occasion. Sight is also more authoritative than even touch (*De Ins.* 460^{b}20f.: perhaps an anomaly). Aristotle therefore rejects the Democritean emphasis on touch (*De Sensu* 442^{a}29f.), and it is sight which provides his main model for intelligence, the awareness of a differentiated whole as it is in itself, not as our desires present it (see V.3.30. VI.10).[2]

18. So far I have been refering to the discriminatory, self-aware aspect of sense-perception. There is also a material aspect. The sense-organ is potentially what its object is actually, and sense-perception is the process of being thus affected (*De An.* 423^{b}30f.). Plainly more is involved in perception than this, for plants, tables, and vats of water can have their temperature raised or lowered (*De An.* 424^{a}33f.) without our immediately concluding that any awareness is involved. Aristotle's claim is that such changes are effects of form-and-matter, that is the concrete individual, whereas sense-perception is an effect of form alone. I do not think we need spend much time in unravelling this: it surely means no more than that in sense-perception we acquire the idea of the individual, in short that we observe the individual (*De An.* 424^{b}16f.). How do we do so? How can the affairs of other entities possibly be made known to us? Quite simply because they affect our physical presence in such a way that we are aware of them: our awareness is so modified as to become them, in a way. Our awareness cannot become just anything: there are some sensual aspects of real entities that our organs cannot reproduce save to their own destruction. There are lights too bright, noises too loud, and temperatures too high to bear. Also, if the sensual aspect in question involves no change in us we cannot distinguish it from the absence of sensory stimulation, and therefore cannot be aware of it.

19. The senses, in short, are means, or rather the sense-organs are productive balances of contrary qualities (*De An.* 424^{a}30f.) such that their normal state lies in the middle of the range of qualities available to the respective senses. It is customary to suggest that this is no more than an uneasy extrapolation from our temperature sense. I suggest that it is rather more. The physiological medium of sight is the water of the eye, considered as transparency (*De Sensu* 438^{b}5f.). The transparent is invisible, save via some actual colour (*De An.* 418^{b}4f.). It is the current modifications of our transparencies of which we are aware. 'The eye tends to accept as white [i.e. as colourless] the general illumination whatever this may be' (GREGORY (1) p.

---

[2] This awareness, of the (whole) thing in itself rather than of its immediate relevance to our interests and desires, is the source in us of love and science (see II.1.25f., V.2.15, VI.5,10).

125). We do not see the colour which has become the stable condition of our sense organ. This and similar results, incidentally, make any simple materialistic theory of vision, in which red is light with a certain wavelength, somewhat problematic. Nor, though Aristotle can hardly be supposed to have known this, are we aware of any visual object which has been stabilized on our retinas (GREGORY (1) p. 44). Similarly the internal medium of hearing is the trapped air in the ear (*De An.* 420ᵃ4f.), which cannot itself properly be heard. It is change in the current pitch of the auditory base-line that we notice, and not just any change. 'A stimulus is only accepted as a signal of an outside event when the neural activity is unlikely to be merely a chance increase in the noise level' (GREGORY (1) p. 88). Similarly we grow used to odours, nor do we taste our own tongues save in some disordered states (*De An.* 417ᵃ2f.; cf. III.1.9). The tactile polarities, save for temperature, are more difficult to handle, though there are polarities even here (cf. *Meteor.* 382ᵃ16).

20. As I shall argue below on the Mean, the word 'mean' has many meanings, and the *mesotes* of the senses can be very variously interpreted. It draws attention firstly to our inability to be aware of that for which there are no capacities in ourselves. We cannot see the ultra-violet or infra-red because our organs cannot reproduce such effects. It draws attention secondly to the manner in which we judge the world from ourselves as central, stationary observers. We are very easily misled on the subject of velocity (*De Ins.* 460ᵇ21f.): only if we are stationary or if we can correct for our motion do we get correct results. And in general 'distortions are sometimes due to the sensory receptors' becoming fatigued, or adapted, by prolonged or intense stimulation' (GREGORY (2) pp. 74f.). Thus also is pleasure dulled (*N.E.* X, 1175ᵃ3f.; cf. VII, 1154ᵇ20f.). It draws attention thirdly to our inability to notice what is always there: *semper idem sentire idem est ac non sentire.*

21. 'The middle is what judges' (*De An.* 424ᵃ6). And only if our middle is in 'the' middle shall we judge correctly. In disordered states we mistake alterations in ourselves for alterations in the world. Only if we are properly balanced and at one with the world shall we see straight. 'What particularly distinguishes the sound man is his seeing the truth in every case, being as it were a rule and measure of them' (*N.E.* III, 1113ᵃ32; cf. *Met.* XI, 1062ᵇ33f.). This aspect of mean theory I take to be basic: the senses are means because sense

is a mean; the critical faculty embedded in sense-awareness assesses
the world as if from the world's centre, and can only be accurate if
it can correct its bias.

22.   This critical faculty is of course no more than the ability of an
individual: it is not a substantial entity, but rather the formal cause
of an individual's sense-awareness, his waking consciousness. There
is more to sense-awareness than this. Perception is in a way 'a kind
of thinking' (GREGORY (2) p. 59), but it is not the same as thinking.
It also involves the element of appearance (LYCOS; MERLEAU PONTY
p. 34). But this element cannot be characterized without recourse to
the categories whose use we have acquired. 'All perception is theory-
laden. Worse still, the perceptual hypotheses can differ from our
most firmly held intellectual beliefs' (GREGORY (2) p. 149; cf. *De An.*
428^{b}3f.; *De Ins.* 461^{b}30f.). We do not first perceive things and then
infer the external existence or future reliability of that of which we
have sensory impressions: we can only perceive them as we do if we
perceive them precisely as external and reliable. We do not see
coloured patches but coloured things—though what the things may
be is another question.

23.   Perception of movement, rest, number, shape, and size is
shared by more than one sense (*De An.* 418^{a}16f.): 'of the common
sensibles we have common awareness, not incidentally' (*De An.*
425^{a}27). 'There is also a common faculty accompanying all the
senses' (*De Somno* 455^{a}15f.). HAMLYN (3) argues that the common
sense is not the same as the common faculty, and has no connection
with the primary sense-organ, but is rather a sense—arguing that
there can only be a *pathos* of the common sense (mentioned at *De
Memoria* 450^{a}10f.) if it is an individual sense (which Aristotle denies:
cf. III.1.6). I can see no force in this argument, though there is a
progression in Aristotle's thought. The passage just cited from the
De Somno implicitly explains the ability which every sense has by
some faculty distinguishable in thought from the senses proper.
Similarly the argument of the *De Anima* that each sense is, as it were,
transparent (III. 1.9), culminates in the *De Somno* with the theoretical isolation of this self-awareness (cf. *N.E.* IX, 1170^{a}29f.). The *De
Anima* invokes this same central faculty to account for intersensory
comparisons (426^{b}12f.) and as marking the unity of the organism
(431^{a}19f.). The *De Sensu* takes this a step further by concluding that
the individual senses are but the diversified activities of the central

sense (449ᵃ8f.). This is confirmed in the *De Somno*: sleeping and waking are states of this primary faculty (454ᵃ22f.), to which the individual senses are posterior (455ᵃ4f.). It is this which is the critical faculty needed to compare and criticize the sensory input (455ᵃ20f.), the judging principle of *De Ins.* 461ᵇ5f., which is already implicit in the *De Anima*: *aisthesis* is one of those faculties 'by which we judge and speak truth or falsehood' (*De An.* 428ᵃ3f.). All animals 'have an inborn critical faculty called sense, and of those that have some remember their sense-impressions and some do not' (*Post. An.* 99ᵇ35f.). We remember with that part of the soul that is conscious of time (*De Mem.* 449ᵇ29: see IV.1.15), which is also that which is conscious of magnitude and motion, and which is responsible for fantasizing (*De Mem.* 450ᵃ10: fantasy is a *pathos* of the common sense). The images of memory and fantasy are housed in the central sense-organ, for subjective, psychological fact is automatically a picture of objective, physical reality (see below on Body–mind): the unity of the sensory soul implies the unity of the vascular system in the heart (*De Part. An.* 667ᵇ21f.; cf. *De Ins.* 461ᵇ17f. *et al.*). Summing up these passages we may surely conclude, with KAHN, that the primary sense is equivalent to the potential of a living being for waking consciousness. Aristotle's anticipation of the Cartesian *cogito* (*N.E.* IX, 1170ᵃ29f.) has psycho-physical entities for its subject, not a bare faculty exalted into a substance. We may also conclude that this potential may be for a more or less aware waking life.

24. The primary sensibles, so to call them, are movement, rest, number, shape, size, and time. Or at least those are all that Aristotle mentions in this context. In the field of scientific investigation there is a parallel distinction between common and proper objects of sciences (*Post. An.* 76ᵃ37f.: cf. *De An.* 418ᵃ7f.). The common propositions are seen to be true whatever the specialized content of the individual sciences, as that if equals be taken from equals, equals remain. We learn the one concept which sums up many facts via experience (*Post. An.* 100ᵃ3f.; *Met.* I, 980ᵇ26f.). 'The [human] soul is such as to be affected thus' (*Post. An.* 100ᵃ13f.). Our human sentience is such that we can isolate the concepts which can interpret the world, and which give us an increasingly detailed and workable picture of that world. *Dianoia*, thinking-things-through, and the common sense are linked to each other and also to our upright posture (*De Part. An.* 686ᵃ27f.). It is by our common sense that we

recognize that a fire means the enemy (*De An.* 431^{b}5f.), or that x is a triangle (*N.E.* VI, 1142^{a}28f.). Similarly we elicit or perceive the moral value of particular things and acts (ibid.). It is because of these abilities that we are ethical and scientific beings (see II.1.22f.). We have these abilities because we can 'became all things' (*De An.* 431^{b}21) in a way that transcends, at least potentially, our own immediate concerns. The nature of that 'becoming' at a noetic level will be the topic of my chapter on Nous.

25.   It is by our primary sense that we can answer the questions 'is it moving?', 'how many are there?', 'how large, what shape, for how long a time?' It is reasonable to conclude that it is also our primary sense by which we answer those questions which Aristotle labels categorial. How much, to what related, where, when, in what position, how disposed, what doing, and what suffering: all are questions posed of the primary sense. So also is the question 'what is it like?', although the answer may often be in terms of the objects of some one of the special senses. 'What shape?' is presumably a sub-question in the field of quality which can be answered in more than one sense (III.1.6). The most important Aristotelian question 'what is it?', or 'what are we to identify it as?', can be answered (and therefore asked) only in a certain way. The sheer particularity of an individual, its being *this*, cannot be received by the soul, but only its sort, its being such-and-such (*De An.* 424^{a}23). The soul becomes the form, not the composite individual, and our knowledge of things qua substance is therefore inevitably general (see IV.2.6). To know what a thing is, substantially (II.3 *passim*), is once again to know its kind. Primary awareness and categorial awareness, in short, come to the same thing: the recognition of the concepts which can interpret the unknowable flood of particular being.[3]

26.   I conclude (i) that Aristotle's psychological and biological works may legitimately be placed towards the later part of his life—his philosophy turns toward the world (see V.3.33f.); (ii) that the relation of primary and special senses, of the critical faculty to the various types of phenomena presented in different sensory dimen-

---

[3] Aristotle's Ten Categories, incidentally, are not as randomly ordered as they may appear: the arrangement is that of a tetractys. *Ousia* comes first—a noun; *poson* and *poion*—adjectival forms; *pros ti, pou, pote*—adverbs; *keisthai, echein, poiein,* and *paschein* —verbs. Our abstract translations for these terms (substance, quantity, quality, relation, location, time, position, state, action, and passion) conceal a point which is not as trivial as it may seem (see IV.1.12n).

sions, is an instance of that relation of whole (or supreme part) to (other) parts which pervades his work (see V.1.19); (iii) that all sensory claims are corrigible in theory, even those restricting themselves to colour identification in cases where there is no obvious public object—claims to be seeing colour are equivalent to claims to be seeing, and though such apparent seeing may sometimes be termed fantasy, there is always some material object which the fantasizer could correctly claim to be seeing (lived experience is the chief evidence for existence: see VI.13); (iv) human senses are variously accurate, detached from immediate pleasure and pain, and grasping of wholes—sight is the paradigm; (v) that the senses are means partly because sense is a mean. The last point, together with the concept of a critical faculty that bridges the gap between 'fact' and 'value', will be of most immediate relevance; the others will recur later.

27. The most general point that follows from all this is a reassertion of the reality of the phenomenal world, the comprehensibility of reality. In denying that there could be a mental seeming without a corresponding physical presence (of some sort), Aristotle at once affirms common reality and denies the body/mind distinction: not in the sense which later materialists have done, but in affirming the phenomenological truism that the world is a matter of experience. A fuller discussion of this must be delayed till my final chapter. Too great a concentration on the theme of a reality that is only mediated to us in our senses, rather than an immediately given reality of which we are a part, leads to a half-horrified belief in a world of monsters through which we pick our somnambulistic way. It does not seem to have occurred to Aristotle seriously to doubt common reality (see V.2.12): the doubt is perhaps pathological.

III.2.   The Doctrine of the Mean

1.   Aristotle was a biologist and a philosopher of biology: he was also a biological philosopher (BURNET (1), GRENE (3), HANTZ), and particularly a medical one. His use of explicitly medical paradigms can hardly be ignored (BONITZ 837ª5f.), and his use of medical information is equally pervasive (JAEGER (2), LONGRIGG, G. E. R. LLOYD (2), PREUS). This is especially true of the ethical mean. In what follows I shall rebut what seem to me quite inadequate readings of this concept, present the biological background, and with this in mind attempt to draw out the form of the various virtues discussed by Aristotle. Once again, my discussion will go somewhat beyond 'the text': my justification must be in the value of the resulting ethical theory. I shall in conclusion suggest that the analogy between moral sense and the primary sense (see III.1.24) is of considerable value.

2.   One common response to the doctrine of the mean might be summed up in the judgement that the Golden Mean is so called because it is both lucrative and ignoble. It is apparently necessary to point out that Aristotle nowhere says that it is always wrong, for example, to be extremely angry (*N.E.* II, 1105ᵇ27 refers to dispositions, not to acts): sometimes, though more rarely than most of us tend to think, this is the appropriate response. Nor is Aristotle urging us to act always in a lukewarm manner: some things should be done with all one's might (*N.E.* X, 1177ᵇ31f.), others should not be done at all (*N.E.* II, 1107ª9). Although there is a connection between the Delphic 'Nothing in excess' and Aristotelian ethics, slipshod use of this parallel has done considerable harm. The gods of the Greek heaven, like the tyrants of Corinth and Miletus, were jealous of mortal prowess: 'you see how the god blasts overwheening creatures and does not permit their appearance, but small things don't bother him' (*Hdt.* VII, 10ᵉ). Aristotle's God is no more jealous than Plato's (*Met.* I, 983ª2f.; cf. Pl. *Tim.* 29 d, *Epin.* 988 b). Aristotle is quite certainly not repeating the weary lesson of Bellerophon (Pindar *Isthm.* VII.44f.), the lesson of much pessimistic Babylonian thought (cf. Etana and the eagle: CAMPBELL (2) II pp. 132f.). Even more sympathetic commentators sometimes avoid these absurdities only to fall into trivialities. For the false, but at least informative,

assertion that it is always wrong to be extremely angry they substitute the triviality that it is always wrong to be more angry than one ought to be. There is a distressing tendency solemnly to draw a short line, label the ends 'vices' and the middle 'virtue' and then to suppose that one's duty to the text has been done. But 'symmetry is homonymous' (*Top.* 139ᵇ21), 'for "the between" and "the mean" have many meanings' (*De Caelo* 312ᵇ2). 'If "having a middle" means many things, then one ought to define in what sense one has a middle' (*Top.* 149ᵃ35f.).

3. The failure even to attempt this is responsible for much confusion. OLMSTED draws a parallel between the aesthetic and the ethical mean, after BURNET (2), but hardly manages more than a general comparison of emotional sensitivity and aesthetic perception, without really coming to terms with the precise meaning of the doctrine in an ethical context. HARDIE (ch. 7) for similar reasons provides no real illumination, though he is entirely right in rejecting ROSS's (1) criticism to emphasize the difference between *enkrateia* and virtue. ALLAN (2) goes some way to unravelling the theory, but does not elaborate his insight as much as he could. How does Aristotle use '*to meson*', the mean, and its cognates elsewhere?

4. 'Nothing of what exists by and according to nature is disorderly, for nature is in everything a cause of order' (*Phys.* VIII, 252ᵃ11). To be *x* is to be ordered as *x*, and departures from that order are degenerations, malformations (cf. II.3.6). 'Should the abnormal increase be one of quality as well as quantity the malformed animal may take the form of another animal' (*Pol.* V, 1302ᵇ38f.; cf. II.2.15). An excessively snub nose ceases to be a nose at all (*Rhet.* 1360ᵃ23f.). To survive it is necessary to preserve the symmetry proper to one's species. 'Harmony then is health and strength and beauty' (*Eudemus* fr. 45; cf. *Poet.* 1450ᵇ37). Any self-maintaining organism precisely seeks to maintain itself, continually correcting divergencies in its chemical and physiological state so as to achieve the mean (CANNON; Pantin: I. T. RAMSEY; cf. II.3.20). Health consists in this ability to maintain the precarious balance essential to any organic whole. 'Symmetry makes, increases, and preserves health: just so are temperance and courage preserved by *mesotes*' (*N.E.* II, 1104ᵃ17f.: slightly different context (?)).

5. This is a standard medical opinion. 'Alcmaeon said that the balance of qualities preserved health, and the rule of one alone

produced disease' (*Aetius* V, 30.1). 'Health is symmetry of heats and chills' (*Top.* 139^{b}21). 'The dry and the wet and suchlike produce flesh and bone and the rest at a *mesotes*' (*De Gen. Corr.* 334^{b}28f.). The dry and the wet are secondary: heat and cold form the basic pair and it is their symmetry that produces health (*Top.* 145^{b}7f.). 'If a lack of proportion in heats and chills makes for lack of health, then their proportion makes for health' (*Post. An.* 78^{b}18f.). Indeed 'everything that happens by art or nature exists by some due proportion (λόγῳ τινί ἐστι)' (*De Gen. An.* 767^{a}16f.): it is this proportion that needs to be preserved. Such 'proportion is also needed in the mixing, *mixis*, of male and female' (*De Gen. An.* 767^{a}22f.). *Mixis* involves an approach to the mean by the reciprocally active elements (cf. JOACHIM (1)), and there are at least two such elements: heat and cold, dry and wet, black and white (*De Sensu* 442^{a}12f.; *De An.* 422^{b}10f.) and the rest are pairs, not differing degrees of some single range (though see App. B. 3). The resulting proportionate mixture has elements of both contrary powers or characters, but is itself 'between' the *pure* characters.

6.   Health, then, consists 'in the blending and harmony of heats and chills either with one another or with the environment' (*Phys.* VII, 246^{b}5f.; see *De An.* 408^{a}1f.). The healthy man can produce from himself the heat demanded of him in a particular environment (see App. A). He can do so because there is heat in him, as also cold: neither power is so predominant that the other is excluded from his make-up. The healthy man can digest as much and wishes to eat as much and as little as is demanded of him in a particular environment: he can be such on particular occasions—can achieve the mean in action—because he is or has a mean. He can do *x* or its contrary because he has the equipment to do so. The same, I suggest, is true of the ethically healthy man.

7.   An organism is preserved by the union of opposite powers: one entity comes to be by combination (II.2.27). And what is thus one is a unit of measurement, and the standard form from which the sick diverge. 'To be one is to be the primary measure of each kind' (*Met.* X, 1052^{b}18; cf. XIV, 1087^{b}33f.). To be one it is necessary to be one something (see IV.2.6n); to be properly something it is necessary to be one (see II.3.5). To fail of the organic unity proper to one's kind is, to that extent, to fail of one's kind. The process of combination into such a unity is attested from medical writers. 'Man is in the

best condition of all when everything is ripened and at peace, showing no particular power preeminently' (*On Ancient Medicine* ch. 19). For the Hippocratic writer *pepsis*, ripening, leads to *krasis*, blending, and so to peace, and in this process 'one must aim at some standard' (ch. 9). Just so ethical virtue is 'aiming at the mean' (*N.E.* II, 1106^{b}28). 'For when it has been ripened, it is completed and has come to be' (*Meteor.* 379^{b}20f.). 'There is only a heap until it is ripened, and some one thing has come to be from its elements' (*Met.* VII, 1040^b,f.; cf. II.3.26 *et al.*). 'Mixing is the coming-to-be one of what is mixed as they are changed' (*De Gen. Corr.* 328^{b}22). The rest, the coming-to-be one (see III.3.6), which the healthy organism achieves is, like any standard, the opposite of all types of motion (*Phys.* VIII, 261^{b}18f.). The 'rest' which the human soul can achieve (rather, as Zen Buddhists have insisted, that which we can realize as having been there all along (see VI.15)) also lies at the end of a process of ordering: 'for by bringing the soul to rest from its natural turmoil something wise and knowledgeable is revealed' (*Phys.* VII, 247^{b}17f.; on connection between *episteme*, knowledge, and *ephist-amai*, I stand still, see *Post. An.* 100^{a}3f.; Pl. *Phdo* 96 b).

8.   Thus: the being of any organism is preserved by the maintenance of correct proportion in the blending of the elements which compose it. Such a healthy organism is a standard for its kind, and therefore lies between the various divergent types. It lies at the mean because it is a mean: 'what lies between is necessarily composite' (*Met.* X, 1057^{b}26f.). The best form of government, for example, lies between democracy and oligarchy precisely because in it the conflicting claims of rich and poor are reconciled (*Pol.* IV, 1294^{a}30f., 1296^{a}22f.). This correct proportion of the relevant contraries is not, of course, one that can be exactly defined: 'the mean is not indivisible' (*De Gen. Corr.* 334^{b}28), and any within a certain range of proportions will do. Circumstances also alter cases, so that neither medicine nor ethics nor, in general, any such effort at proportion can be an exact or abstract science (see *N.E.* I, 1094^{b}14f.). One may show more of heat or more of cold from time to time and still be 'at the mean': what is essential is that one contrary should not overpower the other, for there would then be no organism, and the overpowering contrary itself would be transformed into the overpowered (*De Gen. Corr.* 334^{b}21f.). Just so in Chinese thought Yin and Yang are transformed into each other (see *Book of Changes, passim*): and the Chinese

solution to the problem was the same, I suggest as Aristotle's. 'By "chung", central, mean, is meant what is not one-sided' (Ch'eng Yi: CHAN (2) p. 97).

9. An organism, particularly a healthy organism, should not be and in the end cannot be one-sided. There is need both of the Yin and the Yang. This is also true at the level of spiritual, ethical health. The combination of contraries into an organic whole is no novel doctrine: where Aristotle differs from some Presocratic, 'Orientalist', or syncretic interpreters of the doctrine is in realizing that Good and Evil, Proportion and Disproportion cannot themselves be treated as contraries to be combined in a wider synthesis (*N.E.* II, 1107^{a}8f.). And also in defining more clearly at what level the combination of Yin and Yang should occur.

10. Having outlined the Aristotelian background to the specifically ethical mean, I must now show that the latter can be interpreted in accordance with the model. Also that on this interpretation Aristotle's words are more significant than they have sometimes been made to appear. Before attempting this task, it is worth noting the objections that e.g. HARDIE (ch. 7) brings against the 'blending' theory of virtue advanced by Burnet, and which may also seem to count against my account. One, that to base an ethical theory on obsolete physics and physiology is to vitiate the ethical theory. But the theory of organic equilibrium is far from obsolete (see CANNON; E. S. RUSSELL (2); BERTALANFFY (1); DUBOS). Two, that there can be no blending of giving more and giving less money, nor of pleasures and their absence: but no one said there could (see below). Three, that the two *pathe* involved in courage are distinct: but that is the point. It is precisely because courage is a matter of combining two contrary passions so that neither can utterly exclude the other, that courage is a mean in the sense I have been discussing. Four, that if a virtue is a ratio of contrary impulses then the strength of these impulses can vary independently: it is this last point which provides confirmation of my account.

11. A particular right action is at a mean, relative to the wrong actions in this situation: to do right is to do neither more nor less than one should. This may indeed seem trivial (see *N.E.* VI, 1138^{b}25f.), though it is like Dogen's advice to 'avoid evil' in recognizing that it is often easier to know what is wrong than what

exactly is right (see FOX). 'The mean is not indivisible' and we may well have done as much as can be expected if we have avoided excess or defect. A type of action, however, cannot be declared either right or wrong in the abstract—save where the description of the action-type includes the information that it is unlawful. The right action is the one that a good man would perform. Virtuous action involves a response appropriate to the demands of the environment (see III.2.6); a disposition thus to act virtuously, a virtue, itself involves the capacity to do contrary things when the occasion arises. Virtue is an organic mean because a virtuous action must be a balanced response.

11A. Heat and cold must both be present in an entity, so that their respective excesses are controlled, each by the other (*De Gen. Corr.* 334^{b}10f.). Where one is in excess and the other deficient, there are pure examples of the 'two vices' (in a non-ethical sense) between which the compound virtue stands. Where both are deficient, there is no healthy entity at all. Where both are in excess, so that both heat and cold are present but neither has (yet) controlled the other, we have the paradoxical situation to which Hardie's fourth objection refers. The paradox is not an impossible one: two entities do not make a third simply by their conjunction (*Met.* XIII, 1082^{b}30f.; see App. B. 7). Virtue does not consist in the excessive capacity for both of the relevant contraries, so that (in the sphere of courage) the virtuous man alternates between terror, and berserkery: it is a mean, not madness. How this mean is to be obtained is a matter on which Aristotle has some eminently practical advice to offer.

12. 'Courage, manliness, is a *mesotes* about fears and boldness' (*N.E.* II, 1107^{a}33; III 1115^{a}6f.), specifically those related to death in battle. Aristotle declines to treat it in the Platonic, generalized manner, and restricts himself to the virtue commonly so called (cf. Pl. *Prot.* 358 d, *Lach.* 191 d, 198 b): we must begin from where we are, and not more decorous and firmly distant places. If Aristotle wishes to show the form of virtue he cannot reasonably take artificial virtues as his subject: he must begin from what his public are likely to accept (see III.3.19). In the case of courage, ROSS (1) first observes and then explains away the fact that two *pathe* are involved: *andreia* is 'really' an uneasy compound of courage and discretion (a device extended to cover other virtues by URMSON). Operating with a quite unaristotelian notion of 'one vice, one virtue' Ross entirely fails to

see the point. Given two variables, in this case fear and confidence, and ignoring the doubtful cases where one variable is at its optimum and the other not (these would usually be assimilated to one of the clearly vicious dispositions), there are four faulty combinations. If one fears too little, one may also have too much confidence, or too little: 'he would be crazy or insensible' (*N.E.* III, 1115^{b}26: the latter neither flees nor outfaces apparent danger). If one fears too much, one may also have too little confidence: such is the coward. Or he may fear to excess and also have too much (compensating) confidence: the typically over-confident *thrasus* who so easily proves a coward (*N.E.* III, 1115^{b}32). Only the man who fears real dangers and has a worthy confidence in his pursuit of the beautiful (in doing what he believes worthwhile: cf. TAYLOR/WOLFRAM) is *andreios*. Such a man is not predisposed to fear or to boldness. And how are we to habituate ourselves thus? 'We must consider what we are most inclined to . . . and drag ourselves off in the opposite direction, for by moving from error we shall reach the mean, exactly as they do in straightening wood' (*N.E.* II, 1109^{b}1f.; Pl. *Prot.* 325 d). 'Everything needs some counterbalancing force so that it may achieve the measure and the mean (for it is the mean, and not the extremes on their own, which has being and proportion [*ousia* and *logos*])' (*De Part. An.* 652^{b}16f.).

13.   The second great Platonic virtue, *sophrosune*, is also considered in its demotic form. 'Temperance is a *mesotes* about pleasures and pains' (*N.E.* II, 1107^{b}4; III, 1117^{b}23f.). The pains are commonly taken to be those of frustration: 'pleasure makes his pain' (*N.E.* III, 1118^{b}32; see *E.E.* 1231^{a}31f.). At first glance, therefore, Hardie may seem to be right to say that the 'blending' theory involves a blend of pleasures and their absence: but frustration is different from the mere absence of pleasure—if it were not our state would be disagreeable indeed. But in fact there is more to *lupe* than frustration: it is the cause, object, or condition of finding something disagreeable, as *hedone* of finding it agreeable. It is possible to seek the one and avoid the other quite independently (*N.E.* VII, 1150^{a}25f.). Aristotle restricts *sophrosune* to the sphere of tactile pleasure and pain, and regards it as having more to do with pleasures. The akolastic man finds things more disagreeable than he should (in the absence of his pleasures): his taking of excessive pleasure turns to a finding of excessive pain (see III.2.8). Another variety of *akolastos* (though

perhaps more sick than sinful) likes and dislikes the wrong things (the first only dislikes to excess because he is deprived of his liking). The *anaisthetos*, who likes too little, and is rarely found, may also be deficient 'about pains' or else be positively pained by what ought not to pain him. It is obvious that most of these characters (unmentioned as such by Aristotle) would count as ill, but it is conceivable that men might have such erroneous principles. Another model can be teased from the text: the four characters given above varied in what they found agreeable or disagreeable. What if they varied rather in seeking (tactile) pleasure and avoiding (tactile) pain? John avoids pain and seeks pleasure, both to excess: 'effeminacy'. James avoids pain to excess, but is deficient in seeking pleasure: 'trepidation'. Andrew seeks pleasure to excess, and avoids pain too little: 'profligacy' or perhaps 'decadence'. Simon is deficient in both dimensions, and is either insentient or a Gymnosophist. In these terms *sophrosune* would be a *mesotes* about taking pleasure and avoiding pain. Yet a third model is perhaps most illuminating. Let *sophrosune* be a *mesotes* about taking and rejecting pleasure: thinking it good and thinking it bad. One may think it (all or too much) bad—though it is likely enough that such total rejection will turn, or be expected to turn (cf. *N.E.* X, 1172^{b}1f.), into total acceptance: such is the rare super-puritan. One may think it all good, or too much of it: such is *akolastos*. One may think nothing at all about it, either of good or evil, believing it (perhaps) a complete irrelevance. And finally one may have that muddled set of beliefs which declares pleasure bad (as a matter of principle, perhaps, or as a result of excessive *aidos* (see *N.E.* IV, 1128^{b}10f.)) but pursues it (or would wish to) as a manifest good (*N.E.* VII, 1147^{a}31f.). In this case desire and reason, which should be met together, are at variance. This is the encratic, or perhaps the acratic, man whom most of us resemble. The state in which both contraries are present to excess is not virtue, but something very close to vice. Perhaps even below vice, for the wickedly principled man has at least some claim to unity, even if not stability (see III.3.6). The *sophron* finds a more stable unity in supposing some pleasures sometimes bad, and some sometimes good.

14. 'Liberality is a *mesotes* about giving and taking money' (*N.E.* II, 1107^{b}8; IV, 1119^{b}22f.), not as HARDIE says, following Burnet, a mean of giving more and less money. This virtue is a mean of *praxeis* rather than *pathe*, actions rather than feelings, or beliefs. But this

distinction, although a real one, is not to my present purposes: a man may be no less a coward for being a cool one, nor more a 'liberal' for having pangs of compassion. One may treat any virtue as a *mesotes* either of *pathe* or *praxeis* without undue distortion. It does not become a free man to be too concerned with money, for wealth is only a means (*N.E.* IV, 1120ᵃ5; *Pol.* I, 1256ᵇ27f.; see IV.2.17; V.1.13). But it is at least a means, and to waste it is to destroy one's substance in Greek as well as English. The *eleutherios* is more concerned with the use of money than its acquisition (*N.E.* IV, 1120ᵃ9f.), for the taking of money is largely a matter for the virtue of justice. Most probably the *eleutherios* takes his money from his own, inherited estate (*N.E.* IV, 1120ᵃ34f., 1120ᵇ11f.; cf. Pl. *Rpb.* 330 b 8f.). The *asotos* may give more than he should and take less. Or he may give and also take in order to continue his wasteful career (*N.E.* IV, 1121ᵃ30f.). As the *thrasus* becomes a coward, or as excess of pleasure or *lupe* leads to its opposite, so the *asotos* may become *aneleutheros*. This latter is also double-headed (*N.E.* IV, 1121ᵇ17f.): one gives too little, but only holds his own; another takes from other men as well. Both aim at money as an end.

15.   A variety of *eleutheria* is *megaloprepeia* (*N.E.* II, 1107ᵇ16; IV, 1122ᵃ18f.). Here Aristotle emphasizes the balance with the environment necessary in the individual acts: the expense demanded by the situation and the expense incurred. *Banausia*, vulgarity, and *mikroprepeia*, shabbiness, are thus opposed. We may reasonably suppose that the 'organic mean' involved in this virtue is a balance of the desires for display and conservation (*N.E.* IV, 1123ᵃ18f.). The *megaloprepes*, in any case, needs to be a man of taste (*N.E.* IV, 1122ᵃ34). He aims at the beautiful, 'for this is common to all the virtues' (*N.E.* IV, 1122ᵇ7), not at doing just one, materially defined, sort of thing (like giving money away).

16.   'Great-heartedness is a *mesotes* about honour and infamy' (*N.E.* II, 1107ᵇ21; IV, 1123ᵃ34f.). The precise manner of this *mesotes* remains unclear, for Aristotle is diverted into a detailed description of the great man. The *megalopsuchos* regulates his opinion of himself to his deserts, and his deserts are high. Also he pays little attention to the opinions, good or bad, of his fellows (*N.E.* IV, 1125ᵃ6f.). What confirms his rightfully good opinion of himself he accepts. He has no concern with the trivial surprises of the world, for nothing is great to him (*N.E.* IV, 1125ᵃ3). He accepts life only

on the terms appropriate to his great estate (*N.E.* IV, 1124ᵇ8). It may be that Aristotle's main purpose was to show that the sort of great man admired by many of his day and after was admirable only if he was really good—so that it was the goodness and not the greatness which was to be admired: 'that for which we love something is more loved' (*Post. An.* 72ᵃ29f.). On the other hand perhaps this is what an Aristotelian saint *would* be like—not that we should seek to imitate his manner without his merit. Elsewhere Aristotle marks this character as combining intolerance of dishonour with indifference to fortune (*Post. An.* 97ᵇ16f.).

17.   For most of us it is a lesser virtue which preserves us amid honour and infamy (*N.E.* II, 1107ᵇ24; IV, 1125ᵇ1f; VII, 1148ᵃ28f.). It may sound as if the good man does enough but not too much of what brings honour, which is indeed true—for one can have too much of such a lesser good (*N.E.* VII, 1148ᵃ28f.; see V.1.13)—but does not reveal a balance. But a man may refrain from seeking honour, and avoid infamy or the risk of it, to excess: such in Athenian political propaganda is *apragmon*, a drop-out (Thuc. II.63; Eur. *Suppliants* 576f.; cf. NEIL App. 2). One who neither seeks honour nor avoids infamy, living in complete disregard of others' opinions, must be thought unsocial and either more or less than a man. The *megalopsuchos* is exactly thus, and his virtue is for demi-gods rather than men (cf. *N.E.* VII, 1145ᵃ15f.). Another seeks honour but with too little care to avoid infamy. Another seeks honour in fear and trembling, also avoiding infamy: such is overwhelmed by social pressure, and the virtuous man ought not so to lose sight of the noble.

18.   'Courtesy is a *mesotes* about fits of anger' (*N.E.* II, 1108ᵃ4; IV, 1125ᵇ26f.). This is the only virtue not immediately defined in terms of a doublet and may therefore seem anomalous. There is, of course, a balance between response and provocation: a man who had never had just cause to be angry would not be *aorgetos* if he never was, nor would a man who was, on some occasion, very angry be *orgilos* if he had sufficient cause. The virtuous man is not predisposed to anger, but neither is he slavishly accommodating (*N.E.* IV, 1126ᵃ6). Courtesy is, in a way, rather like *sophrosune*: 'vengeance puts a stop to anger, importing pleasure in the place of pain' (*N.E.* IV, 1126ᵃ21), so that courtesy is a mean about the pleasures and pains of vengeance. One may take too much pleasure in vengeance and be too disgruntled

when one does not get it, or else be too disgruntled at events in general (see III.2.13 on *akolastoi*). One may take too little pleasure in vengeance, whether or not one is also too much or too little pained by events. Other models are possible, which perhaps accommodate Aristotle's own examples better than this. The *pikros* is too much pained by events and obtains relief only by swinging to the other extreme: if he does not so swing, his anger remains hidden. The *akrokholos* is perennially furious and openly revengeful, embodying both excesses. The *orgilos* is swiftly angry, but bears no grudges, embodying the excess of anger most clearly. On this model courtesy is a *mesotes* about taking vengeance and remembering wrongs: one who is deficient in both dimensions is perhaps only a simpleton. A third model, once again, is perhaps most illuminating. Virtue is neither a disposition to anger nor one to accommodation: 'the courteous man is not revengeful but rather tends to make allowances' (*N.E.* IV, 1126ᵃ2). One who is always making allowances is no free man, for he is being lived by others, whether he is merely a simpleton or simultaneously wracked by fury. The free man is 'for himself', and not a tool, but neither is he blind to the point of view of others. The problem which courtesy raises is that of the individual in society. One devoid either of sympathy or of temper fails of courtesy. And this of course is a clue to learning how to control one's temper (cf. *Rhet.* 1380ᵃ5f.)—or one's sympathy.

19. 'The courteous man wants to be unconfused, and not to be dragged about by emotion but to be angry about what and for as long as the *logos* bids him' (*N.E.* IV, 1125ᵇ33). This ataraxic condition is not one lacking in emotion, but one in which there is no bias in favour of some one emotional response. 'One should not corrupt a juryman by making him angry, envious, or sentimental: that would be like twisting what one was going to use as a measure' (*Rhet.* 1354ᵃ24f.). The juryman cannot judge clearly or correctly, cannot respond appropriately, when 'private pain or pleasure obscures his judgement' (*Rhet.* 1354ᵇ10). This is why the human sense of smell is inaccurate (III.1.17). It is easy to be deceived about what we see when in an emotional state (*De Ins.* 460ᵇ4f.; *De An.* 429ᵃ7f.; *De Mem.* 450ᵇ1f.). Passion warps judgement (*Pol.* III, 1287ᵃ30f.) and 'the law is reason (*nous*) unaffected by desire'. 'The law is the mean' (*Pol.* III, 1287ᵇ4). Just as the eye tends to accept the current illumination as its standard (III.1.19), so we tend to accept our current mood as reality, or as the proper response to reality. Not that

we should aim at insensibility in our judgements, but that we should make sure in general that we are not predisposed to a particular sort of reaction, by ensuring that we can also react in the opposite way when that is required.

20. The three means of social life, *aletheia*, *eutrapelia*, and *philia*, confirm my analysis (*N.E.* II, 1108ᵃ9f.; IV, 1126ᵇ11f.). The *philos* steers a course between total good-fellowship and being thoroughly disagreeable—not in the sense that he is mildly disagreeable or has no social flavour at all, but that he apportions his approval and disapproval appropriately. Here too there is the inhumanly indifferent man. There is the man who is deficiently sociable and over-critical, the *duskolos*. There is the man who socializes in order to be quarrelsome, the *duseris* (*N.E.* IV, 1127ᵃ10f.: I do not press the distinction between the terms but there are plainly two types). There is the man incapable of criticism, whether he be amateur or professional. 'Truthfulness is about the truth': not that the honest man only speaks some of the truth or mixes lies and truth adroitly, but that he proportions what he says of himself to the truth. Nor that he simply says no more and no less than the truth: in that case the *alazon* would say more and the *eiron* less, whereas in fact the *eiron* actively denies the truth, and in doing so draws close to *alazoneia* (*N.E.* IV, 1127ᵇ29). 'Wit is about the pleasures of recreation.' Defect of wit may result in an *agroikos* or a *skleros*, boorishness or harshness, depending on the degree to which the man disapproves of others' wit. Similarly with excess of wittiness—though *bomolokhos* and *phortikos* do not seem to have very different connotations.

21. *Aidos*, shame, involves a proportion between action and feeling, though it is not really a virtue, and itself involves no emotional balance (*N.E.* II, 1108ᵃ31; IV, 1128ᵇ10f.). One who has never done anything for which he need blush is not shameless if he does not blush, however young he is. As I noted above (III.2.13), it may form a pair with desire. '*Nemesis*, righteous indignation, is a *mesotes* of envy and rejoicing at evil' (*N.E.* II, 1108ᵃ35). The envious man displays too much displeasure, even at good fortune; the malicious an excess of pleasure, even at ill. This is not very satisfactory, and is omitted in the fuller account: the envious and malicious man seem to be identical (cf. *Rhet.* 1386ᵇ34: the envious man is pleased at others' disasters). A more satisfactory triad would be *nemesis*, malice, and sentimentality, which is pained at all ill-fortune however appropriate and rejoices at all good. This triad is given at *E.E.* 1221ᵃ38f.,

though 1233^{b}19f. gives the Nicomachean version. One who rejoices at all fortune is presumably a maniac, one who rejoices at none a dullard.

22. Justice I shall not discuss at length. The judge must balance the contestants' claims against each other, giving each their proper weight, and any deviation is equally injustice. The contestants must also seek to weigh their own interests properly. Total indifference would mark a robot, not a man; to overweight one's own would be *pleonexia*; to overweight one's opponents' interests is slavish weakness; to overweight both is perhaps no more than a failure in one's sense of proportion—*de minimis non curat lex*.

23. What emerges from all this? A virtuous act is one done as it ought to be, appropriately to the demands of the situation. It is one done for its own sake, because it is worthwhile (this is true of all *praxeis* (*Met.* IX, 1048^{b}18f.; see V.1.13f.)), which truly is worthwhile and as the *logos* bids, as the *phronimos* would define (*N.E.* II, 1106^{b}36f.). By noting that the sort of men we admire are not one-sided, that they incorporate opposite faculties, our attention is drawn to the probability that it is such a balanced man who is most likely to make the correct judgements. The spirited and philosophic types should be combined (Pl. *Rpb.* 411); so also courage and temperance (Pl. *Pol.* 306f.). For even virtues on their own are suspect: 'if temperance and liberality are parted, liberality becomes luxurious and temperance toilsome' (*Pol.* II, 1265^{a}33). The nobility of youth and the caution of age are best combined (*Rhet.* 1390^{a}29f.; cf. *N.E.* VI, 1144^{b}1f. on virtue and *phronesis*). Where thick and warm blood gives strength and thin, cold blood intelligence, the best is obviously thin and warm (*De Part. An.* 648^{a}2f.). Similarly minimizers lower their sensory input and can endure pain more easily, but must seek stimulation by adventure and are easily bored; maximizers boost their sensory input and can therefore avoid boredom but are consequently susceptible to pain. Plainly the best (not in this case the virtuous) man is capable of both activities. And so, I think, throughout. Whenever we find that one group of human beings have one capacity or disposition, and another have the opposite, the chances are very high that both capacities have a part to play in human living, and he will be the most reliable judge who has both. The proper man is the whole man.

24. Such a proper man, the *phronimos*, exercises his good sense, and his emotions respond without constraint. He does what is reasonable—not in the sense that he follows the dictates of economic reason, for it may sometimes be eminently reasonable to give up one's life in a worth-while cause (*N.E.* III, 1117ª35f.). In seeing the moral quality of an act the *phronimos* is doing much the same sort of thing as in seeing that a given figure is a triangle or a given fire means the enemy (cf. III.1.24). The distinction between description and evaluation is not one that can be easily maintained. WARNOCK (pp. 18of.) has observed that an existential claim is not logically implied by any set of sensory impressions, both actual and possible: we are committing no logical absurdity in refusing our assent to an existential claim while granting every sensory claim that would normally validate it—we are none the less being ridiculous. Similarly, I suggest, in the moral sphere: a non-moral, or falsely moral, account of the world is as inadequate as a naïvely phenomenalistic one (see VI.7f.).

25. The question 'how shall I live well?' (II.1.1) has led to the question 'how shall I become a good judge?', and received a partial answer in the concept of balance, of incorporating opposite faculties, and also opposite opinions (cf. I.5,13): those who denounce and those who praise any particular type of action open to men both have some truth in what they say, and the good judge will find a mean between their doctrines (III.2.13).

26. 'Before the faculties of pleasure, anger, sorrow and joy are aroused it is called equilibrium ("chung"). When these feelings are aroused and each and all attain due measure and degree it is called harmony. Equilibrium is the great foundation of the world, and harmony its universal path. When equilibrium and harmony are realised to the highest degree, heaven and earth will attain their proper order and all things will flourish' (*Doctrine of the Mean* § 1: CHAN (2) p. 98). Our worlds at least, the worlds we see, will not be in order, will not be seen straight, until we are thus balanced in disposition and harmonious in execution. Our route lies through *enkrateia* in its various kinds, but its destination is the unforced willing of what is right. And in so far as the good man is the standard of truth (III.1.21) the good man's world shows the form of *the* world. But that is, for the moment, another story.

III.3. Policy and Polity

1.   Man alone is both gregarious and solitary (*Hist. An.* 488ᵃ7f.) and the reconciliation of these two capacities, for togetherness and for solitude, is of course a large part of morality. That we should attempt the reconciliation is at once a consequence of the doctrine of the mean (III.2.23) and a practical necessity. My present concern is to outline an Aristotelian approach to the problem. I wish to suggest that it can be solved, or dissolved, with the help of a 'moral' concept of personal identity, the theory that society has a life of its own, and the fact and nature of love.

2.   Man's nature, as I have already argued (II.1.17f.), is precisely such that he has no precisely determined given nature. Men, unlike the stars and unlike lesser sublunary entities, have a double potential, 'so that continuing in motion is a labour' (*Met.* IX, 1050ᵇ26). Not everything is necessary (*De Int.* 19ᵃ7f.; cf. *Met.* VI, 1027ᵃ29f.; IV.1.8f.). Where there is a capacity for contrary effects it is desire or will that is decisive (*Met.* IX, 1048ᵃ8f.; cf. *Phys.* VIII, 251ᵃ30f.: knowledge is capable of contrary effects). Human nature therefore is seen in this wearisome capacity, indeed compulsion, for choice. Such capacities are '*kata logon*', acquired rather than given and a consequence of our ability to contemplate options in their absence: we must choose because we are linguistic entities—we can be individuals because we are social.

3.   My being a man is shown in my capacity to be what I choose, within limits. My being the man I am is shown in what it is I choose to be. 'A thing's nature is its end and final cause' (*Phys.* II, 194ᵃ28f.; cf. 198ᵃ25). Formal and final cause are identical (cf. II.3.15). Earth is what moves to the centre (*De Caelo* 268ᵇ26f.; *Phys.* IV, 208ᵇ8f.): its motion to its proper place (that is, its coming to a natural stop (*Phys.* V, 230ᵇ26f.)) is also its movement to its proper form (*De Caelo* 310ᵃ33). The direction of an entity or stuff is its identity. 'The soul is clearly the final cause of the body' (*De An.* 415ᵇ15). 'Everything is defined by its *ergon* and its potential' (*Pol.* I, 1253ᵃ23). My identity as a man is shown in my human way of life, and particularly in that which is revealed when the human soul comes to rest (*Phys.* VII,

247^{b}17f.; see V.3.18f.), but whereas a particle of earth has no choice in the matter, I have.

4. 'Conatus quo unaquaeque res in suo esse perseverare conatur nihil est praeter ipsius rei actualem essentiam.' 'The endeavour with which each thing endeavours to persist in its own being is nothing else than the real essence of that thing' (Spinoza: *Ethics* III.7; cf. ARBER, E. S. RUSSELL (2) pp. 190f.). But 'by becoming human, man exchanges the stable material self, native to each biological species, for a countless multitude of possible selves, moulded for the working out of a special drama and plot he himself helps to create' (MUMFORD p. 23).[1] My humanity lies in my maintaining myself as a self-determining being: my being Me lies in my maintaining myself in my particular policy of living. My identity over time is a function of this policy maintenance.

5. This sense of identity, of course, is not intended as a solution to the philosophical problem of identity as commonly posed (cf. WIGGINS, PARFIT): rather it is an admission that this problem cannot be unequivocally solved. There is no one criterion or set of criteria by which we can always pick out one and one only individual as the same person as another, past individual. Philosophers who argue that physical continuity, or memory, or similarity of character constitute personal identity miss the point if they think they are arguing about a matter of 'fact': they are simply trying to suggest standard criteria for ascribing responsibility over time. Personal identity may seem obvious, just as ownership may seem simply identical with physical possession: but ownership is in fact a moral, indeed a legal, concept which may or may not rely on physical possession. So also personal identity. The number of persons (i.e. free men) who exist at any one time depends on the number of wills that are in question: slaves and tools are part of their master. Similarly the number of persons that exist over time. Granted, 'friendship with oneself is like kinship, for neither can be dissolved: even if they disagree kinsmen

---

[1] An entity's form is its form of life (or, in general, being (see II.1.6, II.3.9f.)); its form of life (its interests, desires, and priorities) constitutes the world it inhabits. Men are such that it is up to them what world they inhabit, how they take the world (see VI.9). As I shall argue in V.3 and VI, the 'human world' in terms of which everything should be explained (II.2.28) is The World, of which we have an intuition that surpasses our own personal interests (III.1.17). It is because we know, as e.g. a dog does not, that the world is more and other than our immediate desires define, that there can be no single, immediately given life-world for our species.

are kinsmen and a man is single as long as he lives' (*E.E.* 1240ᵇ34f.).
But kinship is not a strictly factual notion: it too depends on social
norms—such that society will reaffirm the kinship whatever the
kinsmen feel about it. Similarly, such lobotomized patients as show
a failure of self-identification over time (and also a failure of sympathy with others and an inability to handle abstract concepts (cf.
GOLDSTEIN (2) pp. 40f.)) are still counted as single over time, though
they do not themselves feel this identity. The wicked too (see III.2.8)
fail of perfect identity over time, or even at a time, but they too are
held responsible by society for their misdoings. Societies which hold
to different criteria of ascribed responsibility are neither impossible
to imagine nor to discover. To say who I am, to identify myself, it is
necessary to be integrated under a particular policy of living, and if
that policy should lapse it amounts to ontological suicide (II.1.14)
even though my society should, protreptically, continue to consider
me single. What Aristotle specifically says of the identity of cities
through time, I impute to persons.

6.   To be human is to have a share in *proairesis* (II.1.19) for 'a man
seems to be a source of actions' (*N.E.* III, 1112ᵇ31f.). '*Proairesis* is
either desiderative reason or ratiocinative desire, and such a source
of action is a man' (*N.E.* VI, 1139ᵇ4). My identity, my 'what I am',
is my policy of living as it expresses itself in particular decisions.
'For it is by choosing the good or ill that we are the sort of people we
are' (*N.E.* III, 1112ᵃ1): by acting in particular cases we make our
dispositions stable, construct our personalities, become single. Our
unity over time and at a time is therefore largely proleptic—we build
ourselves into single persons just as we build the world into ourselves
(II.3.25). Not to choose consistently is not to be any definite sort of
person. *Akrasia*, incontinence, is like a revolt or civil disintegration
—a failure of the integrative power to control its material. STACK
contrasts Kierkegaard with Aristotle precisely on this ground, that
the former thinks of choice 'as an individuating act through which
the personality is consolidated, unified'. Or as Plato said: 'everyone
ought to do the one task for which he is suited, so that each man may,
in doing his one thing, become one instead of many' (Pl. *Rpb.*
423 d 3f.). 'The inferior man is not one but many, and on the same
day is different and unstable' (*E.E.* 1240ᵇ16f.; *N.E.* VIII, 1159ᵇ7f.).
ADKINS (1) apparently thinks that social pressures ensured that the
Greeks were much more divided personalities than we, and that the

notion of a unitary personality was therefore a long time coming. I think he exaggerates the Greeks' difference from us, but this does emphasize that singleness is a creation not a given fact.[2] It is in fact social pressure which helps to make us single. It is the deciding element in man which is the chief part in man and the criterion for his unity (*N.E.* III, 1113^{a}6). Properly to be friends with oneself, at a time and over time, it is necessary to have a stable policy of living, and the nature of that policy determines what we take ourselves to be: to serve oneself is to pursue one's policy. The question of imputed responsibility over policy-gaps is raised with reference to cities' continuity in the *Politics* (*Pol.* III, 1276^{b}14): there is no real difficulty at the personal level. The responsibilities we accept, the policy we wish to pursue, our vision of ourself, may not be the responsibilities, policy, or vision the society we live in would wish. We are not always allowed to escape our debts by changing our minds.

7. From which I conclude that the reconciliation of our gregariousness and our solitariness may be interpreted as the reconciliation of our self-image and societal, what we intend and what is intended for us.

8. Although the concepts of 'good man' and 'good citizen' are generally distinct (*N.E.* V, 1130^{b}28f.; *Pol.* III, 1276^{b}34f.), and no man's identity can be exhausted by his social role, none the less in so far as he is a man he is social. 'No one would choose to have all good things but by himself, for man is social and born to living-together' (*N.E.* IX, 1169^{b}17f.). Given that men have the desires and structure that they do the wilfully solitary man must be the exception, and most probably degenerate (or conceivably divine) in some way. No reasonable man can plan his life in such a way that he is stripped of all human society, save in very exceptional circumstances. 'Jen is jen: humanity (living-together) is humanity (man)' (*Doctrine of the Mean* § 20: CHAN (2) p. 104; CHAN (3)).

9. Living-together for men involves communication (*N.E.* IX, 1170^{b}10), not necessarily agreement. The pleasures of sleep and of children are vegetable pleasures (*E.E.* I, 1216^{a}3f.); sleep is like

---

[2] Attempts to argue that 'the Greeks', or Homeric Greeks, lacked a concept of the self are misguided. Of what, then, would e.g. 'Odysseus' be the name? Of what did Odysseus speak when he spoke in the first person? It remains true that what I regard as me or as mine is in part a function of my society's doctrines; so also is what I regard as most essential to my self.

embryonic life (*De Gen. An.* 778ᵇ35f.). The pleasures of the senses are beast-pleasures (*E.E.* I, 1216ᵃ3f.; *N.E.* I, 1095ᵇ19). A man who has no *logos* about anything is no more than a vegetable (*Met.* IV, 1006ᵃ14f.). Not that these lesser pleasures are forbidden us, but that we have the option of higher ones. Nor that conversation as such is the end of man: for we can all see that talking for the sake of talking is trivial, and in the end boring. The point must rather be that communication can reveal some good. Men are not for discussion, but discussion is a part of that social life in which individuals find the good. Any city, any state which fails to preserve the good life for its members is deviant (*Pol.* III, 1279ᵃ30).[3] A citizen is one who can share in the city's life, the city's civic activities, judiciary, and rule (*Pol.* III, 1275ᵃ32), but the human being who is the citizen does not exist for the sake of the city (unless perhaps the ideal city). The city is for its members, a *koinonia* or companionship of free men (*Pol.* III, 1279ᵃ21).

10. That the free man is at once self-determining and social has one obvious consequence: 'as the virtue of a man is the same as that of a citizen in the best society [cf. *Pol.* III, 1276ᵇ16f.], clearly one would found a state ruled by the best or by a king in the same way and by the same means that a man becomes good [or 'sound' (*spoudaios*)], and the same education and habits will be found to make a good man and a man fit to be statesman or king' (*Pol.* III, 1288ᵃ38f.). It is the nature of this best society, in which freedom and sociality are reconciled, which is to be investigated. We study societies in order to find the form of the good life to be lived by the individual (cf. Pl. *Rpb.* 592 b 2f.).

11. 'A city is naturally prior to the household and to each of us, just as any organism is prior to its parts' (*Pol.* I, 1253ᵃ19; cf. II.3.26). This does not commit Aristotle to the view that men became human within the social group (though this may well be true), or that families are no more than half-separated parts of the whole body politic rather than the fundamental units which believers in the nuclear family suppose (cf. R. FOX). Rather it is only because men have the capacity to form such structures that they are formed: if any two individuals come together to form a larger individual they

---

[3] Strictly, no state can do more than provide the conditions and encouragement for its citizens' *eudaimonia*, can only do what is *sumpheron*, advantageous: but this latter category is defined in terms of the good life, not merely of economic survival.

must share some form: 'in organic unities there is something identical in both parts, which makes them grow together instead of merely touching' (*Met.* V, 1014ᵇ23f.). This form which we share is most clearly to be seen in a (perhaps imaginary) perfect community.

12. The criterion for a city's identity is its constitution (*Pol.* III, 1276ᵇ10f.), its way of life as shown in its institutions and day-to-day decisions (cf. ROBINSON pp. xv ff.): so far so that 'the state is its constitution', as the heart is the source and centre of an animal's life. In so far as there is a total change of direction in a human group a new state is formed: the goal, and explanation, of democracy is liberty, of oligarchy wealth, of aristocracy culture and right conduct, of tyranny self-preservation (*Rhet.* 1366ᵃ4f.). This is more obvious in the case of states than in the case of individual human beings: for whereas we are not permitted to escape our responsibilities by changing policy there is no higher authority who can prevent a state from doing precisely that (though the individual spectator may reprimand such an action). When a democracy gives way to an oligarchy there is a new polity and therefore a new *polis*.[4]

13. A man may cease to be a man by having no more aims: how is a state to vanish utterly, so that there is no more state, even a different one in the same area or with the same inhabitants, at all? If it deviates from the general end of states it may in the end cease to be one, for change 'will first make the state worse and finally no state at all' (*Pol.* V, 1309ᵇ34f.). On the one hand leagues and economic unions generally are not *poleis* because they have no concern for the vice and virtue of their members (*Pol.* III, 1280ᵇ6; cf. 1276ᵃ18f.)— not the totalitarian point which some have made it (ALLAN (3) ref. *N.E.* V). On the other a *polis* that is totally united ceases to be composed of individuals and therefore ceases to be a society (*Pol.* II, 1261ᵃ18f.; cf. Pl. *Rpb.* 462 c). Like any organism a *polis* is composed of anomoeomerous parts and finds its unity in its policy of survival, which must not be such as wholly to override the policies of its members (*Hist. An.* 486ᵃ5f.).

14. This talk of supra-individual organisms may seem absurd or dangerous. That some varieties of political organicism may be so

---

[4] What Aristotle would make of representative democracy in a nation-state is uncertain: probably he would think that if it had any unity at all this must be in terms of 'consensus politics', the general agreement of all parties not utterly to rearrange the state's priorities and techniques of rule.

cannot be denied, but I hope to show that, properly understood, Aristotle's theory is neither ridiculous nor repellent.

15. Any organism is composed of parts. In some organisms the parts can operate independently (not qua parts), becoming for a time e.g. independent cells. Slime moulds such as Dictyostelium, or sea-squirts such as Leptoclinum occasionally form colonies which act as single individuals (PANTIN pp. 48f.). Sponges squeezed through fine silk reconstitute themselves within five or six days (E. S. RUSSELL (2) p. 140). Many organisms are symbiotic associations of lesser organisms of different types. An animal is like a well-governed state (*De Motu* 703ᵃ29f.; cf. *N.E.* III, 1113ᵃ8f.; *Pol.* V, 1302ᵇ35f.). There is therefore no particular difficulty in the concept of an entity composed of variously independent lesser entities, and it is possible that this is the best description of those insect colonies which so impressed the ancients (cf. *De Gen. An.* 761ᵃ5f.: bees have something divine about them; MARAIS). Unity of purpose is a matter of degree: plants are 'living democracies' (AGAR p. 92), to be described more in terms of biological fields than of the organic integrity proper to higher animals. Their parts can grow and regenerate (*De Long. Vit.* 467ᵃ18f.; cf. II.2.13). Where a community develops a common purpose and responsiblities there can be no harm in supposing it a single organism, in its degree. That the multitude should come together to form 'as it were a single man' (*Pol.* III, 1281ᵇ5, IV, 1292ᵃ11) was a familiar enough motif (Aristoph. *Knights*; 'Old Oligarch'[5]): the city is to be less tightly united. Consider a society of telepaths, communicating their thoughts and feelings faultlessly: the individuals have distinctive tastes and opinions, but they can also co-operate in a common policy which defines the total polity. If we have no difficulty in accepting the organic unity of such a society why should we change our attitude when an auditory or visual medium is substituted for a cerebro-electric (or whatever)? It is the nature of this common life in its purest and best form which we should seek.

16. The best *politeia*, called by Aristotle simply 'the *politeia*' as it is this which best fulfils the purposes of such community (*Pol.* III, 1279ᵃ38f.), is government neither by the rich nor the poor exclusively, such that no section of the community is discontented (*Pol.* IV,

---

[5] One of the earliest political thinkers to show how a state's institutions 'made sense' in terms of its end. He was neither old nor an oligarch. Nor was he Xenophon.

1294^{b}37f.). It can arise only where there is a middle class large enough to prevent the domination of the state by great individuals or by mob rule (*Pol.* IV, 1296^{a}23f.). This does not mean that the best state is one ruled exclusively by the middle classes: rather that where the middle class, generally the most inclined to obey the *logos* (*Pol.* IV, 1295^{b}5f.), is strong enough it can compel rich and poor alike to live in harmony, can adopt institutions which combine elements from the self-interest of both opposing groups (*Pol.* IV, 1294^{a}35f., 1297^{a}38f.). The Greek states had torn each other and themselves to pieces by revolution and counter-revolution: in seeking a Solonic balance the Aristotelian state hopes to reconcile the two parties. The description of mixing institutions to reach the mean at *Pol.* IV, 1294^{a}37f. provides for three methods: (i) where oligarchy does *a* and not *b*, and oligarchy does *b* and not *a*, the *politeia* does both *a* and *b*; (ii) where oligarchy requires a high property qualification and democracy either none or a low one, the mean lies between; (iii) where oligarchy does *a* and *b*, democracy *A* and *B*, the *politeia* does both *a* and *B*. The second method is anomalous, nor does Aristotle explicitly say that the *politeia* would adopt this measure: it amounts to demanding a property qualification for citizenship, and thereby excluding the poor. It falls under exactly the charge made by STE. CROIX against the standard interpretation of Theramenes' constitution: the *politeia* must be describable as a democracy (*Pol.* IV, 1294^{b}14)—a mean produced by compromise rather than combination is not (see III.2).

17. The polity is essentially a companionship of free men, who take it in turns to be ruler and ruled. Unfortunately 'by this time it has become a fixed habit with the people in the cities not even to want equality, but either to seek to rule or to endure being ruled' (*Pol.* IV, 1295^{a}40f.). Once the master-slave relation has been thoroughly learnt, men seem unable to find a way through the middle, a way to relate to each other as free men. Men fleeing serfdom come to a new country and there outdo their former lords in tyranny. But this sort of relationship is not 'what men are for', is not a fully satisfying one. There can be no friendship between master and slave, qua master and slave, though there can be 'in so far as they are both men' (*N.E.* VIII, 1161^{b}5), and though the master can have friendship for the slave as part of himself (*Pol.* I, 1255^{b}12; *E.E.* 1242^{a}28f.). But to recognize our common humanity

in reciprocal friendship is to transcend master-slave categories. True friendship arises under the rule of law, which is the mean (III.2.19).

18.   This companionship is what the state exists for, not merely for survival on the economic level (*Pol.* III, 1280ᵇ30f.; VII, 1328ᵃ36f.). Consequently in the perfect state only those classes with leisure and undulled sensibilities should be citizens, sharing with each other the military, counselling, and priestly functions (*Pol.* VII, 1328ᵇ33f.). Mechanics, merchants, and farmers are but the necessary incidentals. In the absence of gods or demigods (*Pol.* I, 1254ᵇ34f.; III, 1284ᵃ3f.; VII, 1332ᵇ16f.; cf. *E.E.* 1215ᵃ26f.), the proper rulers of the state must be those free men who have time and ability to look up from their immediate economic concerns (like the Egyptian priests (*Met.* I, 981ᵇ13f.)). Ideally the whole sub-citizen class, including slaves, should be replaced by automata, as Aristotle envisages at *Pol.* I, 1253ᵇ33f. Neither slaves nor children have any share in *eudaimonia*, as neither lead a free and responsible life (*Pol.* III, 1280ᵃ32f. *et al.*; cf. II.1.19): slaves and children have virtues indeed, but only with reference to the fully developed beings who are their authorities (*Pol.* I, 1260ᵃ31f.; cf. *N.E.* VI, 1142ᵇ34f.). These incomplete men think, as it were, with someone else's head. So also, with some qualifications, do women. Finally, it is only the fortunate Greek who is capable of free and responsible citizenship. The European tribes are spirited but stupid: the Asiatic nations are intelligent but lethargic. The Greek, because he is a mixture, is a mean (*Pol.* VII, 1327ᵇ23f.). Vitruvius thought the same of the Romans (VI 3–11; cf. Pliny *NH* II, 80.110f.): probably every thinker secretly considers his homeland to be the mean. With his judgement, or concession, that war against natural but unwilling slaves is just Aristotle rises from mere racist and male chauvinist pig to rank imperialist (*Pol.* I, 1256ᵇ25). His moral sense is too suspect for any of his words to have any authority with us.

19.   Or perhaps not. Aristotle remarks that nobility is not a reliably hereditable characteristic (*Pol.* I, 1255ᵇ2f.), and the main thrust of his remarks about barbarians and natural slaves is not to demonstrate that barbarians *are* natural slaves but rather to argue from standard Greek opinion to a deeper analysis of exactly what is to be despised in the non-Greek. Barbarians are revealed as slavish by their treatment of women as slaves (*Pol.* I, 1252ᵇ5f.). They are not to be despised simply because they are non-Greek but because they fail, or

are alleged to fail, under certain categories of value: it is these values therefore which are to be admired, not the mere fact of Greekness (cf. *Post. An.* 72ᵃ29f.). 'It must be admitted that some are slaves everywhere, and some nowhere' (*Pol.* I, 1255ᵃ31): there are men who cannot make up their minds, who are manipulated by external influence, who can obey but cannot internalize the law (probably if they cannot do so *at all* they cannot even speak (cf. II.1.23)). War against such men is just, nor is it illiberal to suppose so—what else is the fight against crime? Slavery as an institution may be an evil, and Aristotle admits as much, but it cannot be outlawed by metaphysical dogma: if we could infallibly discover those men who will never live their own lives it were surely as well that they should be able to serve some good master. For those who cannot rule themselves, slavery is both expedient and just (*Pol.* I, 1255ᵃ1f.). They do not therefore have no claim on us, nor are they simply to be ordered without regard to their feelings (*Pol.* I, 1260ᵇ5f.; cf. Pl. *Laws* 777 e). The easy rejection of Aristotle on this point (e.g. SCHLAIFER) is a sign of superficiality. JONES' (cf. RIFKIN) emphasis (pp. 22–3) on the dynamic and liberating effects of Aristotle's discussion is more to the point.

20. What then is left? Firstly, that the life of drudgery and banausic work cannot be thought the best life for men: there must be something better than that, something perhaps revealed in the lives of those who have been relieved from drudgery. Making and mending do not exhaust our possibilities; the life of the community is revealed elsewhere. Secondly, there are almost certainly some men who cannot wholly rise above this level, nor wish to. It is not impossible, and Aristotle perhaps pays too little attention to this, that free men should enjoy craftsmanship and the like, but a man who was utterly engaged in such a task would not be a suitable model for the free-man-in-society.

21. By finding for ourselves what societies we can endure, by finding the categories under which we admire men, we discover the implicit valuations which restrict the scope of the good life. We could not reasonably want to be slavish, or to be wholly engaged in mercantile affairs. The good life is to be found in or within the life of self-determination and mutuality.

22. 'Man's being lies in community, in the unity of man with man— a unity which rests, however, only on the reality of the difference

between I and Thou' (FEUERBACH 59). This basic friendship is possible only between good men, who like each other not for pleasure or utility but for each other's worth (*N.E.* VIII, 1156ᵇ7f.). In corrupt states true friendship, and justice, hardly exist (*N.E.* VIII, 1161ᵃ10f. *et al.*). It is the nature of this friendship, therefore, which is of prime importance in working out how to live (*N.E.* VIII, 1155ᵃ22f.).

23. If there were men as distinguished even physically as the statues of the gods all men would serve them (*Pol.* I, 1254ᵇ34). The exceptionally virtuous are as gods before the law, and in a perfectly good state would be the rulers (*Pol.* III, 1284ᵃ3f.). Gods and heroes would justly be permanent rulers (*Pol.* VII, 1332ᵇ16f.). In the absence of such beings, with whom there could be no ties of law nor therefore of friendship in the fullest sense (cf. *N.E.* VIII, 1161ᵇ6), no one group of people can claim total superiority: all men with whom we can converse at all must have equal rights as far as rule is concerned. 'Reciprocal equality is the salvation of cities' (*Pol.* II, 1261ᵃ30f.). The encroachments of the powerful are more to be feared (*Pol.* IV, 1297ᵃ11f.), and democracy is to be preferred to oligarchy (*Pol.* V, 1302ᵃ13). It is the friendship of free men, the greatest of goods for cities (*Pol.* II, 1262ᵇ7; *N.E.* VIII, 1155ᵃ22), that is to be preserved. What is the nature of this friendship?

24. Aristotle's discussions are to be found in *Nicomachean Ethics* VIII and IX, *Eudemian Ethics* VII, and *Rhetoric* 1380ᵇ33f. I do not want to discuss them in detail, though they merit it, but rather to draw out an aspect which is commonly ignored (as by ADKINS (2) (3)). Friendship lies more in loving than in being loved (*N.E.* VIII, 1159ᵃ27; *E.E.* 1237ᵃ37f., cf. 1239ᵃ26f.). To love *x* is to find pleasure in *x*, whereas to be loved is not itself to be pleased, though one may be pleased to be loved. Considered in themselves it is therefore better to love than to be loved, better to know than be known (*M.M.** 1210ᵇ5f.). It is better to love without return than only to be loved: it is of course even better to be loved in return. Therefore, by an argument applied to a related set of concepts at *Prior Analytics* 68ᵃ39f., that if *A* prefers *x* and not-*y* to *y* and not-*x*, he prefers *x* to *y* and might reasonably pursue *y* as a means to *x*, we must conclude that we cannot pursue being loved over loving: 'being loved is either no end at all or is one relative to the end of loving' (cf. V.1.5). Aristotle is of course aware that some men prefer to be loved than to love (*E.E.* 1239ᵃ26f.; see below), but these are deviant cases, para-

sitic on the norm: the natural end of friendship is active—it is better to give than receive, though human pride being what it is it is sometimes more praiseworthy to accept a gift gladly (cf. *N.E.* IX, 1171^{b}25f., 1169^{a}32f.). What is the use of prosperity when one has no one to share it with (*N.E.* VIII, 1155^{a}7f.)? So also do benefactors love their beneficiaries more than they are loved (*N.E.* IX, 1167^{b}17f.).

25. 'Parents love their children as themselves, for having been split off from them they are as it were other selves, selves at a distance' (*N.E.* VIII, 1161^{b}27). Reproduction is an aspect of growth and continuance (*De An.* 415^{a}22f.), and the logic of semen in particular (*De Gen. An.* 734^{b}14f.) reveals the child as as it were the handiwork of the father. And all handiwork is in a way he that made it, in activity (*N.E.* IX, 1168^{a}7; cf. II.3.25): the child, until it reaches a certain age, is part of the father (*N.E.* V, 1134^{b}10). All friendship and friendly association arise from one's 'relation with oneself' (*N.E.* IX, 1166^{a}1f.), for the bad man is not well disposed even to himself (*N.E.* IX, 1166^{b}25f.). One for whom life is good (*N.E.* IX, 1166^{a}19f.) can find an equal friendship with another such. Selfishness is not loving oneself, but loving oneself more than one ought (*Pol.* II, 1263^{a}41f.). Proper care for one's future and for one's friends is to find life good, to find a good life. On the one hand: 'one life' (*N.E.* IX, 1168^{b}7; Diogenes *Vit.* V, 1.11) and similar phrases reveal an important aspect of love (cf. *E.E.* 1240^{a}36f.). 'Bene quidam dixit de amico suo: "dimidium animae suae". Nam ego sensi animam illius et mei unam fuisse animam in duobus corporibus.' 'Well did he say of his friend, "half of my soul"; for I felt his soul and mine had been one soul in two bodies' (Augustine: *Confessions* IV 6). On the other hand: this life is not simply one's own, for that would be to treat one's friends as mere appendages. Kings get many eyes, ears, and hands by making colleagues of their friends (*Pol.* III, 1287^{b}29), but one who is treated as a tool, for utility or for pleasure, is not being treated as a free man, one who is for himself (*N.E.* VIII, 1156^{b}9f.). True friendship is to love someone for himself, to esteem him because he is worthy of such esteem, to care for him for no ulterior purpose. In doing so we find a wider life than our own. The *homonoia*, unanimity, which marks the political unity of a state (*N.E.* IX, 1167^{a}22f.) is of similar effect. We are more able to think and act with friends (*N.E.* VIII, 1155^{a}15f.); in friendship we can grow in goodness, whence the expression 'splendid deeds from

splendid men' (*N.E.* IX, 1172ᵃ11f.). We grow in community, partly because our friends assist us in the making of our identities, partly because having friends is to be introduced to a wider world. 'Self-hood is social or it is nothing' (HARTSHORNE p. 151). The happy desire solitude least of all, for they want to share their success (*N.E.* VIII, 1157ᵇ21f.). The manner of this sharing must be such as to retain the individuality of the sharers: sharing is impossible unless there is first distinction (*Pol.* II, 1263ᵇ6f.)—and too extreme a success on the part of the Aristophanic lovers of Plato's *Symposium* would result in their destruction (*Pol.* II, 1262ᵇ10f.).

26. Complete, reciprocal friendship is only possible between the good, but there are other, unequal friendships of a praiseworthy sort in which men can appreciate each other for themselves (*N.E.* VIII, 1158ᵇ11f.), and these too involve assessments of the loved one: a change in the loved one must alter the friendship qua esteem (*N.E.* IX, 1165ᵃ36f.), even to destruction—though there may still be good will or sorrow for old time's sake, or the general human sympathy felt even for the wicked (*Poet.* 1453ᵃ2f.; cf. Diog. *Vit.* V, 1.11: Aristotle's remark in reference to an act of charity to an undeserving cause—'I gave not to the man but to humanity'). Our responsibilities vary with the degree of friendship we have accepted or are expected to accept (*N.E.* VIII, 1159ᵇ35f.; cf. 1162ᵃ29f.). Aristotle would certainly have agreed with the opponents of Mo Tzu's doctrine of universal love (FUNG I 76f.) that this would be to obliterate necessary distinctions and, most probably, love itself. Each of us is surrounded by circles of friendship and obligation, varying in degree: and it is in accepting such responsibilities that we make ourselves.

27. Although community is natural to man, still there is always difficulty in living such community (*Pol.* II, 1263ᵃ15f.). The good man is not at discord, but a friend to himself, and 'a man is like that by nature, but a wicked man is contrary to nature' (*E.E.* 1240ᵇ12f.): our difficulties lie in making a unity of ourselves and a true commun-ity of our society. They are the same problem. It is the responsible lover who best combines the various human capacities.

28. The good man, he that achieves the good life, does not pri-marily serve his bodily appetite, his political ambitions, or such lesser class-functions: rather he seeks to preserve himself in love, to find and maintain that life which may be served by all men in their

degree and for which there is no competition. Drinking-companions too share what they take to be their lives, but their companionship is contingent upon there being a sufficiency of drink. True friends may compete in virtue, but not in such a way as to deprive the other of virtue. By recognizing that we desire and admire true friendship we direct our attention to the sort of identities we need to achieve it. To permit our friends to have lives of their own is to find a perspective in which we too may have lives of our own. I cannot be free unless I let others free (cf. III.3.17), and in doing so within love I find that which is common to all who can be friends (cf. III.3.11)—namely *nous*: 'the man who loves and gratifies this is especially a lover of self' (*N.E.* IX, 1168ᵇ33), for it is this for which our structure is what it is.

29. On Aristotle's terms a truly self-reflexive activity is impossible, as I shall argue below (V.2.9, V.3.12), so that any claim to self-reflexivity must unpack in terms of a separate subject and object. Loving oneself therefore amounts to caring for one's future, qua some self-image, or esteeming that in oneself which is counted good. The proper variety of self-love is to esteem *nous* and to care for oneself qua noetic being. I do not wish to admit the common locution which equates *nous* with reason, for 'reason' commonly means the calculative faculty, which itself moves nothing (*De An.* 432ᵇ26f.; cf. *N.E.* VI, 1144ᵃ7f.) and which now carries implications of a particular sort of self-concern, namely the economic. For the moment I prefer to employ '*nous*' more as a dummy term, to mean whatever it is which is common to all men such that to care for our future qua noetic beings is to care also for all good men in their degree, and indeed for all men.[6]

30. The good life is the same for city and for individual (*N.E.* I, 1094ᵇ7f.; *Pol.* VII, 1324ᵃ5f.): both must retain their balance, see things as they are, abide by their obligations, treat others differently when they are relevantly different (cf. *Pol.* VII, 1324ᵇ32f. *et al.*), serve the most divine element in themselves (cf. *N.E.* IX, 1168ᵇ31). Both aim to achieve peace: movement is for the sake of rest, and is

---

[6] To love oneself is to do what is right. This is not to define right action by the known phenomenon of self-love: it is to analyse self-love in terms of action. Being is doing (II.1.18, V.1.2f.), so that to love what one is is to love what one *does*. Similarly in Buddhist thought, 'true knowledge is self-knowledge' does not define knowledge as introspection but the Self as the supreme object of knowledge (V.3.32).

completed upon achieving somewhere to rest (*Phys.* V, 229ª25f.);
war is for the sake of peace, all the changeful for the sake of the
unchanging (*Pol.* VII, 1325ª5f., cf. 1333ª21f.). 'The highest good is
neither war nor civil strife . . . but peace with one another and
friendly feeling' (Pl. *Laws* 628 c 9).

31. There are alternatives. Aristotle distinguishes between the
philetikos and the *philotimos*, the loving and the ambitious (*E.E.*
1239ª26f.). The denial of tenderness, the preference of honour to
active loving (love consists in loving more than in being loved
(III.3.24)) is at the root of robotic theories of human personality, the
inability to see people as people (SUTTIE; cf. II.1.7). The *philotimos*
does not 'love himself' more than the *philetikos*: he does so less.
For 'to love oneself' is do what is right, or what one thinks right:
there is no self other than that served in such right-doing. And it is
the man who sees and does what truly *is* right, who loves himself,
and others, most truly. In seeing what 'men are for', what explains
and justifies their given nature, he so acts as a loving society would
enjoin. In doing so he finds humanity. To act otherwise than rightly
is to find no stable self at all.

32. 'The mind of heaven and earth, which gives birth to all things,
is love (jen). Man, being endowed with Ch'i (matter), receives this
mind of heaven and earth, and thereby his life. Hence tender-
heartedness and love are part of the very essence of his life' (Chu
Hsi: BRUCE (1) p. 182; NEEDHAM (1) II 488).

33. Right living is to serve the true polity in which love engenders
equality and the rule of law. In doing so we serve our 'true selves',
that which explains our natures (cf. II.1.25f.). Only those who can
thus love without exploitation (III.3.25) can be good men, for only
they can appreciate things and people as they are in themselves, and
so see the 'mind of heaven' (see V.3 and VI).

34. The good sense, *phronesis*, displayed by the good man in
organizing his life is essentially one with that shown by the good
householder or the good statesman (*N.E.* VI, 1140ᵇ10f., 1142ª9f.;
E.E. 1218ᵇ13). We must take account of the responsibilities enjoined
on us in the highest form of society. Different men value life, create
their lives, under different descriptions and it is that pursuit which
is for them the chief meaning of existence which they most wish to
share (*N.E.* X, 1172ª1f.). Only that form of life which we can suppose

or endure to be shared is a suitable life for us. I shall have more to say on the architecture of the lives we build (V.1), on the techniques of judgement we must employ (IV.2) and on that most divine of things whose presence in us provides both for love and science (II.1.30; V.3). My present conclusion is that the reconciliation of man's capacities for solitude and togetherness, for self-service and altruism, lies in realizing that the self we serve is one that we create, and that the only reasonable self to create is a loving one.

35. 'Man is love' (BLAKE p. 743): the fact that individual men are so obviously and so frequently not, is precisely our problem.

IV.1. Time

1. In laying such stress on the dynamic aspect of being I may seem thoroughly unaristotelian. For though no serious student of Aristotle could fall into this trap, it has become orthodox in other and wider circles to speak of Aristotle's 'structure' as if it were equivalent to 'shape' (e.g. MOULYN; cf. II.1.7). We are earnestly informed that 'Aristotle could not grasp reality as time and change' (GUNNELL p. 235; see App. C. 6), though this would surely be a rather peculiar variety of ignorance. In fact, of course, Aristotle devoted much of his philosophical attention to the fact and nature of change, development, and activity. Against Parmenideans who held that true being was unchanging he declared that 'we take it for granted that all or some of what exists by nature is in motion' (*Phys.* I, 185ª12). Against those determinists who held that past and future were equally fixed he affirmed the double potential of what existed: a given cloak may be cut up, or it may wear out first (*De Int.* 19ª12). As we shall see, it was essential that he should do so: if an entity can be nothing, or do nothing, except what it actually does (throughout its 'life-time'), the whole distinction between an entity's being of a certain sort and its accidental features must collapse (see II.3.8f.). As PRIOR saw (e.g. (1) p. 64), a metaphysic of substances (rather than events or stuffs) goes along with limited indeterminism (that some, but not all, alternatives are possible) and with tensed propositions (rather than the untensed, timelessly true or false propositions of ordinary modern logic). My purpose in this chapter is not to contribute to the running debates about the value of tense-logic, or the *A* and *B*-theories of time (though it will be obvious enough that I prefer the *A*-theory, approve of tense-logic, and believe that Aristotle was on the same side). I wish only to outline what I take to be Aristotle's account of temporal change, and give at least some prima facie reasons for thinking it reasonable. Without such an account his metaphysic of substance, his concept of human freedom, and his affirmation of the reality of the world of sense (see also VI) remain incomplete. Our temporal model, furthermore, is closely related to our other qualities and personality traits (KNAPP/GARBUTT, FRAISSE): an outline of Aristotle's

model will therefore assist the understanding of his canonical man (see VI.9).

2.   McTaggart divided temporal properties into the *A*-series, which consists of past, present and future, and the *B*-series, which consists of events earlier than, or later than, other events. The *B*-series is unchanging: the death of Alexander is (timelessly) before the death of Napoleon. The *A*-series is perpetually changing: what was future, is present and will be past. *B*-theorists contend that the *B*-series is the more basic, and that true propositions should always be expressed in timeless terms if we are to speak accurately. *A*-theorists contend that our understanding of the *A*-series precedes the construction of the *B*-series, which is no more than an abstraction from lived reality, and not its transcendent ground. Different philosophers have introduced different qualifications into this broad division, but the opposition between *B*-theorists (or dimensionalists) and *A*-theorists (or operationalists) still stands. My thesis is that Aristotle was, within the limits of his time (for the question had perhaps not been fully formulated: cf. IV.2.21), an *A*-theorist, and that common objections to his account stem from *B*-theory assumptions on the part of his critics.

3.   Aristotle's account of time in *Physics* IV has frequently been summarized (e.g. CALLAHAN; see also CONEN). After posing an assortment of questions, in his usual manner (how can time exist when what is past is no longer and what is to come is not yet? how can moments come to be or pass away—when do they do so? how can 'now' remain always the same without making all event simultaneous?), and quickly outlining current solutions to the nature of time, Aristotle suggests that 'time is the number of motion with respect to the before and after' (*Phys.* IV, 219ᵇ2). The 'now' is, in one sense, always the same and, in another, different (*Phys.* IV, 219ᵇ12f.). Just as a point, or a body, may be carried from place to place and remain the same, though differently described, so also 'the now' is differently described as we are aware of 'the before and after' in motion (*Phys.* IV, 219ᵇ18f.). Time and the now are interdependent (*Phys.* IV, 219ᵇ33f.). What does this amount to?

4.   The obvious objection to Aristotle's definition of time is that it is circular. Surely there could be no change if there were no time, so that we can hardly analyse time in terms of change? Surely the relevant sort of 'before and after' relationship (see *Phys.* IV, 219ᵇ15f.)

can be defined only in terms of time? In fact, the first objection does not quite work, for epistemological and ontological priority are distinct (*Met.* V, 1018ᵇ9f.): we may know of change before we know of time, even though time is a *sine qua non* of change, and may therefore introduce the concept of time by way of change. But Aristotle denies, by implication, that time is a *sine qua non*: it is an attribute of change which is dependent on the possibility of a counter (*Phys.* IV, 223ᵃ21f.). Similarly the objection to introducing 'before and after' into a definition of time fails if 'time' and 'before and after' are interdependent concepts—it is no objection to the definition of e.g. logical symbols that the definiens can equally be taken as the definiendum. But the objector may still feel uneasy: for my answer is as much as to say that temporal concepts are irreducible to non-temporal concepts, that time is an immediately intuitable phenomenon (see III.1.23f.). If we do not know what it is we cannot be told (cf. V.3.1).

5. ROSS (2) raises the question of circularity (with reference to 'before and after') and the alleged possibility of change's existence without time (p. 68). He also urges that the 'static now', the dated moment, is inconsistent with the dynamic, the 'now' which always is the same in being (p. 601), and that 'now' can only be specifically the same from moment to moment—'now' is applicable to only one moment at a time and to all moments at those moments (p. 67). If this latter point be true then time, or the temporal spread, is made up of 'nows' (against *Phys.* IV, 220ᵃ18, *De Caelo* 300ᵃ12f., cf. Pl. *Pmn.* 156 d). Ross declares firmly that time should be considered a dimension in which motion is extended (pp. 65, 607). This is the crux of the matter. If time *is* a dimension in the sense which Ross apparently intends, it is made up of moments which are all (timelessly) present; there could be empty time into which motion is *not* extended (against *Phys.* IV, 218ᵇ21f.); 'the now' would not change at all, for all truths are timeless; difference of date is to be cashed as difference of location in a quasi-spatial 'direction'. We may reasonably conclude, not that Aristotle is simply mistaken, but that he would refuse Ross's account of time as a dimension. What would he put in its place?

6. There is a sense in which the most fanatical *A*-theorist may admit that 'time' is dimensional: namely that it is measurable. In this sense time may be continuous or discrete (Aristotle supposes it more

probably continuous (*Phys.* VI, 237^a15 *et al.*)): that is, we may measure in ever smaller units or may find that there is some smallest possible unit of measurement in the natural world. Having measured the time, that is to say having seen how many times some standardly repeating process has occurred during the course of the relevant event, we may represent this relationship as a divided line. The present is then seen to 'move' from one end of the line to the other: it was at time t^0, is at time t^i and will be at time t^{ii}. There is nothing mysterious about this, nor do we need a second time-series to accommodate the 'movement of the present': for this is only a sophisticated rewording of the simple chronicle 'My time-keeper has now completed (i) revolutions since I started counting and will soon complete (ii)' (see PRIOR (4) pp. 17f.). If this operationalist interpretation is refused, we are asked to conceive of Newton's absolute time (see SMART pp. 81f.), time as a container of events in a sense more literal than Aristotle's (*Phys.* IV, 221^a4f.). But if dates are literal, or 'quasi-literal' places, we must abandon all talk of the present's moving up them (as ROSS (2) p. 68). For the present has got to t^0 at t^0, and to t^1 at t^1, and so throughout: the present is time-lessly at all dates in the temporal spread. Past and future are purely relational concepts, equivalent to 'before this utterance' and 'after this utterance' respectively: in whichever direction we point, towards the Battle of Megiddo or towards Armageddon, events are equally and symmetrically fixed.

7. In short: the *A*-theorist takes tensed experience to be basic both epistemologically and ontologically—as far as his logic goes there is no need for him to think that the future is as fixed as the past; he constructs his chronology out of his experience of entities' 'behaviour'. The *B*-theorist considers that Reality is, strictly, untensed: he may not think that this actual universe, from t^0 to t^n, is the only *possible* universe (there are other possible worlds which offend against neither logic nor natural law), but descriptions of that universe whether to the past or the future are equally fixed—if God cannot change the past (as *N.E.* VI, 1139^b5f.; *De Caelo* 283^b7f.), neither can He change the future. 'There is some sense, easier to feel than to state, in which time is an unimportant and superficial characteristic of reality. Past and future must be acknowledged to be as real as the present, and a certain emancipation from slavery to time is essential to philosophic thought' (B. RUSSELL p.166). There is

a sense in which Aristotle would agree (IV.2.23), but perhaps not the sense which Russell, and the *B*-theorists, intended.

8.   'If it be true to say that *x* will be (*estai*) it must sometime be true that *x* is. But if it be true now that *x* is going to be (*mellei*) nothing prevents it from not happening' (*De Gen. Corr.* 337ᵇ4f.). We cannot in general argue with anything like certainty from past to future for there are too may incidentals to any system that we might pick (*Post. An.* 95ᵃ34f.; *De Div.* 463ᵇ23f.): what is going to be may not happen, what happens may not have been going to happen (as meeting one's debtor in the market-place (*Phys.* II, 196ᵃ2f.)). That is to say, common sense would suggest that some future events are not implied by, made unavoidable, or even made expectable by the present situation. The *B*-theory, at a popular level, tends to fatalism: all the meetings that will occur (of which it is sometime true that they are occurring) are inevitably going to occur, just as those that have occurred are now ineluctable. At a more sophisticated level this fatalism may be rebutted: the mere fact that we have made or will make certain decisions does not mean that the decisions are fated. Where future event depends upon our will and not upon the inevitable consequences of present fact, our will is a factor in event. There is, none the less, a real difficulty here. For there is surely *one* present fact which does inevitably imply that *x* will be: namely, that '*x* will be' is true. Granted, I will not assert that *x* will be unless I have strong grounds for thinking it inevitable, but I do know that it is either true to say that *x* will be, or it is false. If it is true, inevitably *x* will be; if it is false, inevitably *x* will not be. And although what inevitably follows from a given proposition may not itself be inevitable (for the given proposition may itself be avoidably true), in this case the proposition given is a present fact, and 'whatever is, necessarily is, when it is' (*De Int.* 19ᵃ23). What is or has been is ineluctable: we cannot do anything about past or present fact. And therefore we cannot do anything about future fact either: for what follows inevitably from an inevitable truth is itself an inevitable truth.

9.   The argument I have given, with deliberate sketchiness, represents Aristotle's argument in chapter nine of *De Interpretatione*. I say only 'represents', for I have no assurance of understanding Aristotle's own train of thought: the passage is one of which it is more than usually true that we need to come to some conclusion about

his meaning before we can decide what he has said. The topic has been discussed by Anscombe (MORAVCSIK), Rescher (GALE), ACKRILL, (2) pp. 132f., PRIOR ((4) ch. 7), BUTLER, HINTIKKA (1), and many others. I do not think that any, save perhaps Hintikka, need complain of any distortion in the argument given above. In brief, it declares that if (i) the truth of future singular propositions is a present or past truth ('if Fp ("x will be"), then it is true now that Fp'), and if (ii) all present or past truths are necessary (given, ineluctable), *then* if Fp, 'Fp is true' is a necessary truth from which Fp necessarily follows: Fp is therefore a necessary (given, ineluctable) truth in exactly the same way as past and present truths (or else of course its contradictory is). There seem to be several possible answers. Firstly, we might deny that Fp can be taken as a premise, as Aristotle seems inclined to do (*De Int.* 19ᵃ39: ACKRILL (2)). Or more exactly: statements are true according to how the actual things are (*De Int.* 19ᵃ32f.), and unless the actual things are already such as to make the future event inevitable the future-tensed proposition is *not* true, but false. So also is the denial of the future event, if this is equivalent to an assertion of an inevitable non-event: what is true in this situation is NFp rather than FNp. This is to treat 'x will be' as equivalent to 'x is inevitably going to be'. Alternatively, we might say that Fp, if not inevitable, is (as yet) neither true not false. This is to admit a class of statements which express non-inevitable futurity without actually being false. In either case, Fp can be true only if it is inevitable: the first variant denies that 'either Fp or FNp' is exhaustive (they being contraries rather than contradictories); the second denies that Fp, having as yet been made neither right nor wrong by the some-time truth of p or Np, has (so far) any truth value at all. Taking another line entirely, we might deny (i) declaring that 'Fp *is* true' is only a specious rewording of Fp itself, which precisely reports or predicts a future truth: future truths are not to be taken as part of the present situation. To say that a truth is 'necessary' when it *is* a truth does not mean that it is a necessary truth *tout court* (*De Int.* 19ᵃ23f.). This may seem like an evasion: for it either accepts the first line of attack that a non-inevitable Fp is *not* true now, or rather oddly denies that a present truth (or a future-perfect truth, which is normally held to be equivalent to a past, present, or future truth) is part of the present situation. This approach therefore tends to dissolve into the third major solution, the denial of (ii). Only those present (past) truths which we can do nothing about are necessary: if Fp turns out to have been true at t^0, it was not necessarily inevitable then—'turning out to have been true' is like the retrospective legalization of a hitherto debatable act. Whether Fp was true or not, whether X's doing a was legal or not depends on us. We can affect, if not the past, at least the status of past event, including that of past prediction. On this interpretation it is true that Fp or FNp, but 'not this or that, but whichever happens' (*De Int.* 19ᵃ38): neither has been made unavoidably true as yet, although one must be.

10. It is obvious that any of these approaches can find some support in the Aristotelian text. What is common to them all is the thesis that what happens need not happen, that the difference between the expectable future and the actual future is not a function simply of our ignorance, but a real feature of reality. Leaving status claims aside, what has been will always hereafter have been, without hope of alteration. What will be has not always been, symmetrically, indeterminable by our action or by incidentals. 'Fp is true' is an inevitable truth only if Fp is inevitable in its own right: Fp cannot acquire inevitability from the ineluctability of present and past truth. How precisely we formalize this denial does not, for my purposes, greatly matter: the different approaches are often difficult to distinguish, nor is there any obvious way of choosing between them.[1] What matters is that past and future are asymmetrical; and not all possibilities in any given case are realized.

11. In view of this last conclusion, it is surprising to find HINTIKKA (2) attributing the Diodoran modalities to Aristotle, the claim that the possible is what is true some-time and the necessary what is true always. If this be so, and if p's present truth implies that it will always be that p was true, and that it was always true that it would be, then 'p at t^0', being true for all time, is also necessary. On this view Aristotle's problem is posed by the timeless truth-values of most modern logic. The consequence, obviously, is to render the

---

[1] It seems *marginally* preferable to suppose that Aristotle wished to reject Fp as a possible premise in this argument (as ACKRILL (2) pp. 137f.). It is not so clear that such a rejection would have taken the form of attributing a third truth value to Fp and to FNp. It is not necessary for 'Socrates is ill' and 'Socrates is well' to be one true and the other false—not because both are indeterminate, but because both are false (*Cat.* 13ᵇ14f.: IV.1.12): though once there *is* a Socrates one is true. Once, we might say, there *is* a tomorrow (i.e. tomorrow) it will be sea-battlish or un-sea-battlish—it is neither now. This is not to imply that instants are entities (against *Met.* III, 1002ᵇ5).

term 'necessary' useless. *A*-theorists may well respond, for example, that even if *Fp* turns out to have been true there are some propositions which could not have been uttered until the subject had come into being, so that these at least were not true, for they did not exist at all (see II.3.27: PRIOR (1) ch. 7). *B*-theorists might respond that '*p* at t^0' is not true-at-all-times, but true timelessly: it is not true *now*, at t^i, any more than Caesar exists at t^i simply because he exists (timelessly) at t^0. Of these alternatives Aristotle would probably prefer the former: we cannot know what a thing is until we know that it is (*Post. An.* 93ᵃ20), for until it is it has no nature at all. It is also notable that Aristotle expresses the determinist argument in terms of people's saying things, not in terms of metaphysical 'propositions' that are waiting for their subjects. But Hintikka does not demonstrate that Aristotle would accept the Diodoran modalities. To say that we cannot say that 'this is capable of being but will not be' (*Met.* IX, 1047ᵇ3f.) is not to say that every possible *must* be true some time, still less as a matter of definition: it is simply to say that if we admit the possibility of *p* we cannot simultaneously deny it, and conversely, if *p* will certainly not come true we cannot declare it possible. Probably Aristotle would agree that if *p* (some fairly general thesis, as 'a cat is eating margarine') is possible, then it is incredible that it should never, through all time, manage to be true (see IV.2.14). It does not follow that possibility resides in 'some-time fact'—in that case we should apply the rule in particular as well as indefinite cases, and conclude that if Tabitha never eats margarine she couldn't have. Possibility resides in present entities' powers, which are evidenced in the acts of those entities' congeners (II.3.13). What is never evidenced cannot be believed to be a potential of that sort: what is always happening must be supposed a potential of some sort of entity (II.3.27). Some realized events are aspects of the development of a given form of entity (as an acorn's growing to an oak); others are aspects of that entity's material nature (an acorn's decaying: V.2.6), which in turn is a function of some *other* entities' development and movement in the world.

12.   What is indisputable in all this is that Aristotle is concerned chiefly with the tensed statements of ordinary discourse. He is concerned with what we can truly, or at least reasonably, say about our position in the world between determinate truth and determinable futurity. The present tense is basic, and only present-tensed verbs

are *verbs*, as against verbal inflexions (*De Int.* 16ᵇ16f.).[2] To be is to be *now*: 'moments will not be simultaneous with each other, for the former moment will always have passed away' (*Phys.* IV, 218ᵃ15). Homer is a poet, truly, but it does not follow that Homer *is* (*De Int.* 21ᵃ25f.). If there is no Socrates, then both 'Socrates is ill' and 'Socrates is unwell' are false, while 'Socrates is not well' is true (for Socrates is nothing at all (except a philosopher?)). This is true even in syllogistic: for although some syllogistic premises of the universal sort must be true without temporal limitation (*Prior An.* 43ᵇ11f., *Post. An.* 73ᵃ28f., 96ᵃ14f.), many must depend upon the time of utterance. When there are no Eskimos all claims about them are false and all denials true: the square of opposition is made consistent by taking both universal and particular affirmative forms to carry existential (presently existential) force, and neither negative form (Thompson: MORAVCSIK)—this, at least, is the most plausible framework for Aristotelian syllogistic. Such present-tensed claims become true or false according to the current state of the world: propositions become true (false)—that is, entities 'behave'. And they behave in the only moment available to them, namely the present. The *B*-theorist describes change in such terms as 'The cat is on the mat at t^0 and not on the mat at t^1, which is itself an unchanging truth: the *A*-theorist, and Aristotle, describe the same 'event' as the changing of one proposition, 'the cat is on the mat,' from true to false, not the juxtaposition of two different propositions. This change is, of course, only the reflection of the cat's getting off the mat.

13.   Some universal propositions never stop being true, and are therefore not 'in time' (*Phys.* IV, 221ᵇ3f.). But this is not a *B*-theorist's worship of timeless truth (as Donald Williams: GALE p. 99). The point is that the 'span of truth' of such propositions, the period during which they are true, is not contained within any longer period of their untruth. Similarly the *aion*, the period of the whole heaven (and therefore of the totality of things) includes all time (*De Caelo* 279ᵃ25): on this eternity all lesser things depend, within this 'period' all lesser periods fall. *Aion* always is, ἀεὶ ὤν; *aither*, the fifth and divine element, always runs (*De Caelo* 270ᵇ23; 279ᵃ27; Pl. *Crat.* 410

---

[2] This is to anticipate PEARS's suggestion that temporal characteristics are adverbial: 'is past' does not mean that the subject *is* (even timelessly), still less that we need a second temporal dimension to accommodate the change from being future to being past. 'Is past' means precisely that the subject *is not*.

b). The world has always existed and always will exist (*Phys.* VIII, 250ᵇ11f.) for if the world could ever not have existed there is no reason why it should now exist, and it cannot be in an entity's nature to cease to exist (see V.2.3). The world is therefore eternal, and its life is always complete. God makes coming-to-be uninterrupted (*De Gen. Corr.* 336ᵇ32); God, being God, cannot (or would not) destroy or remake the world (*Peri Philosophias* fr. 19ᶜRoss). This eternity does not imply that there is any actual infinity of past time (*Phys.* III, 206ᵃ1; *De Gen. Corr.* 318ᵃ19f.; *Met.* XI, 1066ᵃ35f.), but rather that it has always been the case that something was the case before. We have completed an infinite series of events culminating in the present but that series does not now exist, and we cannot grasp all of it because there is no 'all' to grasp. We have completed the series, but the series is nonetheless infinite, for it had no beginning. In counting the years of the past we must begin from the present (*Met.* V, 1018ᵇ14f.), and in so counting we would never have to stop: in this respect the Greeks' lack of a standardized chronology (FINLEY) worked in Aristotle's favour—he was not tempted to begin counting from an imaginary 'first year'. The heavenly life, which contains all events in some sense, does not contain them in any Boethian *totum simul* (for not all events are simultaneous (*Phys.* IV, 218ᵃ25f.) nor is there perception without change (see III.1.20)). It contains all else because it outlasts all else, and because all wholes are 'in' their motive and their end (*Phys.* IV, 210ᵃ21f.).

14.   Aristotle has other arguments for the eternity of the world which may suggest a more metaphysical approach. Time will not end as long as there is motion (*Phys.* IV, 222ᵃ29f.). For the only condition under which motion could exist without time, that is without being countable in respect of the before and after, is a world without the possibility of a counter (*Phys.* IV, 223ᵃ22f.). And counters are impossible only where life (and self-movement) is impossible: but in that situation motion too is impossible (*Phys.* VIII, 254ᵇ12f. *et al.*). Time is an attribute of motion which is brought into being by the same fact as is motion. And once motion has started an infinity of pastward time is created which cannot reasonably be considered 'empty'. Likewise an infinity of futureward time. *B*-theorists might draw erroneous conclusions from this sequence of arguments: firstly, that the initial possibility of motion without time refers to the same concept as Russell's claim that without minds no one moment

of the temporal spread has any pre-eminence (only minds are de-
luded into thinking what is later than themselves is less real that
what is earlier). Time as a container is prior to change; time as the
experience of becoming is an error of the human mind. But this
is not Aristotle's point: things certainly become, and there is no
illusion (see III.1.27). Rather, time is the *number* of change, and
numerables are not Platonically conceived, but as possibly being
enumerated. Time does not exist without this possibility because
numbers do not. Aristotle would more likely say that time as the
possibility of becoming is, in a sense, prior to change; time as a
container is an abstraction of the human mind. A second error would
be to suppose that imaginary 'empty time', the initial possibility of
which is created by the fact that we can go on counting indefinitely
once we have standard units (we can talk of 'a million years before
the formation of the Sun' without paradox even though a year is in
the first instance dependent on the existence of the Sun), is a metaphysical container. The point is rather that once anything exists we
can reasonably ask 'what happened before?'. A third error has more
immediate support. Time cannot come into being or have an end,
'for there could be no before and after without time' (*Met.* XII,
1071^{b}7f.). Surely this is an admission that time is a *sine qua non* of
becoming? But there is no need to suppose so: to come into being
is not to have existed before, to have an end is not to exist after. It
might be possible to devise a tense-logic in which beginnings (ends)
did not imply previous (subsequent) non-being: it is hardly surprising that Aristotle did not do so. There might be thought to be
a slight inconsistency in his method: he insists that a purely potential infinity, such that one may divide a line in whatever ratio one
pleases, is good enough for geometers, and proves nothing about an
actual spatial infinity (*Phys.* III, 207^{b}27f.). Chronological infinity,
on the other hand, is held to demand an absence of temporal limits.
One might reply that, just as space may be unbounded yet finite, so
also may time: particularly as all processes are cyclical (IV.2.13). Is
not the same time continually coming round for this very reason
(*Phys.* IV, 223^{b}24f.)? Aristotle firmly denies the suggested moral:
time is not a circle, for the present would then be the beginning and
the end of the same process (*Phys.* IV, 222^{b}1f.). Once again, this
reply only works if the present alone is real: otherwise, by analogy,
the America reached by going east from Europe would have to be
counted as numerically distinct from that reached by going west.

B-theorists have no general ground for rejecting the view that time might be unbounded but finite. Aristotle pins his faith on the experience of the (present) world which exists as a given fact with continually realized possibilities of development.

15. At *De Memoria* 450ᵃ17f. Aristotle insists that an awareness of time is necessary for memory. We may have images in our mind's eye but unless we recognize these images of something that was and is no longer, we are not really remembering. Unless we can put our 'memories' into some sort of order, there is only a confluence of images.[3] If we cannot number events in respect of the before and after, our images of them might be predictions or visions of some currently existing reality, not of the soil from which the present situation is developed. We can go further: to see the world intelligibly at all we must be aware of time. Consider the creation of a stretch of sand, level save where it is indented into hollows about nine inches by two, rounded at one end and ragged at the other. So there is some sand in a particular configuration. But do not be so detached: it is not merely a particular configuration—look with the eyes of humanity and see that there are footprints in the sand. GOSSE (see BORGES (2) pp. 22f.) seems to have been the first to point out that the creation of any configured universe, that is of any universe, necessarily involved the creation at least of the idea of its past. To see an entity as structured in a certain way is to see it as *having developed*. '*Ek*' may signify both causal and temporal sequence (*Met.* V, 1023ᵃ26f.; *De Gen. An.* 724ᵃ21f.); not unreasonably, for they are unintelligible without each other. 'Before and after' similarly bridges temporal and ontological priority. Both orders arise from our single experience of change in which we recognize one and the same entity under different attributes (see PRIOR (2), Piaget: FRASER). 'The sand has a past' is a general way of reporting that the sand's present configuration arises by due process from something's action. The *B*-theorist sees the identity through time of enduring individuals simply as the (timeless) connection of three-dimensional slices by a temporal 'worm'—he sees successive *bits* of a timeless individual. The *A*-theorist sees one and the same individual as having done

---

[3] In connecting memory and time-awareness (i.e. awareness of entities as at once given and completable according to certain discoverable principles (see II.1.22)) Aristotle is laying the groundwork for a rejection of the simple engram theory of memory (STRAUS pp. 59–100).

such-and-such and possibly going to do so-and-so. This historical seeing cannot be cashed in material terms: it is an aspect of the 'moral' vision of the world of being (see III.3.5), a matter of seeing 'what is going on' (see IV.2.8).

16. The *A*-theory is an attempt to expound the actual structure of our lived reality, taking our judgements of irrevocability and possibility with due seriousness. The *B*-theory must hold that we are in practice systematically mistaken: the past is not prior to the future (except trivially—as one might say that the earlier is earlier than the later), nor are we ever directly acquainted with entities but only with bits of entity (see II.3.6n). Unfortunately the *B*-theorist has exactly the same starting-point as the *A*-theorist, namely our lived experience: he is therefore in the familiar philosophical bind of explaining the explicanda to destruction. If the world is timelessly what it is and only *happens* to be such that each instant 'maps' or 'remembers' earlier instants rather than later, what possible assurance have we that any map is accurate? If our maps, memories, are fallacious to the extent of imputing no-longer-being to the past, causal priority to the past and so forth, why should we think them more accurate in detail? Perhaps the instant 'earlier' is the year 512 of the restored Han dynasty, and the instant 'after' inhabited by intelligent lizards? We cannot reply that if the first had been so things would be different now, and if the second were to be so things would have to be different now—for we have abandoned causal priority in favour of an alleged, and incomprehensible, 'consistency' between instants for which *we* have no evidence at all however much a Boethian God (aware *of* every instant *at* every instant) might have. The *B*-theorist has copied down our ordinary memories and expectations onto a chronological grid constructed by our experience of numbering events: he has then asserted that this represents timeless reality, whereas it is at best no more than a partial account of how things are at one instant of that timeless reality. It would be a strange coincidence if one sector of Hadrian's Wall should contain in little a replica of the wall to that sector's westward, and no one would assert that it did without having seen the wall as a whole. Yet the *B*-theorist apparently feels no qualms at an equivalently rash claim—rightly, for we are assured, if of anything, then of past existence: but in being assured of it we are also assured that it is no more. The *A*-theorist is bound to think it wiser to stick to the world of common day (see VI).

17.   In certain respects Aristotle's account resembles modern physical theory, at least as expounded from an operationalist standpoint
(as CAPEK pp. 272f.; see Beauregard *versus* Capek: FRASER). To begin
with the simplest resemblance, he holds that infinite velocity is
impossible (*Phys.* VI, 231^{b}28f., 234^{a}24f.), for there can be no motion
(or rest) purely at an instant (see II.3.17n). Simultaneity, being such
at the same instant as something else's being so, is therefore undis-
coverable—instead we have contemporaneity: two processes are
contemporaneous if their limits are the same (*Phys.* IV, 223^{b}6f.;
CAPEK ch. 13). None the less there is only one time everywhere
(*Phys.* IV, 220^{b}5f.), for change also is single. This doctrine, which
seems at odds with modern relativity theory in insisting that there
is some overall dating system which could assign numbers unequivocally to all the processes that make up the universe, is in fact connected with a way of considering change which is not so at odds.
Against the later Plato's claim that locomotion is the primary form
of change (Pl. *Laws* 893 b, 897 a; against *Tht.* 181 d *et al.*), Aristotle
hesitates, half-convinced that locomotion is analysable in terms of
the qualitative change of the universe (cf. MORROW). It is only if
locomotion is taken as primary that we are tempted into taking
literally the talk of the present moving through the chronological
grid: if change is the realization of potential we no more need
dimensional time than we need empty space. Where an operationalist interpretation of relativity theory goes further than Aristotle is in
arguing that clock-time, which we have constructed in such a way
that its units do not change their length according to our mood (as
we have constructed a physical universe whose shapes and sizes and
colours do not change according to our mood and our position (see
VAN DEN BERG (2)), cannot wholly escape from that relativism. We
ought then to be less eager to lay down that clock-time as absolute
reality, rather than as a device for keeping appointments (see VI).

18.   We are perhaps now in a position to sum up Aristotle's approach to time. Time, as such, is nothing mysterious or forceful.
Time is destructive, to be sure (*Phys.* IV, 221^{a}30f.), yet not *time*
itself (for numbers are not causes (*Met.* XIV, 1093^{b}8f.)), only the
processes which occur in time (*Phys.* IV, 222^{b}19f.): 'all change makes
things depart from their former state' (see IV.2.9). Time is change
with respect to the before and after, qua numerable. It is what is *now*
that alone truly is, though we may truly say that Homer has been,

and something or other will be (*Phys.* IV, 221^{b}31f.), and that both
are contained by time—that is that a number can be put to them.
'Change', the realization of something's potential, is a more difficult
concept, to which he gives the concentrated attention that other
philosophers have given 'time'. 'What an entity is', is, for Aristotle,
a dynamic concept which yet admits the possibility that the entity
will *fail* to 'become what it is'. On a *B*-theory taken in its most
interesting and serious form, a kitten that does not in fact become a
cat could only have been said to have been going to be a cat by
virtue of our ignorance of its fate. We infer (as I have remarked the
inference is very weak) that this creature is of the class of things that
are adult cats at some point in their span, but we are in fact mistaken:
'being a cat', as that concept is applied by us at any time prior to the
creature's adulthood is therefore either a (possibly mistaken) claim
of fact, or a claim that it looks as if it might be a fact: in either case
it comments merely on a resemblance to a given set of creatures, and
not on a real feature of the creature itself. In so far as a kitten does
not turn into a cat, it was not going to be a cat, or 'going to be a cat'
must simply be a statistical truth about its supposed congeners. The
case of turtle eggs, most of which do not turn into turtles, makes it
increasingly difficult to isolate an entity's real being. The moral is,
as Quine quite consistently holds, that there is no such thing as an
entity's real being. Neither then is there any convincing subject-
matter for biology (see II.3.19). Only if possibly unrealized potential
is a real feature of the world, not a product of our ignorance (that is,
only on an *A*-theory), can formal as against positive description (see
IV.2.6n) be more than a chimera. Only so can failure to 'conform'
be given a convincing sense. Only so can our 'freedom' be real: the
B-theorist need not be a fatalist, but a determinist he is.

19.   The complexity of entities is such that they may develop or
decay or be consumed. The eternally necessary truth of the principles of being does not imply, as it has for other philosophers and
mystics, that everything is, in reality, just what it is, and that
absolutely everything is perfect as it is. Accidents happen, failure
to realize being happens: we may not achieve the completion which
is truly available to us. That completion is available not simply in
the sense that others of our apparent kind have achieved it (though
this may be the evidence that we could (see II.3.13; cf. *N.E.* III,
1110^{a}25f.)), nor that there is no contradiction between the imagined

future and the known past (though there is between the imagined and the real future), but that there is a real doubleness in such entities as we (III.3.2; V.3.9). That eternal Being which is unbounded by chronology (IV.1.13, IV.2.23) and exists unchanging in its eternal Now, does not require that all else be unchanging and utterly determinate (VI.15). The now is one and the same in being whatever its changing description (*Phys.* IV, 219^{b}12f.): necessarily, for there is only one world, and that a completable one (II.3.17f.).

IV.2. History

1. It is occasionally suggested that past-tensed statements are made true solely by the present evidence for them, so that in the absence of any relic of the past event referred to no such statement could be true, or false (assuming no counter-relic). On this view the past can perhaps be undone, and the objects of historical investigation can only be the documents and traces selected as historically relevant by the investigator: our past would then change with each historiographical generation. Aristotle does not seem to have been concerned with this possibility. For him the past is as 'necessary' as the present: what is done cannot be undone (*N.E.* VI, 1139^{b}5f.; *De Caelo* 283^{b}7f.), and the objects of historical research are historical events. Past-tensed statements have been made true or false by the course of events, and now remain so (even if we do not know which they are, and even if there is no remaining evidence on the subject).[1] Whatever his views on history and its investigation—the topic which I now wish to discuss—he seems to have no doubt about the existence or stability of the subject-matter. It may be, however, that he considers historical investigation somewhat inferior for other reasons, and there has been no lack of commentators to make this claim (cf. IV.1.1.).

2. Aristotle has been attacked (or commended) on four points which seem to me worthy of discussion: (i) that historical investigation is held to be trivial, in that it deals only with individual events or characters; (ii) that he lacks a concept of progress in history, believing rather in unavoidable decay; (iii) that he holds to a cyclic picture of history in the archaic manner; (iv) that his biological and teleological presuppositions distort the historical evidence he considers. In examining these issues I hope to emphasize the importance of the judgement of the experienced man in descrying what is happening or has happened (cf. II.1.22), to hint at a certain emo-

[1] Or following the suggestion of IV.1.15: '*X* (currently existing entity) did *a*' means that *X* is in a state of having done *a*, *X* is thus structured. Where there is (no longer) an *X*, the claim that *it* did *a* is to be unpacked as a claim about the universe. That is to say: events are not eternal entities with changing properties, nor with relational ones—they are not entities at all.

tional detachment from the course of events as a consequence of
Aristotle's historical model, and to add somewhat to my earlier
defence of his organic view of the state (cf. III.3.15).

3. I begin from the notorious view that 'poetry is a more philosophical and serious thing than history, as poetry speaks rather of the
general, history rather of the particular' (*Poet.* 1451ᵇ5f.). Here we
are clearly faced by the Greek preference of the ideal to the individual, rationalism over empirical investigation. Aristotle, although
he constantly urges us to investigate the appearances (*De Caelo*
306ᵃ5f.; *De Gen. An.* 760ᵇ30f. *et al.*), has no idea of empirical
method. Although he is the champion of the individual in both
ontology and ethics he can think only of abstractions not of concrete
individuals as being a fit study for the philosopher. Or perhaps not.

4. 'The general is honoured because it reveals the cause' (*Post. An.*
88ᵃ5). History deals with the events of a given period, a given local-
ity, 'of which each part has no more than a contingent relationship
with the rest' (*Poet.* 1459ᵃ23f.).[2] It does not deal with coherent
wholes with a beginning, middle, and end. Such histories are mere
aggregates of isolated facts, and fail to reveal the causes, the organic
forms involved in the process of time. Historians such as the Atthidographers, who merely recount whatever happens in a given period
(*chronos* rather than *aion*), are not philosophical. To speak only of
particular events, failing to isolate those aspects of event which are
the general, marking the sort of thing that is always happening, is
not enough. There is nothing to prevent someone from revealing
the general via some actual rather than invented event: 'even if some
man should depict actual happenings he is no less a poet; for nothing
prevents some actual events from being the sort of things that are
likely to and can happen, which is what makes him a poet' (*Poet.*
1451ᵇ29f.). Poetic, philosophic history or historical poetry is written
for 'whoever may want to get a clear picture of what has happened
and of the sort of thing, or very similar, that is to be expected, being

---

[2] Bywater's text of *Poetics* 1459ᵃ21 reads μὴ ὁμοίας ἱστορίας τὰς συνήθεις θεῖναι—(one
should not) count usual histories as like (narrative stories). If this reading is correct,
and it is certainly a little difficult, Aristotle is here admitting, by implication, that
there are *unusual* histories. Dacier's emendation, μὴ ὁμοίας ἱστορίαις τὰς συνθέσεις
εἶναι—poetic compositions should not be like histories—is both easier and safer. But
it is no part of my argument (see IV.2.6) that 'poetic history' (that is, the discovery
of the forms of event: as that 'similar causes have similar results' (*Rhet.* 1360ᵃ5f.)) is
purely poetry. None the less one can show the general in the actual particular, and it
is this effort which Aristotle and Thucydides alike were making.

in human nature' (Thuc. I, 22.4; cf. Polybius XI, 19ᵃ).³ It is the story of universal application that is sought in philosophical history (cf. *Pol.* I, 1259ᵃ6f.; V, 1312ᵃ1).

5. This division between chronicle and history proper is not exact: even to count as a chronicle there must be some implicit theory of causation and significant action which dictates a particular selection of events. No historical catalogue is *just* a catalogue (witness: 'she had a baby and got married' and 'she got married and had a baby'), but there is a difference of degree: chronicles are only the beginning of history. '[Aristotle] conceived it his task [in the *Athenaion Politeia*] not merely to give a factual description of the various historical developments in the Athenian constitution, in the manner of the Atthidographers, but to go beyond their annalistic accounts and interpret the facts of Athenian constitutional history with reference to the contemporary democracy' (KEANEY p. 117). Not that it is possible 'just' to say what happened. 'His definition of art as the revelation of the universal in the particular applies as well to this kind of historical writing as it does to literature (ABELSON p. 168).

6. Even 'poetic history', however, so long as it remains within the historians' camp, cannot achieve a purely scientific status, for the historian is confronted by the irreducibly contingent. Whereas a poet deals with types, with organic situations in which extraneous, intrusive episodes are an artistic fault, the historian begins from events which are not wholly organic, nor wholly such as are to be expected. He may abstract stories which serve as devices for organizing his material, but that material cannot be totally organized. The accidental is always incidental (cf. II.3.27) and not to be predicted or explained, at least within the system currently being considered. 'We have scientific knowledge when we know the cause (*Post. An.* 71ᵇ30f.; cf. *Met.* I, 981ᵃ30f.), and the class of accidental events do not reveal any one cause, qua that class (*Met.* XI, 1064ᵇ30f.; cf. *Prior An.* 32ᵇ18f. *et al.*). But any individual is partly accidental: it has features which cannot be expected, which were not implicit in its development, which belong to it as *this* individual and

³ PIPPIDI perhaps goes too far in arguing that Aristotle actually had Thucydides in mind as an example of the historian who seeks material for political science. He certainly goes too far in remarking that Aristotle lacked the concept of 'l'absolue rationalité du réel' (p. 484), unless this means only that Aristotle did not necessarily impute significance to accidents.

no other. We discern the essential element by observing what it has in common with the other members (or most) of its apparent class, its congeners (cf. II.3.13). Considered purely as individuals individuals cannot be scientifically known, for they have no one cause. A unique individual could not be significantly counted as one: for there would be no way of distinguishing essential and accidental features, nor any way of determining how many things were under consideration (cf. *De Gen. An.* 773ᵃ8f. on monsters). Nor would it be significant to say of an individual qua its individuality that it is good or defective. To be one is to be one something, and if there is no generally revealed sort of thing like this, this is not one of a kind, nor one. Certainly we may arbitrarily define such a kind into existence, but it will have no priority over indefinitely many other pseudo-kinds. The sun and moon are contingently unique, and it is correspondingly difficult to be sure what they are: if they were wholly unique, rather than both being examples of heavenly globes, they would be wholly unknowable, because indefinable (*Met.* VII, 1040ᵃ1f.). One swallow does not make a species.[4]

7. There is no science of individuals qua individuals (*Met.* VII, 1039ᵇ27f.; XIII, 1087ᵃ10f.; *Post. An.* 81ᵇ6f.; *N.E.* II, 1109ᵇ22). 'Individual cases are so infinitely various that no systematic knowledge of them is possible' (*Rhet.* 1356ᵇ31f.). 'He that produces a house does not produce all the attributes that come into being along with the house, for these are innumerable . . . and the science of building is not aimed at them' (*Met.* VI, 1026ᵇ6f.). No individual thing can be exhaustively described, for an indefinitely large number of things can happen to it (*Poet.* 1451ᵃ17f.) and be said about it, but only pointed out: and history, which can only describe, is therefore inevitably selective. So also is mathematics, but the mathematician need not fear that his abstract results will be too far vitiated by the contingent—the historian is interested in more than abstractions and is therefore trapped. He must make assumptions which he knows to be falsified at some point of his study: he cannot count on accident to explain events, but accident has undoubtedly played a considerable

---

[4] This point, that there are no individualized forms (A. C. LLOYD (2)), also solves a possible difficulty in the doctrine of the mean: if there were, if any uniquely identifying description could count as a form, then any such identified object would already be *one* under that description, and ordered as such (see III.2.4f.). The doctrine of the mean would then be vacuous. Only *some* descriptions are properly to be taken as formal (see II.3.11f.).

part in those events. He must be a man of experience, as must the *phronimos* (*N.E.* I, 1095ᵃ2), not the mere applier of general principles: he must be able to guess when the principles do not apply, should not be applied (cf. *N.E.* V, 1137ᵇ26f.). We are not entitled to regard human history as no more than a tale told by an idiot (cf. *Poet.* 1451ᵇ33f.), for the observed facts show that nature as a whole is 'not a series of episodes, like a bad tragedy' (*Met.* XIV, 1090ᵇ19f.), and human history is a part of nature. But the Whole itself is no subject of science (there being no foundation on which to learn it (*Met.* I, 992ᵇ24f.; *Post. An.* 71ᵃ1f.)), and in any case allows considerable indeterminacy on its lower levels (see IV.1)—we cannot escape the category of the accidental.

8.   History, therefore, cannot be a fully scientific discipline, and DAY/CHAMBERS (pp. 43f.) are right to lay stress on the importance of the incidental for Aristotelian and Thucydidean thought. Although Aristotle does not explicitly connect historical research with *phronesis*, the object of both is what could be (could have been) otherwise, the doubly potential. His 'poetic history' attempts to descry the forms of virtue and vice in the given material, to see what it was that was going on. *Phronesis* similarly deliberates on what to do for the best, using exemplars from the agent's or other men's past, so as to see what is going on. The historian, precisely, exercises his common sense (III.1.24) to understand his material, and he can only do so effectively if he has a sound grasp of what to do in a given situation. The *phronimos*, seeing the present situation, works out what to do, and can do so effectively only with a proper understanding of the sorts of things that happen. For the historian to restrict himself to 'what happened' is as futile as for the biologist to prefer material descriptions of the multitude of living things (cf. II.3.10f.): in both cases an understanding of value is essential. The 'annalist' or the reductivist biologist both miss the point: 'history', in either case, is the ground of *phronesis* and impossible without the sense to see the best (cf. II.3.8).

9.   What of the charge that Aristotle (and the Greeks in general) believed history to be the story of unavoidable decay? He certainly says (*Phys.* IV, 222ᵇ19f.) that time is in itself the condition of decay rather than growth—left to themselves changeful entities decay, whereas improvement requires definite action. But this early intuition of the Second Law of Thermodynamics is hardly to the point.

VAN GRONINGEN's use (p. 8) of such isolated comments as 'what is long established seems like second nature' (*Rhet.* 1387ᵃ16f.) is unfortunately typical of most attempts to demonstrate 'the typical Greek's obsession with the past' (cf. MOMIGLIANO). That the Greeks found self-images in history hardly needs demonstration: so do we all in our degree. That Aristotle was hide-bound to the past, I see no reason to believe (cf. VERDENIUS (1)). So far from thinking that any given past was automatically preferable he declares that 'improvement has occurred in every art and craft, including politics, as is shown by the fact that old customs are exceedingly simple and barbarous' (*Pol.* II, 1268ᵇ34f.): our ancestors were ordinary or even foolish men, and their words are not to be taken as absolute commands (*Pol.* II, 1269ᵃ4f.). I grant that this statement is only the first half of an *aporia*, but the second only follows Cleon (Thuc. III.37.3) in warning against too frequent changes in the law: the equality of our ancestors and ourselves in point of sense is not disputed. Granted that long-lived doctrines must have some sense in them, we may still improve on them. 'When the Ionian philosophies had had their day, as they were found inadequate to generate the nature of things, men were forced by the truth itself to inquire into the efficient cause' (*Met.* I, 984ᵇ8f.). 'Anyone is capable of carrying on and articulating what has once been outlined, and time is a good discoverer or partner in this: to which facts the advances in the arts are due' (*N.E.* I, 1098ᵃ22f.). What is true of the arts may also be true of social institutions and manners, though improvement is certainly not inevitable. Aristotle and the Greeks cannot be proven pessimists by invoking Hesiod, nor can we take Plato's more cynical remarks as typical even of him, let alone of 'the Greeks' (as BURY pp. 7f.). WEIL (1) (2) is more to the point in noting that Aristotelian time is active as well as destructive: rather, that things develop as well as decay.

10.   History is not the story of unavoidable decay: indeed it cannot be, for change had no beginning and shall have no end (cf. IV.1.10). Believers in the non-historical character of Greek thought may be induced to accept this, but only because they wish to maintain that history was cyclic for the Greeks. They were, it is alleged (Puech: CAMPBELL (3) pp. 38f.; ELIADE (2) pp. 89f.; cf. MOMIGLIANO), dominated by the myth of the eternal return, in which cycle follows cycle without real change or novelty. This is what reconciles perpetual time and perpetual decay, that the world is always returning to its

beginning: otherwise everything would end up like Endymion (Pl. *Phdo.* 72 b 11). There is perhaps some truth in this but it may not have the moral that is claimed for it.

11. Aristotle asks himself why, if everything passes into not-being, the totality of things has not long since been exhausted (*De Gen. Corr.* 318ᵃ13f.), and replies that things pass not into sheer nothingness, but into not-being-such-and-such, and can as easily come thence (*De Gen. Corr.* 319ᵃ22f.). There is an unending cycle of becoming and decay: unending, because every step is a sufficient condition for its predecessor's return (*Post. An.* 95ᵇ38f.; *De Gen. Corr.* 336ᵇ25f.). Mist rises to form cloud, and the cloud descends in rain, and the earth is moistened into mist (cf. II.3.23; KATZ/KAHN pp. 93f.). It is thus that all sublunary things imitate the celestial wheel, by the continual reinstantiation of a type, and the consequent perpetuity of motion. Similarly with human affairs, 'for nothing human can be continuously active' (*N.E.* X, 1175ᵃ4f.): 'they say that human affairs go in a circle, as well as whatever else has natural motion' (*Phys.* IV, 223ᵇ24f.). 'There is a certain number of the sun's motions and of the moon's and indeed of the life and maturity of every living thing' (*Met.* XIV, 1093ᵃ4). Everything has its *aion*, its period, outside which no natural development can fall (*De Caelo* 279ᵃ23f.; *De Gen. Corr.* 336ᵇ10f.; *Meteor.* 339ᵃ21f.), for there is an order controlling all things (*De Gen. An.* 777ᵇ18f.). The seasons follow the sun, which follows the heavens, and living things, in their turn, follow the seasons (*De Gen. Corr.* 338ᵇ1f.; cf. II.2.14, II.3.1).

12. In so far as life has evolved on and adapted to this earth it is hardly surprising that it should share in the natural rhythms of day and night, winter and summer. Astronomical cycles do not precisely determine the cycles of living things, for there are too many interrelated systems each with their own periods, too much potential for otherness, to allow for accuracy (*De Gen. An.* 778ᵃ4f.). That astronomical cycles do have an effect on human life (*De Gen. An.* 777ᵇ18f.; *Phys.* II, 194ᵇ13 *et al.*) is at once a piece of traditional metaphysics, a truism, and a doctrine occasionally substantiated by modern research (cf. Knoll: CAMPBELL (3); Hamner: FRASER). It is not superstition (see also App. D).

13. The doctrine of natural periods also applies to the earth as a whole: 'the innards of the earth, like the bodies of plants and animals,

have their zenith and decline' (*Meteor.* 351ᵃ27f.). Sea and land
change places over infinite time and every geographical configuration
has occurred before. A periodic cosmic upheaval, the great winter
(*Meteor.* 352ᵃ28f.), reduces mankind to a tiny remnant (*Pol.* II,
1269ᵃ4f.; cf. *Phys.* III, 206ᵃ25) and the great year then begins again.
The great year as calculated by Heraclitus incidentally equals
10,800 solar years (22 A13 D–K), which is the Chinese cosmic
month: a doctrine from which Chu Hsi drew the same moral as
Aristotle (NEEDHAM II 485; cf. HEATH p. 61, GUTHRIE (1) pp. 63f.).
Mythological tradition is the residue of art and philosophy long ago
developed to their peak (*Met.* XII, 1074ᵇ10f.): a consoling thought
for one who thought that the lover of myth was in a sense a philosopher (*Met.* I, 982ᵇ18; Diog. *Vit.* V. 1). Proverbs particularly so:
'proverbs are the remnants of philosophy that perished in the great
disasters that have befallen mankind, and were preserved for their
brevity and wit' (*Peri. Philosophias* fr. 8 Ross). Everything has
already been discovered, and forgotten, an infinite number of times
(*De Caelo* 270ᵇ19f., *Meteor.* 339ᵇ27f.; *Pol.* VII, 1329ᵇ25f.; cf. Pl.
Tim. 21 e f., *Pol.* 269 c 4f.). The common opinions of men are to be
respected, even those which seem foolish, for precisely this reason
(*Pol.* II, 1264ᵃ1). Everyone of us, as Plato observed (Pl. *Tht.* 174 e f.),
has infinitely many kings, philosophers, and crooks in his ancestry.

14. The cyclic nature of change can be taken still further. *On
Philosophy* emphasized the 6,000 year period between Zarathustra
and Plato—a sum apparently deduced from the Zoroastrian great
year of 12,000 solar years (Xanthus of Sardis 765F32: WEST p. 32):
VOEGELIN III p. 285 seems to go too far in inferring that Zarathustra
and Plato initiate parallel historical periods, but some connection is
being made (cf. CHROUST (1)). In the peripatetic *Problemata** (XVII
916ᵃ18f.) the author, perhaps after Aristotle, notes the possibility
that if human history is cyclical then we live before the, or rather a,
Trojan War—not numerically the same war as that fought upwards
of 3,000 years ago, but the same sort of war. That it should be
numerically the same is out of the question, as the now would then
be the beginning and end of the same process (*Phys.* IV, 222ᵇ1f.; cf.
IV.1.14). I see no reason to conclude that Aristotle would necessarily
agree with the exact repetition professed by the Pythagoreans: 'if
we are to believe them, that numerically the same events recur, I
shall be telling stories to you as you sit so, with the rod in my hand

and everything else just so' (Eudemos: Simplicius *Physica* I, 732.26f.): where there is exact, specific repetition there ceases to be any way of dating a given event unambiguously, so that our temporal schema becomes effectively circular. But though in infinite time all possible combinations of climate, opinion, and the like, being finite in number, must be repeated (for though there are e.g. infinitely many temperatures if we wish to say so, we do not discriminate such things so exactly), it is open to Aristotle to insist that individual substances, and particularly individual men, are infinitely various. I do not think therefore that we can legitimately expand Aristotle's cyclicism into the view adopted by Plotinus (V.3.12), by Nietszche, by certain modern physicists (cf. Watanabe: FRASER), and by some Hindu doctrines. That this was toyed with by some Greeks may be true: I do not see it in Aristotle, nor is it the only possible view, nor is it maintained by many of the historians to whom it is attributed. The programme of Thucydides, for example (Thuc. I.22.4; cf. IV.2.4), is no more an expression of a rigid cyclicism than Christ's remarks on past and probable persecution.

15. It is fairly clear, however, that Aristotle would expect no novelty in history: there is no utterly new thing under the sun, nothing utterly unlike what has gone before, though it does not follow that he would have concurred with M. Aurelius' claim to have seen everything at forty (*Meditations* XI.1). Nor does he look forward to any end or consummation of history. If this lack proves him non-historically minded, then he was, but it seems a somewhat arbitrary use even of this amorphous concept. It may also seem a little hard that he should be criticized both for not having a teleological view of history (though see below) and for interpreting historical events on a teleological model. In what sense is he guilty of the latter crime?

16. 'He who considers things in their first growth and origin, whether a state or anything else, will obtain the clearest view of them' (*Pol.* I, 1252ᵃ24). Communities are natural growths, and are to be understood in the same way as any organism—not by viewing them in their decline but in their development. KEANEY, after Else (ed. *Poetics*), has drawn attention to a trick of style which Aristotle frequently uses, and particularly in the *Athenaion Politeia* (doubtless also in the other, non-extant, *Politeiai*): there is a beginning, big with possibilities, a gradual development and expansion leading to some sizeable result (cf. *Ath. Pol.* 41.2, 23.1, 25.1). He does find it natural

to speak in this way of institutions, so that they grow, suffer, and (if fortunate) reach their final end, which is the final cause of their development (*Pol.* I, 1252ᵇ30). Just so, 'tragedy left off its continual changes when it attained its natural form' (*Poet.* 1449ᵃ14f.; cf. 1449ᵃ8). Not every actual end-state is a final cause, or reveals one, for accidents happen: we should rather consider the line of development, and see what *telos* best sums up that line.

17.   DAY/CHAMBERS appear to find this technique either politically or philosophically offensive. They believe that Aristotle would claim that 'the natural is good, the unnatural bad' (p. 40). Aristotle would surely respond 'Good for what?' Usury is unnatural because it interferes with the purposes for which money was instituted, namely to facilitate the sharing of goods (*Pol.* I, 1258ᵃ37f.). It is at once parasitic upon that institution, for money which was used only in the stock exchange would cease to have any meaning (save a ritual one), and bad for that institution. And since the latter is a necessary element of anything approaching the good life, usury and the market economy are a cancer on the body politic. Where the economy is exalted to an entity in its own right, with laws of its own that disrupt social ordering, the life of the community is endangered. Any social mechanism which has grown a life of its own in separation from the life of the community is to be opposed: 'when separated from man or humanity . . . they are thieves and rebels, they are destroyers' (BLAKE p. 571). I do not know whether POLANYI ((2) p. 68) is right in his claim that 'Aristotle divined the full-fledged specimen (of market capitalism) from the embryo'; he is certainly right to draw attention to the way Aristotle embeds economic arrangements in the general social ordering of society (see HUMPHREYS (2)). Prices are to be related to the hierarchical status of the craftsmen in the community (*N.E.* V, 1133ᵃ8f.) not to laws of supply and demand operating independently of political control. Private ownership is to be conjoined with public use (*Pol.* II, 1263ᵃ37f.; MEAD p. 31). That is natural to man which best satisfies his needs: what does not is bad, though it may be the best available compromise in some anomalous situation. The market economy and the doctrines of *laissez-faire* involved in it are manifestly bad for man: they are therefore to be held unnatural.

18.   Day/Chambers also object to using a biological model for the state at all, arguing amongst other things that 'no-one is in doubt

whether the part called the mouth of an animal has been correctly identified', such identifications being purely descriptive, while class-identifications are evaluative (pp. 62–3). This is an error in biology: to identify any part (at least any anomoeomerous part) is to evaluate it: that is, to say what its value, its function is in the economy. One may well hesitate as to which part is the mouth (cf. II.2.3). The 'parts' of an organism are not materially distinguished, but function-ally (see II.3.26). A state is certainly living, for its parts are; nor is it merely an aggregate of persons, for it has laws of its own which govern the interaction of its citizens, nor are they what they are independently of the community (cf. II.3.11). Even if it were theoretically possible to analyse the behaviour of states wholly in terms of the behaviour of individuals, no historian has yet accomplished this analysis—for it is simply too complex. Analyses of living beings solely in terms of their material causes are no more than fantasy (BECKNER (1) p. 46; BERTALANFFY (1) pp. 154f.): so are analyses of states in terms of their membership—only by ignoring most of their members in favour of a few picked out as leaders (a social concept) can we imagine otherwise. A proper history can only be of an organic whole, as against a mere aggregate (IV.2.4), whether it be a state, a civilization or only an economically united region. If we are to talk of such things at all we must talk of them as wholes, whether as machines or as living things: I think the second model is more reliable.[5]

19.   But Day/Chambers insist that the organic model ensures that Aristotle leaves no room for individual decision as an effective power in history, imputing change to natural development or the accidental (p. 64). They simultaneously wonder 'why Aristotle has not left fulfilment of natural states to nature', rather than advising politicians on what to do (p. 53)—as if his advice was not also part of nature. This is to pile fallacy upon falsehood (cf. GILLIARD). An institution is likely to develop in a certain way if the situation is such as to allow the will of certain people to prevail: in developing thus it will consolidate their will and accelerate the process until some balance is achieved. Events not predictable within the terms of this situation may intervene and may, or may not, have a lasting effect. When they are past the situation may revert to the norm, as happened several

---

[5] The one error of FRITZ's otherwise excellent study is to suppose that it was only Aristotle's followers who 'confused' history and biology. They may have made the 'confusion' worse confounded: in origin it is neither unaristotelian nor a confusion.

times in Athenian history, simply because the previous pressures were still there. It does not follow that any institution is inevitable nor that it happens without the will of men. Some changes are not purposed but occur independently, and of these some are viable and even profitable (*De Gen. An.* 774ᵇ16f. on Nature's use of residues: see BALME (3)). Changes that are merely incidental, the product of armed invasion or individual caprice or natural disaster, are likely to survive only if they chance to find confirmation in the dominant wills of the relevant group. Unless the state's institutions permit the will of all free men, all naturally free men, all men with wills, to be heard the state has little chance of fulfilling the purpose for which states exist (in the absence of a supremely intelligent and virtuous ruling class). In falling away from the mean (III.3.16) the state adopts progressively inferior goals (cf. II.2). If political institutions are to survive at all they must make some sense in terms of men's desires and powers within the given situation—if they do not, they are as vestigial and as potentially harmful as an appendix. Political history is the story of the consolidation of desire in the midst of the unpredictable. It is not inevitable.

20. Day/Chambers, despite their philosophical *naïveté*, may be right in thinking that Aristotle's philosophy has caused him to distort certain events—that is, to describe them in other terms than Day/Chambers would have used. It is a criticism to which most historians are open. All history is selective, and employs standards of what is to count as reasonable, or as plausible, that may be wholly parochial (cf. Hume: *Enquiry into the Human Understanding* X: 'On Miracles'; see above, I.2f.). We are all forever reinterpreting our own or humanity's past in accordance with what we *now* see ourselves to be.[6] Aristotle at any rate does not make the common mistake of supposing that exactly the same desires must have been operative in the past as are now either operative or fulfilled. The desires which move in the development of institutions develop with the institutions. Not every move which in fact served to promote democracy was made with that end in view: though the fact that it did serve that end may explain why it did not lapse. Aristotle and Thucydides alike are occasionally castigated for their stress on the accidental: accident at

---

[6] Compare BERGER chs. 3ff. on the way in which past episodes are seen as crucial in the growth of what is currently taken as one's identity: our society's norms are a major element in this. To see things 'as they truly are' is to escape from our society's conventions (see VI.10).

least prevents exact prediction, forestalls anachronism, and permits historical explanation to possess a necessary indeterminacy. Aristotle may not have been a good historian—we have too little of his definitely historical work to give a reliable judgement on that matter —but it is surely impossible to maintain that he was not interested in historical development (witness the corpus of *Politeiai* and *Physikon Doxai*), or that he was unaware of the changes which time brings about. To understand what constitution is currently desirable it is well not only to study the efforts of other nations but also the past history of one's own (*Rhet.* 1360ᵃ30f.). We should not disregard the experience of ages (*Pol.* I, 1264ᵃ1f.). His interest in history is indeed largely practical, not only for the sake of knowledge: he has better things to contemplate than man (cf. II.1.1). It is political and personal understanding, the ability to discern the signs of the times and to assess the situation under the categories of ethical insight (cf. III.2.24), which he desires. He seeks to make sense of what happened, or what has been said, but does not forget that some things simply do not make sense.

21.   What is true of the history of institutions is also true of the history of ideas: we should go over the sayings of past thinkers, to find either a corrective or a confirmation of our own views (*Met.* I, 983ᵇ4f.). In doing so we must often 'interpret according to the meaning and not to the lisping expression' (*Met.* I, 985ᵃ4f.; *De Gen. Corr.* 314ᵃ13f.; see I.2f.); we must assume that our subjects *would*, if pressed, have said things which they did not make explicit (as Anaxagoras: *Met.* I, 989ᵃ30f.). Sometimes, 'seeing that we have investigated (such and such a matter) to the best of our ability, we are entitled to treat our results as representing facts' (*De Caelo* 295ᵃ1f.). Aristotle, like any good philosopher, is interested not merely in the texts but in their possible significance, in what can truthfully be maintained in such a form. His practise is first to say what a given thinker is reputed or reported to have said, and then to conjecture what he might have meant by this, and what we might mean in reaffirming it. The general form of culpable scholarly inaccuracy is not, as Cherniss and his followers appear to suppose, the suggestion of contexts for the subject's beliefs or of coping stones for his system, but the assumption that the subject meant only what one would oneself have meant by his words and was concerned to answer all and only the questions which one asks oneself (see I). Aristotle was

aware that, just as institutions have been founded by men who sought practical answers to questions other than those which the institution is now seen as answering ('how to solve the problem of debt-slaves', or 'how to exclude one's political rivals', rather than 'how to let the people rule'), so also are philosophical and scientific systems to be understood both 'in their first growth and origin' (IV.2.16), as answers to single questions like 'what do things come from?', and in their eventual development as elements of a reorganized system seeking to answer e.g. 'what is being?' Tragedy answers the implicit cravings of dramatist and people, though its founders did not know that Sophocles would 'result' from their labours. Not to be aware of this relation between seed and adult (see II.3.18) is not to understand the temporal processes which have preserved the development: the struggle of pressure-groups within a particular technical and economic context, the desire for a ritual imitation of moral action at once plausible (as possible fact) and illuminating (as possibility: IV.2.3), the vagaries of a natural universe which will not conform to inadequate systems (*Met.* I, 984^{b}8f.: IV.2.9).

22. There are two questions involved in this: firstly, did Aristotle falsify historical facts (in his political history) or philosophical theories (in his history of ideas), and secondly was he right to see political or philosophical history as a struggle to give expression to moral or scientific opinions which could at first be expressed, if at all, only haltingly? Our only answer to the first question is a plea of ignorance, conjoined with doubt that Aristotle is really likely to have been more in error than ourselves (as GUTHRIE (2)). My answer to the second has already been given: we cannot in the end understand anything except in terms of what we believe to be true, and though we should not prejudge an issue of interpretation, neither should we refuse the task (see I.5). Initially muddled claims 'make sense' within the complete system which is their *telos*. Our gratitude must go to those who did not know what they were saying or doing, and from whom we are grown (*Met.* II*, 993^{b}11f.): in giving thanks, we may also note that we too may one day be thought ignorant.

23. Aristotle's view of history reveals on the one hand his practical concerns, enshrined in the concept of the reasonable man of experience, and on the other a slight detachment from the course of history—where there is no end of time one's expectations are inevitably slightly detached from the millennial future, for that too will

pass. I see no grounds for believing that he attempts to reproduce
the conditions of an imaginary primordial prefection, *tempus illud*
(cf. ELIADE (2); Van der Leeuw: CAMPBELL (3)). But in making *nous*
the most important feature of our life he serves that which is out of
time, that 'which lives through all time unchanging with the best and
most self-sufficient of lives' (*De Caelo* 279ᵃ20f.), which all men,
knowingly or not, must serve in their degree. It is in the now, the
present that is not a part of time (*Phys.* IV, 220ᵃ18f.) that *nous* is to
be found, having neither memory nor desire (*De An.* 408ᵇ27f.). 'The
first *nous* thinks itself forever, without parts and without date, in the
undivided now' (Ps.-Alex. *Met.* 714.23H). Incarnate *nous* is temporal, existing in a length of time (*Met.* XII, 1075ᵃ8f.): discarnate
nous, *nous* in itself, has nothing to do with such categories. Truth is,
after all, timeless (in a sense: cf. IV.1.13): and it is because it is the
same for all peoples and times that we can see history as a struggle.
Without such a standard, there could be no meeting between philosophers and their opinions: with it, we lose our critical prerogative
to denounce Aristotle's own struggle to make sense of past contributions to the community of love (politically) and knowledge
(scientifically). What the standard is, is another story.

24.   The author of *Problemata** XVII quotes with apparent approval a saying of Alcmaeon, 'that men perish for this reason, that
they cannot join the beginning to the end' (916ᵃ33f.; cf. ELIADE (1)
pp. 98f.). If the circle could be closed we would be self-caused and
eternal: there would then be no before and after. Our apotheosis is
the destruction of time: the latter is impossible—so therefore the
former. We as individuals are embedded in the contingent and the
temporal: only *nous* stands somehow above the flux—and it is in its
light, as I shall argue, that we make as much sense as we do of
the brute complexity of pure event.

V.1. *Eudaimonia*

1. What then is the good life for man? It is one that *we* must put into practice (cf. II.1). Human life is too complex an affair for simple obedience to rules that can be unambiguously applied to profit us: we need powers of judgement and for that we must be balanced (cf. III.2, IV.2). The sort of identities we should 'reasonably' make for ourselves must be social ones, or we lose a great good and the source of our humanity (cf. III.3). 'Self-interest' is no unambiguous ground for morality, for the self concerned is a creation of our interest (cf. III.3.28f.). What architectural plan should the self we make adhere to? I wish to demonstrate that Aristotle's opinions on this subject can be given an entirely coherent sense with the help of the two concepts, of self-creation and of organic wholeness (cf. II.3.5f.), that I have introduced above. I would not wish to deny that other senses could be provided, particularly ones that involve Aristotle in contradiction (cf. I): I prefer to outline a sense which seems reasonable, and of some use.

2. 'What is it that we say political science desires and what the greatest of all goods obtainable by action? Most people agree on the name, for both the many and the sophisticated call it *eudaimonia*, and suppose that living well and doing well are the same as being *eudaimon*. But as to what *eudaimonia* is, they disagree' (*N.E.* I, 1095ᵃ15). Living, for men, is doing (cf. II.1.19).

3. How then are we to act well? 'The reasonable man, at least, (ὅ γε νοῦν ἔχων) always acts for a purpose, and this is a limit; for the end is a limit' (*Met.* II*, 994ᵇ15). To act non-purposively, in fact, is not really to act. The reasonable man thinks what he is doing and what to do. It does not follow that the reasonable man has only one purpose in mind in all his actions. Aristotle, however, 'in speaking of the good for man . . . hesitates between an inclusive and an exclusive formulation' (HARDIE p. 23). Some of his words suggest that *eudaimonia* is simply the proper ordering of those various goods which men desire; others that it consists in some one, paramount end. I suggest that there need be no contradiction here. In order to do so I shall offer my interpretation of certain cruces in *Nicomachean*

Ethics I. Before doing so, it may be useful to note the etymological background of the term '*eudaimonia*': it is basically the possession of a good *daimon*, a good distributor. In practice '*eudaimon*' was the equivalent of 'lucky', and even if some power were thought responsible for the luck, whether *Tuche* or the gods, it was too capricious to serve the purposes of a moral philosopher, or of anyone seeking what goods were in his power: luck, as such, is not obtainable by any effort of man. Heraclitus determined that 'a man's *daimon* is his character' (22B119D—K). Similarly Xenocrates: 'he who has a sound soul is *eudaimon*, for the soul is each man's *daimon*' (*Top.* 112ᵃ37f.). Aristotle clearly thinks this a trifle strained: for him a *daimon* is a spirit, a god in a more literal sense. 'He says that all men have *daimones* which accompany them throughout their bodily existence' (fr. 193 Rose: cf. LAMEERE). The *daimon* is something a little distinct from the individual: a sort of helmsman, it would be ridiculous to think it loved any but the best and wisest (*E.E.* 1247ᵃ27f.). For Plato, it is *nous*, the direct creation of the demiurge, that is the *daimon* in each of us, and to look after this, devoting oneself to knowledge, is to pursue true *eudaimonia* (Pl. *Tim.* 90).[1] This is the model, I suggest, which best handles Aristotle's claims.

4. In outlining some of the arguments from *Nicomachean Ethics* I I shall refer generically to *technai, methodoi, praxeis* and *proaireseis* (arts, inquiries, acts, decisions) as pursuits, save where there is some distinction to be made.

5. All pursuits aim at their respective goods, but there is no one thing at which they all aim (*N.E.* I, 1094ᵃ1f.): if there were they would be one single pursuit, defined by its end. What there is is the phenomenon of architectonism. Horsecraft is a pursuit subordinate to generalship. This does not mean that there would be no horsecraft were there no generalship, nor that generals always need horses. Some pursuits perhaps are thus related, e.g. horsecraft and bridle-making, though even in this case some and perhaps all bridles could be ornamental, or magic. What is being denied is the reasonableness of fighting wars in order to exercise one's horses. Generalship occasionally regulates and (in the then state of military knowledge) comprises horsecraft, while the reverse situation would be grotesque. Similarly wars are to be fought if at all for the sake of peace and the

---

[1] It is of interest that Plato derives '*daimon*' from '*daemon*', knowing one (Pl. *Cratylus* 398 b; see below on *Nous*).

preservation of the community's life: peace does not exist for war in any reasonable ordering of ends (*Pol.* VII, 1325ª5f., 1333ª21f.). The argument of *Prior Analytics* 68ª39f. (cf. App. B.8) concludes that as being loved is preferable to having intercourse, 'intercourse either is not an end at all or is for the sake of being loved': not that intercourse is not an end, for it plainly is, but that it is subordinate to affection in our ordering of ends. Since we value affection more, we may reasonably decide for or against intercourse in terms of that higher end. Such subordinate and superordinate ends are not always in such a means–end relationship in any particular case: it is important to know that they may be. The architectonic end is more choiceworthy (*N.E.* I, 1094ª14): that is why it is taken as architectonic.

6. If (i) there is some end of action which we seek for itself and other ends for it, and if (ii) we do not choose everything for something else (the desire would then be empty—just as motion without a term is either no motion or a series of separate motions (*Phys.* VI, 237ª12f.)), then this end is the good, and indeed the best (*N.E.* I, 1094ª18f.). There is no need to suppose that Aristotle is here trying to argue that there must be some one end: if he is, he is guilty of the fallacy frequently alleged, that if everyone had a father then there is someone who is everybody's father ((All x)(Some y)$Rxy \neq$ (Some y)(All x)Rxy). That the desire would be empty is a consequence not of there being no single end, but of everything's being sought for something else. Without the second antecedent it would remain a formal possibility that we should seek the one end for which we seek all else for one of its own subordinate ends: x for y, and y for x. There must be at least one end of action which is sought for itself— there may be more than one, standing in no architectonic relationship to each other. If there is such a single end it is clearly what the most architectonic of pursuits, the art of politics, is aiming at. The politician, quà politician and ignoring such accidental characteristics as ambition, seeks to regulate lesser pursuits under the pursuit of what he takes as best. So does the free individual in his deliberations. The political art and practical deliberation are not merely the set of lesser pursuits, any more than is generalship: they have their own identifying ends. And the fact that there are such architectonic pursuits bears witness to our belief that it is possible so to order the things we do.

7. Men agree to call the chiefest of all goods *eudaimonia*, but do

not agree as to what it is. But why should there be any one such good? 'We cheerfully subscribe to, or have the grace to be torn between, simply disparate ideals—why must there be a conceivable amalgam, the Good Life for Man?' (AUSTIN p. 29n). Inconsistency of belief is a good, for we may often have equally good evidence for both *a* and *b* where *a* implies not-*b*; it is then reasonable to acquiesce to both and hope to avoid conflict. Similarly with ideals. But the world being what it is we cannot always hope to avoid crisis situations where our values and beliefs are shown to be in conflict, where we must make some tortured moral or epistemological decision. And if we are to make these decisions on any basis more stable than immediate impulse, it must be in terms of some overriding value which (perhaps) we were not aware of until that moment. If we can avoid crisis we may live our lives well enough, and some commentators have urged that *eudaimonia* is to be interpreted thus inclusively, so that our lives are organized and contain various activities that are desired and well performed but lack any paramount end. Certainly Aristotle himself sometimes gives weight to this conclusion. He notes that men do not have a simple nature, and that no one thing is always pleasant (*N.E.* VII, 1154^{b}20). Even in praising the highest life, that of *theoria*, he adds that such a life on its own is too high for man, that men need friends and all human society and bodily necessities as well (*N.E.* X, 1177^{b}26f.). The good life is one in which perhaps one devotes more time to *a* than to *b*, if that is reasonable, but not one that admits a single end.

8. But this cannot be all that there is to *eudaimonia*, for such straightforwardly inclusivist interpretations ignore the end-ambiguity of 'reasonable' (cf. I.2). It is impossible to make 'reasonable' choices between activities without some conception of the goal of one's life. I have suggested that it would be absurd to fight wars to give one's horses exercise (slightly less so to keep horses to give one's bridles a suitable background), and so indeed it would. But consider a tribe devoted to the worship of the Stallion: might not such a tribe think it grossly irrational to fight wars for any other purpose? War is for the sake of peace perhaps: but could there not be a tribe devoted to fighting and organizing their social lives for precisely this end? Murderous certainly, but why unreasonable (cf. *N.E.* X, 1177^{b}9f.)? What is reasonable under one set of assumptions about the relative importance of activities may be insane under another. The right

ordering of ends and activities is the one which the truly 'reasonable' man adopts: the man, that is, who is not one-sided, seeks to love and understand, attempts to run his life as a free man in society. To take it for granted that such a man will simply adopt the unthinking assumptions by which an average citizen runs his life is absurd: the 'reasonable man' must have a reason also for his ordering of ends, his counting one activity more important than another. Someone who has no such reason, who simply takes what comes and hopes to avoid crisis, has no claim to be *phronimos*, even if he is, overtly, an impeccable citizen of his state. The hippophilist and the Aristotelian may, if they have made their priorities clear, be held 'reasonable' by their friends (by those who share their ends): they are truly so if they are right.

9. Certainly we may prefer not to make our assumptions clear, not to put them to judgement; may prefer to live from moment to moment without any general plan of life. Let us not then pretend to be running our lives. And why should we run them, as distinct from planning parts of our lives? 'Everyone who can live according to his will should place some target of good living on which to concentrate in doing all his acts (as not to order one's life *vis-à-vis* some goal is a mark of considerable lack of sense)' (*E.E.* 1214ᵇ6f.). One who does not attempt this, 'being obedient to his passions will find his study in vain and without profit' (*N.E.* I, 1095ᵃ4f.). One who does, will follow Plato's advice, and by doing his one thing will become one instead of many (Pl. *Rpb.* 423 d 3 f.; III.3.6). It does not follow, though Aristotle's language as he wrestles with the full ordering of ends may sometimes suggest that he thinks it does (as at *N.E.* I, 1102ᵃ2f.: even here we are not said to act for *eudaimonia* on every occasion), that the *eudaimon* never acts for a reason other than the paramount one (see below).

10. The Greek language is perhaps disposed to recognize this making of unity, of one's identity, more easily than English or any other modern Western tongue. Japanese contains very many ways of referring to the first, second, or third persons, depending on relative social standing, situation, and the like. It is correspondingly difficult to express an individuality that is more than the social (though it is possible). English and other Western tongues isolate the subject from his action at the same time as stressing his sheer humanity—or more exactly, requiring no comment on his social

position. We say 'I', 'je', 'ich', 'io' and attach the action or state to this as subject. We are encouraged to find our identities as creatures of God, or in a transcendent ego which is simply I, a pure cogitative substance. Greek does not compel this isolation of the subject from the act: the subject is in the verb grammatically, and in the act semantically. The Greek-speaker is correspondingly encouraged to find identity in action, to think of the soul as life rather than as a detachable ego, to find unity not merely given in the fact of consciousness, but created in act. PLATT's suggestion (p. 104) that we should unite the subject with the verb to emphasize the dynamic and interactionalist nature of identity is anticipated in Greek. Not that Greek, English, Japanese compel these responses, or forbid the speaker to think otherwise, but simply that our languages encourage us to emphasize certain features at the expense of others. The Greek-speaker *can* employ personal pronouns to isolate the subject: he does not need to. Accordingly, if he seeks a unity in his living he is encouraged to find it in some one *praxis* in which he can chiefly be. Being is doing (III.3.29n): to be single is therefore to act singly, to make one's choice coherent. Without such an effort I remain only 'a heap' (cf. *Met.* VII, 1040^{b}8f.): one only protreptically, and proleptically. *Eudaimonia* is *praxis* (*Poet.* 1450^{a}17; *Phys.* II, 197^{b}5).

11.   This is not to say that other acts are good only if they serve the central act, that other ends are good only as a means to this further end. There are many things that are good independently of each other and of any one central thing (*N.E.* I, 1097^{b}1f.; *E.E.* 1218^{b}22). Intercourse, being loved, and loving form an architectonic series, but the lesser ends are desirable in themselves. One does not always seek things to subserve the central good—any more than it is senseless to breed horses in peacetime for peaceful purposes. One does not seek health to achieve whatever constitutes *eudaimonia*: it may be appropriate to disregard one's health in the name of *eudaimonia*, but not the reverse. It has been urged, in apparent contradiction to this account, that seeking *x* for its own sake and seeking it for *eudaimonia* are exactly equivalent. It must be admitted that there are parallels for this usage: to love someone for his own sake and for his goodness are identical; a virtuous act is done both for itself and for the beautiful; sight is esteemed both for its usefulness and for itself, for it is our best help to knowledge (*Met.* I, 980^{a}22f.); science's being chosen for itself is the same as its being chosen for the sake

of knowledge (*Met.* I, 982ᵃ14f.). In all these cases something is chosen or esteemed as itself being worthy under some description (good, beautiful, giving knowledge (sight is a form of knowledge: *Protr.* fr. 7 Ross; cf. III.1; Pl. *Tim.* 47 a ff.)): by analogy to choose some thing for itself is to choose it as being the right thing to do. Or at least this is so if the choice is 'a matter of principle'. So that to choose some action for its own sakҽ is to choose it for the sake of right-doing, *eupraxia*, and therefore for *eudaimonia*. One may *want* something for its own sake without having *eudaimonia* in mind, for one may be a Eudemian fool, acratic or encratic. One may even *do* it with full willingness, as an amusement. One cannot *choose* without supposing the chosen the right thing to do. But this interpretation ignores the problem of what *is* the right thing to do—a problem whose solution depends on the sorting-out of priorities that I have been discussing. Further if *eudaimonia* consists simply in 'doing-the-right-thing', it becomes trivial to declare that one chooses *eudaimonia* always for its own sake and never for a further end, and false that one always wants it for its own sake. *Eudaimonia* is indeed right-doing, action in accordance with virtue, but it is most especially action in accordance with the most important virtue. In the first sense, honour and the rest are chosen always for the sake of *eudaimonia*; in the second, they may not be. And it is the second situation which helps to reveal what chiefly ҁconstitutes *eudaimonia*. Lesser ends cannot constitute *eudaimonia*, for they are *not* always the 'right thing to do' (III.2.11): some end can.

12. A merely general description of what is selected as one's life-work does not exactly determine the sort of choices one makes at a lower level. John and Peter may both be building themselves around the pursuit of honour, but John may count marrying as subordinate to making money, while Peter does the reverse. What sort of honour does each seek? The answer (there may be none till he decides on one) reveals his kind, and, given that he wishes to marry (as an end), may determine what particular marriage he makes. His wish to marry could not similarly fix what sort of honour he preferred. It may of course be that the only consistency he will ever know will be to be inconsistent (*Poet.* 1454ᵃ26f.).

13. For people do disagree, even with themselves, as to what *eudaimonia* is, as to what they take to be architectonic (*N.E.* I, 1095ᵃ20f.). Some say sensual pleasure and live apolaustically; others

say *time* and go into politics. Wealth is dismissed as even a plausible end (cf. IV.2.17). The argument against it (*N.E.* I, 1096ᵃ5f.) does not seem to be that whoever seeks it does so for an ulterior end: Aristotle and the New Comedy alike are aware of misers (cf. III.2.14). Nor does it depend on the possibility that a man may use wealth for an ulterior purpose: so may he philosophy. Consider only a man who practices *theoria* in order to get a lucrative university appointment and live in (semi-) Sardanapallan luxury all his life. Admittedly he might be a bad philosopher: but a non-miserly capitalist might equally be a bad capitalist. The point is rather that the acquisition of wealth simply does not make sense as an ultimate end, does not arise from the natural interests of man save by perversion. The art of acquisition in its natural form has a limit (*Pol.* I, 1256ᵇ26f.): one exercises the art to obtain a sufficiency of goods for living well, and then stops. It is possible to have too much money. Whereas the art of medicine knows no limit to its pursuit of health (or perhaps it does), the proper art of wealth-getting has a limit: of the means there is a limit, for the end is always the limit (*Pol.* I, 1257ᵇ25f.; cf. V.1.3). If we can suppose it possible to have too much of a good thing then we cannot suppose that this is an appropriate ultimate end. We are in search of *praxeis*, and no *praxis* with a limit is an end, or even a *praxis* in the strict sense—for a *praxis* is necessarily done for its own sake (*Met.* IX, 1048ᵇ18f.).

14.   This fact provides another way of considering architectonism. When we ask what it is that John is doing, we will not be satisfied with a perfectly correct description of John's motions which leaves out the *end*. 'He is testing for dry rot' is a more adequate description of events than 'He is sticking a knife into the wall', if that is why he is sticking the knife in. One description is overriden by another. But we do not permit just any description to be overridden by just any other; 'he is fishing for shark' cannot override 'he is killing babies' (cf. *N.E.* III, 1110ᵃ26f.). This matter is an extremely complex one, but part of the trouble is caused by the sort of priorities we have. Any momentarily overriden description may at some time by an ultimate description (perhaps he just likes sticking knives in walls), and it can be overridden only by descriptions that embody higher priorities, or at least not lower ones. 'He is advancing human knowledge' cannot override 'he is torturing people to death': a fact which may seem to make difficulties for Aristotle's choice of paramount

end. By describing *outré* circumstances to oneself, applying the rules suggested above, we can get an increasingly detailed picture of the architecture of the sort of life we can reasonably make for ourselves.

15. The arguments against Plato's position are lengthy, and I shall not discuss them here (*N.E.* I, 1096ª11f.), except to suggest that the point at which they aim in terms of Aristotle's general discussion is a denial that there is any one reason for the goodness of the colossal diversity of things that are desirable for themselves; least of all a reason that could itself count as the good for man. The architectonic good does not create the goodness of the lesser. If these arguments are valid at all they would seem to me to count also against any view of *eudaimonia* as the satisfaction of desire.

16. Once Plato has been dealt with, Aristotle begins a fresh sequence of arguments (*N.E.* I, 1097ª15f.) that sometimes duplicates what went before. Instead of pursuits he talks mainly of ends, and introduces the concept of *teleiotes*, completeness. Most importantly he concludes that whatever is to count as of the essence of *eudaimonia* must not only be more choiceworthy and therefore architectonic, but also adequate. Adequate not merely for the individual who has it but also for his relatives, friends, and fellow citizens (*N.E.* I, 1097ᵇ8). This surely cannot mean merely that a necessary condition of a man's being *eudaimon* is that his associates should be well and happy, and that the former state is therefore a sufficient condition of the latter (*CCNpNqCqp*). The point is rather that a man's *eudaimonia* benefits his associates: he is a good man to have around. Nothing can count as eudaimonic that cannot thus be shared (cf. III.3.24).

17. The passage that follows (*N.E.* I, 1097ᵇ16f.) is too compressed for its meaning to be entirely clear.[2] The currently orthodox

---

[2] ἔτι δὲ πάντων αἱρετωτάτην μὴ συναριθμουμένην, συναριθμουμένην δὲ δῆλον ὡς αἱρετωτέραν μετὰ τοῦ ἐλαχίστου τῶν ἀγαθῶν. ὑπεροχὴ γὰρ ἀγαθῶν γίνεται τὸ προστιθέμενον, ἀγαθῶν δὲ τὸ μεῖζον αἱρετώτερον ἀεί. Note that ἔτι δὲ introduces a new point, not merely a repeat of the 'lacking nothing' criterion. When Aristotle wishes to express the *Philebus*'s argument (as at *N.E.* X, 1172ᵇ28f.), he does so clearly, and what it proves is that pleasure, or any other single good, cannot itself be goodness (cf. V.1.11). It does not prove that there is no paramount good. The sense in which pleasure is not *tagathon*, the good, is not that in which *eudaimonia* is—as Aristotle reveals by following Plato's argument with a renewed plea for a practical good rather than the Platonic Goodness (*N.E.* X, 1172ᵇ34f.). The argument of *M.M.** 1184ª16f. is no more helpful to the orthodox position. *Eudaimonia* is not itself one of the goods which compose it—it does not follow that *eudaimonia* is not commensurate with other goods, such as longevity or chocolate creams, which are not parts of it. Nor would Aristotle have accepted that it could not be one of its own parts most especially (cf. II.1.26, III.3.12).

interpretation, after an argument of Plato's *Philebus* (60 de), runs: 'we think *eudaimonia* most choiceworthy of all, not counting it with anything else—if it were so counted it would clearly be more choiceworthy with even the least of goods added: for the additional good becomes an added layer of goods and the greater good is always more choiceworthy: (which is absurd).' That is, *eudaimonia* must include all possible goods. This interpretation is supported by the preceding dictum that whatever counts as *eudaimonia* must on its own make the *eudaimon*'s life choiceworthy and lacking in nothing. Also Aristotle later argues that it would be absurd not to admit that the *eudaimon* has friends, which are the greatest of external goods (*N.E.* IX, 1169^{b}8f.). He also speaks of *eudaimonia* and its parts (*N.E.* V, 1129^{b}18; *Rhet.* 1360^{b}8f.). The interpretation is none the less to be rebutted on the following grounds: (i) there is, to my ear, no trace of the counterfactual force that is necessary; (ii) that *eudaimonia* should comprise all possible goods must surely be an impossible condition, and such as to remove the discussion from the realm of practical decision—also an absurd one, for who is seriously incommoded by the occasional lack of chocolate creams?[3] (iii) that *eudaimonia* makes the *eudaimon*'s life lacking in nothing only in the trivial sense that he is not *eudaimon* if he does lack anything makes the discussion inane. To impute this grotesque notion to Aristotle would be allowable only if there were no other interpretation that was even remotely feasible, and orthodox interpreters can continue to do so only by failing to consider what would be involved in such a wholly inclusive good that cannot be improved by any addition.

18. The alternative, developed from KENNY, runs as follows: 'we think *eudaimonia* most choiceworthy of all when it is not counted with anything else—clearly when it is so counted it is more choiceworthy with even the least additional good ... (which is not at all absurd)'. The point is rather that of Plato's *Republic* (II, 357 a f.), that the ultimate good cannot be chosen simply because of incidental goods it carries with it: it must be more choiceworthy than any other good even on its own. With certain additions, the result may be

---

[3] The orthodox might reply that the elements of *eudaimonia* are not e.g. chocolates and knighthoods, but more generally, pleasure and honour and so forth. But this is to give up the game: for the contemplative has his own pleasure (*N.E.* X, 1177^{a}23f. *et al.*) and virtue (of which honour is only the recognition (*N.E.* I, 1095^{b}26))—so that a single activity may lack no general good, and the present passage ceases to provide any support for inclusive interpretations.

superior, but these additions are often not in our command. There is some reason to believe that Aristotle does envisage superior states: though *to makarion*, blessedness, is usually more or less the same as *eudaimonia*, the term does have a more felicitous ring, and he occasionally seems to intend a contrast. One who is *eudaimon* can never be *athlios*, but neither will he be *makarios* 'if he should have Priam's luck' (*N.E.* I, 1101ᵃ6f.; cf. X, 1179ᵃ1f., *E.E.* 1215ᵃ9f.).[4] How does this interpretation handle the apparent evidence for the orthodox one? That *eudaimonia* lacks nothing (*N.E.* X, 1176ᵇ5) surely means no more than that the *eudaimon* is not in need, that there is no further good which is required to complete the good life, though such further goods undoubtedly exist. The belief that a given life would not be self-sufficient if some addition could make it better, as well as the use made of *eudaimonia*'s having parts, merely demonstrates that orthodox commentators have entirely failed to understand the nature of the whole-part relationship (cf. II.3.5, III.1.7).

19.   For we are not concerned simply with abstract *eudaimonia*, but with the *eudaimon*, who is an organic whole. Wholes are not mutilated by the privation of just any part (*Met.* V, 1024ᵃ23) and the *eudaimon*'s life is not mutilated by being deprived of chocolate creams, any more than his body by being clean-shaven. His claims to *eudaimonia* may be shaken by the loss of friends and other such goods, as his life may be threatened by the loss of limbs, but there are certain essential organs which are of the essence of his life (*De Part. An.* 640ᵃ33f. *et al.*) and likewise certain essential activities well performed. He is not invulnerable, and to claim that a man may be *eudaimon* even on the rack draws close to absurdity (*N.E.* VII, 1153ᵇ19f.): if *eudaimonia* is compatible with just any public state it gives us no guidance in determining our public course—where the good life is entirely a matter of 'spiritual' attitude anomie is the only course (and ennui). If a thing's removal from an organism makes no real difference to the organism, it was no real part (*Poet.* 1451ᵃ34f.). If a condition is only a *sine qua non* of an organism's existence it is no real part of the whole (*N.E.* V, 1129ᵇ17f.; cf. *E.E.* 1214ᵇ26f.). *Eudaimonia* does have parts, but not all are equally important to the

---

⁴ Luck, as such, is unobtainable by man: God is both *eudaimon* and *makarios*, without need of external goods, but for a man to be *makarios* he must also be *eutuches* (*Pol.* VII, 1323ᵇ23f.).

life of the *eudaimon*, nor are all conditions parts. Even where all commentators admit that he is speaking of 'dominant' *eudaimonia* he insists that it requires a complete term of life to reveal itself (*N.E.* X, 1177^{b}25; cf. II.3.17); longevity is not therefore a part of *eudaimonia*, for it is not in our gifts. The whole inclusive/dominant dichotomy in fact serves only to darken counsel: there is indeed room for many different sorts of activity in the good life, though not literally for all sorts; this does not prevent there being one activity which is central. Just as the universal end, which is God, exists both as ruler of the hierarchy and throughout it (*Met.* XII, 1075^{a}12f.), just as the ruling element in any entity is that entity most especially (cf. III.3.6), so there is one good which is of the *eudaimon*'s essence: *eudaimonia* is that good most especially, but also the whole life of the living man.

20. This is also of importance in the *ergon* argument: 'the good for man is activity of soul in accordance with virtue, and if there is more than one virtue, according to the best and most perfect' (*N.E.* I, 1098^{a}16f.; cf. I, 1098^{b}30, VII, 1153^{b}9f., X, 1177^{a}12f.). That is, the good for man is living well, and if there is more than one way of living, because more than one sense of 'living', then the good for man is primarily to make a good job of his supreme activities. Not that he is thereby instructed to make a bad job of his others, but that the higher are more important. Fleetness of foot is a virtue of sorts, as is a good digestion, but it would be absurd to count these as of equal status with the virtues of higher activities.[5] Similarly, in connection with the problem of overriding descriptions (cf. V.1.14), that a man did *x* swiftly does not excuse his doing it wickedly. Ideally we should do everything well, but ideals often conflict (cf. *Pol.* VIII, 1338^{b}9f.). It may be (though there is no certainty that it is) that some of us cannot achieve the highest for ourselves: it does not follow that we should not serve it (V.1.33n, App. B.9).

21. What then must a good be like if it is to be of the essence of *eudaimonia*? It must be such as to be chosen against any other single good, or even combination of other goods. It must be such that

---

[5] 'The less principal virtues are . . . called less principal, not because they are indifferent or may be accounted useless, for then they would not be virtues: but because though their practice be of extraordinary importance in their place, they are more remote, and less avail in the way to felicity, and are more confined in their operations' (T. Traherne, *Way to Blessedness*, ch. 3).

whereas it could never reasonably be merely a means to some further end, other goods may be (though they need not be) obtained, or rejected, as a step towards it. It must be such that one cannot envisage having too much of it. It must be sufficient not merely for that abstraction, the pure individual, but for the real, social being that is the individual-in-society. It must be such as to provide a stable identity for that individual, though this stability need not be, because it cannot be, an absolute stability. It must be dependent as little as possible upon what other people do or the state of the environment, but rather on the individual—for only so can it be something practically obtainable by him (*N.E.* I, 1095^{b}25, X, 1177^{a}28f.). It is also pleasant, 'for to each man that of which he is called a lover is pleasant' (*N.E.* I, 1099^{a}7f.), and therefore needs no further pleasure to make it complete. There are inevitably conditions that are more or less necessary for its attainment (*N.E.* I, 1099^{a}31f.), but as far as it is possible it should be practical and not the gift of chance (*N.E.* I, 1099^{b}20f.). *Eudaimonia* is activity in accordance with virtue, and if there is more than one in accordance with the best and most complete (*N.E.* I, 1098^{a}16f.): one who lacks the material for such activity cannot actually be *eudaimon*, cannot actually be doing right, though presumably he may be potentially so.

22. One thing *eudaimonia* is not, is happiness, in the sense of felt contentment (Austin: MORAVCSIK). 'Both evil and good are thought to exist for a dead man, as much as for one who is alive but unaware of them' (*N.E.* I, 1100^{a}18f.). Although nothing can be allowed to alter a dead man's status from *eudaimon* to *dusdaimon*, or vice versa, yet some effects must be admitted (*N.E.* I, 1101^{a}21f.). *Eudaimonia* is a status rather than a state. The point about the *eudaimon* is not that he is pleased—though there is pleasure in any unimpeded natural activity (*N.E.* X, 1174^{b}15f.)—but that he is doing his thing well, and that the thing in question really does have (in the eyes of a 'reasonable' man) the properties required by the concept of *eudaimonia*.

23. A familiar sophism is that all human acts are performed for the sake of one's own pleasure: if John expends time and energy in helping his friend he can only be doing it to get a certain sort of pleasure. As Aristotle observes, this merely compels us to redefine what we mean by 'self-serving activity' in the opprobrious sense (*N.E.* IX, 1169^{a}12f.). As Aristotle's account of pleasure makes clear,

it also misunderstands the situation: John may well be pleased at having helped his friend, but the pleasure is not a further state which might also be obtained by taking a pill—it is precisely the pleasure of having helped his friend. He would not be thus pleased were he not glad, and if his friend's being helped were not therefore at least a possible motive for his action. The pleasure of natural activity is real, and a real good, but it is a supervening one—a point not unconnected with the paradox of hedonism, that one is more likely to get pleasure if one is seeking something other than pleasure (cf. III.1.17). Men find their identities in many ways: they cannot unambiguously be said to find it in happiness, pleasure, satisfaction (cf. V.1.11), for these concepts are as vacuous as goodness itself, or self-preservation (cf. III.3.29). Nor is it possible that they should reasonably find or create themselves with reference to any more specific pleasure, of an apolaustic sort. Which would you prefer, to be sensually pleased and not know it or know your condition and not be sensually pleased? Suppose we could infallibly stimulate our own pleasure centres with a small machine: would you accept permanent and solipsistic addiction to this device? If you would not, and I suspect that only the suicidal would choose otherwise, then pleasure is not a suitable paramount end. Pleasure and life go together (*N.E.* X, 1175^{b}18f.), and all men aim at life, but 'life' means many things. Aristotle is certainly not saying that all men do or should aim at their own contentment. The perceptible is prior to perception (III.1.13), the enjoyable to enjoyment: a thing's value is prior to our recognition of that value (see VI.11). Aristotle's ethical system is not subjectivist.

24.   Some activities are engaged in for their own sakes, others for their product: the latter are not really activities, *energeiai*. Now it is not appropriate to find one's purpose in being in the production of some one thing, for what then shall we do when we have produced it? What of the time before we have produced it? The future is uncertain, whereas the good for man should be something difficult to separate from the self—clearly, for it is the self. It is important therefore that *eudaimonia* is activity, desirable in itself and without natural term. 'Of this nature virtuous acts are thought to be; for to do noble and good deeds is a thing desirable in itself' (*N.E.* X, 1176^{b}8). Pleasant amusement is also such, but 'to exert oneself and work for the sake of amusement seems silly and utterly childish; for

amusement is a sort of relaxation' (*N.E.* X, 1176^{b}32). 'Everything that wakes must be able to sleep, for it is impossible to be always active' (*De Somno* 454^{b}7f.). Relaxation is enjoyable, but hardly a life's work: consider the man who hits himself with a hammer because it's so nice when he stops.

25. 'No-one would maintain that he is *makarios* who has not in him a particle of courage or temperance or justice or prudence' (*Pol.* VII, 1323^{a}27f.). These virtues are prior to more material goods, partly because the latter are (generally) consequent on the acquisition of virtue and not vice versa (*Pol.* VII, 1323^{a}40f.). They are more of the essence. But a man or a society who had no more than these civil virtues would still not have reached as far as is possible for man. We cannot achieve the purely theoretic life enjoyed by the gods (*N.E.* X, 1178^{b}8f.), but we should not forget it. The heart and vascular system cannot survive on their own; they are still the material centre of our lives. A civil life in which one merely gets along with one's neighbours does not seem satisfying: not so much that it seems pointless, for any ultimate end is strictly pointless—it points nowhere—but that it does not engage all our attention. 'All men naturally reach out for knowledge' (*Met.* I, 980^{a}23; *Poet.* 1448^{b}13), and it is knowledge, primarily knowledge of the Whole, that is the central good of Aristotelian man. 'For deeds many things are needed, and more, the greater and nobler the deeds are. But the man who is contemplating the truth needs no such thing, at least with a view to the exercise of his activity; indeed they are, one may say, even hindrances, at least to his contemplation: but in so far as he is a man and lives with a number of people, he chooses to do virtuous acts; he will therefore need such aids to living a human life' (*N.E.* X, 1178^{b}1f.).

26. A fuller analysis of this supreme activity must await my discussion of *nous*, but some points may be made immediately. Firstly, there is the problem of fanaticism (cf. V.1.14). If the pursuit of knowledge is a higher end than the civil life are we to conclude that it must be reasonable to engage in social intercourse for the sake of research, and not vice versa? And do we in fact admire, or even refrain from condemning a scientist or scholar who compels all to serve his single end? Who abets murder for scientific purposes? Who prefers research without love to love without research? It is

undoubtedly this problem which has caused some moralists to specu-
late that *eudaimonia* is simply inclusive, but it cannot in fact be solved
by the inclusive model—this would merely result in competing
values with no decidable priorities. We should rather consider the
sort of knowledge of which Aristotle is speaking. 'He was being
affectionate' cannot override 'he raped her', not (as at V.1.14)
because intercourse is more important than affection (it is not: App.
B.8), but because the two statements cannot be simultaneously true.
It is unreasonable to rape for love. It is no less so knowingly to
disregard one's fellows to their hurt for the sake of theoretic truth.
A supposed *theoretikos* who is thus antisocial (he may well of course
be 'outside the law' in *some* sense (cf. III.3.23)) is no true contemplative, for that divine thing in him is also that which is in all good
society (III.3.11: see V.2.15). Civil and theoretic *eudaimonia* meet
in this, that the really good civil life is actually or only subjectively
within a really good polity, one where the highest is served (cf. App.
B.9). The problem of fanaticism does indeed outlaw certain varieties
of research as appropriate paramount ends. It does not, I think,
outlaw *theoria*. It is sometimes appropriate to abjure some society
for the sake of *theoria*: it can never be so to abjure *theoria* for the
sake of society—for a society in which the *theos* is no longer served
is one already dead. That *theoria* is theo-ria, the service of the god
(and a pun no worse than most of Plato's), I shall seek to justify
below (V.3.28). Likewise that love and knowledge are here united
(cf. II.1.25).

27. 'We must as far as possible make ourselves immortal and strain
every nerve to live in accordance with the best thing in us . . . that
would seem especially to be each man' (*N.E.* X, 1177^{b}31f.). It would
be strange not to choose one's own life, but that of something else.
Our own life is the life of sight and knowledge (cf. *Protr.* fr. 7). This
life is that which is in accord with the divine in us. Perhaps all things
seek it in their degree, 'for everything has in it something of the
divine by nature' (*N.E.* VII, 1153^{b}32), but only men of all sublunary
things have a chance of obtaining it. 'None of the other animals can
be *eudaimon*, for none have any share in *theoria*' (*N.E.* X, 1178^{b}27f.).
We need a share in something divine to be capable of *eudaimonia*
(*E.E.* 1217^{a}26f.). Morals (*N.E.* III, 1115^{b}12, IV, 1122^{b}6f.) and
mathematics alike (cf. *Met.* XIII, 1078^{a}32f.) aim in their degree at
the beautiful, and he that thus aims, whether in the 'community or

on his own, whether actually or subjectively in the *koinonia* of free men, is most truly *eudaimon*. 'We ought to practise virtue for the sake of wisdom, for wisdom is the supreme end' (*Protr.* fr. 11). Wisdom is the formal cause of the good life (*N.E.* VI, 1144ª4). For Aristotle, as for Plato, the *daimon* of *eudaimonia* is *nous*.

28. This said, we must also remember that we cannot immortalize ourselves. We may wish for immortality, but we cannot achieve it (*N.E.* I, 1111ᵇ22; *E.E.* 1225ᵇ34). Indeed no man could even wish to be a god if he saw what was implied in such a transformation (*N.E.* IX, 1166ª19). I shall have more to say about death and immortality below; for the moment I wish only to say that desire without a term is no desire at all. A reaching out that cannot reach, and does not wish to reach its purported end, is no more than a gesture. The pursuit of divinity enjoined on us is therefore no movement valued for its separate end: it is an activity whose end is in itself. It is life, not life's consummation, to which Aristotle pledges himself: *eudaimonia* is not a possession (*N.E.* IX, 1169ᵇ29f.). What one has can be taken away; what one hopes for one may never get. What one *is* is inseparable from oneself, and one is one's activity. True *eudaimonia* lies not in having obtained any external good, however spiritual, but in our continued approximation to that unobtainable, inimitable divinity. 'One thing has and shares the good, another approaches it quickly via few steps, another through many, while a fourth does not even try, except to come sufficiently near the term' (*De Caelo* 292ᵇ10f.). Men cannot, physically and logically, obtain that which is best for more than a moment (cf. *De Caelo* 279ª12f., *Met.* XII, 1072ᵇ13, *N.E.* X, 1174ᵇ31f., *De Part. An.* 644ᵇ32f.), and therefore it is not this best which is man's good, but the living of a life in which he sometimes does.

29. 'Think immortal and divine thoughts and in so far as human nature can share in immortality lose no part of it' (Pl. *Tim.* 89 e). Similarly Zen disciples are urged to discover the Buddha, or produce their souls, or say 'what at this moment thy own original face doth look like, which thou hadst even prior to thy birth' (Hui-neng: SUZUKI (1) p. 70). They are asked to do the impossible.

30. Aristotle has no conclusive argument, least of all any speciously deductive one, to compel us to make ourselves in the Aristotelian mode. He has some argument to show that it is this which is most

natural to men. In so far as it is the divine element which enables us to live and act humanly together it is the divine which makes us men. 'One must always seek the highest cause of each thing' (*Phys.* II, 195^{b}21f.). 'For the cause of an attribute's inherence in a subject always itself inheres in the subject more firmly than the attribute, for example the reason for which we love anything is dearer to us than that thing' (*Post. An.* 72^{a}29f.). That element by which we are human, almost human, is therefore most especially ourselves (*N.E.* X, 1178^{a}4f.).

31. 'Man's pleasure is a short time growing and falls to the ground as quickly, when an unlucky twist of thought loosens its roots. Man's life is a day. What is he? What is he not? A shadow in a dream is man; but when God sheds a brightness, shining light is on earth and life is as sweet as honey' (Pindar *Pythian* VIII.92f., Bowra).

32. In this, his last extant poem, Pindar touches from a different direction and with a different mood, an Aristotelian point. 'Pleasure perfects the activity, not as an immanent disposition, but as a sort of extra end, like the bloom of youth on those who are in their prime . . . all human things fail to maintain their activity . . . and so pleasure too is dulled' (*N.E.* X, 1174^{b}31f.).

33. There is nothing that we can keep up for long, and the life we live is bound by this. All things grow dull, but the life of *nous* gives pleasure more abiding than any other (*N.E.* X, 1177^{a}25f.). We must live in accordance with the best in us, with that which we cannot wholly obtain. 'The possession of knowledge might justly be regarded as beyond human power; for in many ways human nature is in bondage, so that according to Simonides "God alone can have this privilege"' (*Met.* I, 982^{b}28f.). Yet it is this, and truth, which is supremely worth having in Aristotle's eyes. There is a right answer to the question 'what is right-doing?', for there is a right answer to the question 'what are men?' To love oneself is to do what one thinks right; to do what is really right is to love one's true self (see III.3.29n). I may identify myself, say what I am in terms of my chosen life-work, as I choose (barring interference from my society); but if I do so wickedly I fail of my potential and achieve no stable self. Men are creatures that can receive God, and only the man who strives so to do can say truly what men and the world may be: for only he comes even close to seeing what the world is in itself (see V.3.28). Those

men, if there be such,[6] who are naturally free (II.1.19f.) but who cannot realize the presence in time of *nous* even for a moment may still do right by following their state's suggestions—if their state's governors have intuited the god. If the state and its citizens alike are blind, all alike are *dusdaimones* (cf. VI.6).

[6] There may be free men who do not know the god: I doubt if Aristotle would allow that they *could* not—they are only free because they are slightly emancipated from immediate reality by an intuition of the world apart from themselves (cf. II.1.30).

V.2. Death

1. We plan, or at least it is sensible to plan, our lives. In so doing we create a life, but in another sense it is death that so creates, nor does it wait upon our desire. Our situation is such that it may seem merely pompous to speak of making one's life, and any philosophical anthropology must attempt to come to terms, or at least to blows, with this most universal and also most particular of facts, that I am going to die. In what follows I shall try to show how Aristotle resolves the tension between the two major views of death, as an intrusion and as a completion. I also hope to counter the difficulty inherent in any ethical theory that bases itself on the desire for survival, namely that ethical values may sometimes require our demise.

2. 'The nature is the end or "that for the sake of which". For if a thing undergoes a continuous change and there is a stage which is last, this stage is the end or "that for the sake of which". That is why the poet was being absurd when he said "he has the end, i.e. death, for which he was born". For not every stage that is last claims to be an end but only that which is best' (*Phys.* II, 194ᵃ27f.). This may seem a contradiction: having said that the last stage is the final cause he argues that for this reason death cannot be the end. Emendation is possible, but unnecessary: rather the last natural stage is the goal. With this proviso the argument makes sense, if we can assume that Aristotle thought death unnatural on all occasions. If I am run over by a bus, or drowned in a boating accident, this plainly cannot count as the goal of my existence: as far as my specific essence goes it is precisely accidental. 'But all of us alike are dying, though our fates are not the same' (Pindar *Isth.* VII.7.42). How can death as such be unnatural, particularly if the natural is what happens always or usually?

3. 'All weaknesses in animals, such as old age and decay, are unnatural' (*De Caelo* 288ᵇ15f.). Disease is adventitious age, old age a disease (though here a 'natural' one) (*De Gen. An.* 784ᵇ33; cf. *Probl.** XIV, 909ᵇ3, XXXVIII, 967ᵇ15). Death and decay are ends only analogically (*Met.* V, 1021ᵇ25f.). Corruptions, as of wine to

vinegar, are accidental (*Met.* VIII, 1044ᵇ34f.). Nothing can be the cause of its own decay (*De Motu* 700ᵃ35f.). These claims may reasonably be linked to a doctrine I have mentioned before (cf. II.3.4), that a dead eye is not really an eye (*Meteor.* 389ᵇ32; *De Gen. An.* 735ᵃ6f.) nor is a corpse a man (*De Part. An.* 640ᵇ34) nor is a finger apart from the living body a finger (*Met.* VII, 1035ᵇ24f.). Now that which is incapable of completing its coming to be *x* cannot be in process of coming to be *x* (*Met.* III, 999ᵇ9f.; cf. V.1.28). In Aristotle's biology caterpillars do not become but give birth to butterflies (*De Gen. An.* 758ᵇ6f.). Men are not in process of becoming dead. Dying is not an activity of the organism, nor is decay. Destruction arises from impotence, not potency, and therefore not from the victim's nature (*Met.* V, 1019ᵃ28f.). 'The human person is not, in its true essence, an existence towards death' (LANDSBERG p. 22). Nor is any living being. The final form of an organism is not a corpse, for that is no form of the organism at all, but the adult being (cf. II.3.15).

4. But though dying is no activity of mine (cf. *N.E.* V, 1135ᵃ33f.), it is none the less certain that I shall die. Every creature has its own natural period (*Met.* XIV, 1093ᵃ4f.; *De Caelo* 279ᵃ23f.; *De Gen. An.* 777ᵇ16f.; *De Gen. Corr.* 336ᵇ11f.), and anything left to itself decays (*Phys.* IV, 222ᵇ19f.; cf. IV.2.9). 'The end of everything put together by nature is decay, unless it perishes by violence' (*Meteor.* 379ᵃ5). Birth and death are characteristic of all living creatures, and in the case of natural death, where the source is in the entity, 'the structure of the animal involved this from the beginning, and it was no extraneous disease' (*De Resp.* 478ᵇ26f.). Nature provides us with teeth that last until old age: if we were to live longer the teeth would have to be bigger (*De Gen. An.* 745ᵃ32f.). Old age is a natural event (*E.E.* 1224ᵇ32f.). Growth and decay are regulated by the natural solar rhythms (*De Gen. Corr.* 336ᵇ17f.; cf. *Meteor.* 346ᵇ20f.; *De Gen. An.* 716ᵃ16, *Phys.* II, 194ᵇ13, *Met.* XII, 1071ᵃ15). Growth, maturity, and decay alike are functions of the soul (*De An.* 411ᵃ30f.): it is for this reason that wind-eggs are to be counted as living (in a vegetable sense), that they can decay (*De Gen. An.* 741ᵃ20f.).

5. The resolution of this paradox, that death is at once unnatural, against our nature, and an aspect of natural rhythm, is not merely a problem in Aristotelian scholarship. The opposition has been traced to the primitive division between hunters and farmers: the

former seeing death typically as an act of violence, the latter as the way of the world (Frobenius: CAMPBELL (2) I pp. 125f.). It recurs in modern medicine and psychology (cf. CHORON). Plessner (CAMPBELL (3) p. 254) recognizes the division and declares that the entity 'inclines toward death but it must still be overpowered by death'. The question whether to fight or submit to age and death is the ethical aspect of the same problem. It is no accident that men find the image of the wheel both comforting and hateful.

6. How did Aristotle resolve his dilemma? Metaphysically there may be no real problem, at least if we allow for a certain looseness of expression in some of the texts quoted above. Death is unnatural *kata to eidos*, in respect of the form, but natural *kata ten hulen*, in respect of the matter (cf. *De Gen. An.* $770^b16f.$; see II.3.28); it is a product of material necessity, not of the definition of the entity in question (cf. *De Part. An.* $663^b22f.$). Death is not an action but rather something to be suffered. The elements which go to form any concrete individual each have their own period, and the single form must eventually fail to constrain its parts (*De Caelo* $288^b15f.$). Natural death is the decay of the 'first cooled part' (cf. *De Part. An.* $653^b3f.$), 'from length of time and completeness' (*De Resp.* $479^b2f.$). It is a failure on the part of the heat of life to regulate its material (*De Gen. Corr.* $329^b24f.$; JOACHIM (2) pp. 205f.), a victory of matter over form (*Meteor.* $379^a11f.$). Old age is a slackening of the heat (*De Gen. An.* $783^b6f.$; *De Long. Vit.* $466^a20f.$), and death is its destruction (*De Vit.* $469^b19f.$). Entities are organic (cf. II.3.5), and only the Whole itself, whose parts maintain both their being and its own, is immune to this material revolt. All that lives, except the Whole, must one day die, but only by material necessity. Decay is not a function of an entity qua its unity, but qua its multiplicity.

7. In short, I shall die because I have parts which have other laws to obey than the laws of my being—laws, for example, of chemical reaction, gravity, and levity. A very similar discovery issues from the realization that 'death is not an event in life: we do not live to experience death' (WITTGENSTEIN (3) 6.4311, (1) p. 75). My own death is unimaginable because it will not be an event in my world (cf. PEIRCE IV p. 148, FREUD p. 289)—unless, of course, death is not what we think it is (see below). Certainly I can imagine what the world will be like when I am dead for those that still live and for The World itself, but not what it will be like for me. I know what

it is for my foot to have gone dead: to be paralysed, to be separated from me. But what is it like for Me to be separated from me? Once again, I can die because there is a world larger than my world in which I can have ceased to be, and in facing the certainty of my on-coming demise I realise the survival of that larger whole (see V.2.15).

8. The relevance of the above paragraph will perhaps not be entirely clear until my next chapter: for the moment let it stand as pre-face to Plato's arguments for personal immortality, which in turn may help to explicate Aristotle's attitude to death and immortality. For it is at least half-true that Aristotle's attitude arises from his response to and partial acceptance of Plato's arguments, though not of his thesis.

9. The argument from self-movement (Pl. *Phdr.* 245, *Laws* 895; ascribed to Alcmaeon at *De An.* 405ᵃ30f.), that the soul keeps itself going, and is therefore *causa sui* and immortal, collapsed when Aristotle decided that literal self-movement was impossible, in that it implied the simultaneous actuality and potentiality of the same entity in the same respect (*Phys.* VIII, 255ᵃ15; *De An.* 405ᵇ31f.). In concluding that only the unmoved was independent of contingent influences Aristotle at once took Plato's belief in the simplicity of the soul to its conclusion, and effectively removed it from the sphere of personal continuance. Plato's more subtle arguments, in the *Phaedo*, have a similar effect when seen through Aristotelian eyes. In this dialogue, Socrates argues first from the cyclical nature of all natural processes (*Phdo.* 70 c 4), suggesting that as we depart into the void of death, so must we return from the void at birth: otherwise everything would end up like Endymion. Aristotle uses a similar argument at *De Gen. Corr.* 319ᵃ22f. but does not permit anything more than the reinstantiation of the type to follow from it (cf. IV.1.14, IV.2.11). Socrates' next argument purports to show that as certain concepts are not obtainable from sensory experience they must have been acquired prior to all sensory experience, i.e. before birth (*Phdo.* 72 e 3f.). And if we existed before our births it would be ridiculous not to admit our *post-mortem* existence as well. The doctrine of *anamnesis* is rejected in Aristotle's analysis of the acquisition of concepts: the soul is such as to acquire them. Re-learning is not remembering (*De Mem.* 452ᵃ4f.), and the only element that Aristotle does allow as immortal in the human soul has no memory at all (*De An.* 430ᵃ22). None the less, in analysing our

knowledge of certain concepts as he does Aristotle appeals to something more than the empirical self—a light from beyond (see V.3.23). Similarly with Socrates' third argument: if the soul is probably immortal because it resembles the divine (*Phdo.* 79 a f.), is it not that which causes that resemblance, as most especially divine, that is most probably immortal?

10.   Socrates' final and most difficult argument is easily parodied in the form, 'there is no dead soul and therefore no one can die' ('there is no sleeping waking-man, and therefore no one can go to sleep' (cf. *De Soph. El.* 166ᵃ22f.)). I am deathless while alive (WITTGENSTEIN (3) 6.4311), and presumably insomniac while awake. There is more to it than that. If dying is a process or an act of becoming dead then something which is essentially alive cannot die, any more than water can become dry. A particular pool can of course 'dry up', a particular fire can go cold, a particular human body can die (or a particular lump of flesh). Fire, water, and soul themselves can only 'withdraw or be extinguished'. But if fire is the hottest of all things, as making all else hot (*Met.* II*, 993ᵇ24), soul, which is the cause of life in all bodily entities, is itself alive and cannot put off that life so as to be extinguished. Soul is therefore immortal.

11.   The conclusion follows only on two assumptions: (i) that there is at least some part of the soul which is more than the mere harmony of bodily parts, more than the formula which defines the entity's mode of being (for if soul is not itself alive there is no problem in its being extinguished); Plato supposes himself to have proved this (*Phdo.* 91 c 6f.); (ii) that this soul-from-outside is not itself a concrete individual, for if it were its material substrate could put off it and life together. In short immortal soul must be at once living and a form. The resolution in Aristotelian terms of this seeming paradox must be delayed. For the moment it is enough to note the actual, if not the intended, goal of Plato's arguments. Taking them all together, they suggest the immortality of that in us which is the formal cause of our life, our ability to learn and categorize, our intimations of the divine, which is the centre of our apparent self-movement and the one enduring thing in the ceaseless rhythms of the world (it alone *lives*, and is, perpetually, while all else perishes and comes to be). It may be that there is no such thing; if there is it seems to have little enough to do with our ordinary selves. Themistius suggests that the arguments were intended to prove no more than

an ideal, rational immortality, and not personal continuance, that all other Platonic descriptions are merely myths. I suggest that Aristotle too followed the arguments in that direction: my immortal soul is no other than yours.

12. Plato's beliefs probably involved more than this ideal immortality, though the *Symposium*'s begetting of true excellence on Beauty (*Symp.* 211e; cf. *Rpb.* 490b2f., *Ep.* VII, 341d, *Tht.* 176a5f.) also seems more ideal than personal. The life beyond death is one of conversing with the gods, perhaps with men dead long ago, paying penalties and receiving due reward for earthly crime and virtue, in a world not more abstract, more attenuated than this one, but by far more real: a world as far above ours in clarity and beauty as ours above the world beneath the sea. Granted, 'those who have been sufficiently purified by philosophy live altogether without bodies and reach homes even more beautiful than these' (*Phdo.* 114 c 3f.): it may be that, like some Indian sects, Plato distinguished between the 'bodily' heavens obtainable by the multitude and the solitary splendour beyond the cycle of rebirth obtained by philosopher or kevalin (see ZIMMER (2) pp. 305f.). On this interpretation what is essentially immortal is the ideal self, but earthly accretions weigh it down to the world of rebirth: the Self, Purusa, has dreamed itself a variety of forms from which even physical death does not necessarily release it. On the other hand, living without bodies, 'not stuffed with flesh and colours and a great deal more perishable nonsense' (*Symp.* 211 e), does not seem to involve in Plato's mind living without contact or impersonally, and it may be that even philosophic beatitude is 'bodily' in the sense of being social. In either case (and it is no part of my present purposes to resolve the issue) we clearly need some model which will accommodate 'survival after death' in the standard meaning attached to this phrase. Such a model will also make clear what Aristotle rejected. There are well-known difficulties about *post-mortem* continuity, notably those associated with personal identity. I have already argued that personal identity is never a purely descriptive notion (III.3.5), so that such difficulties are far from decisive. None the less mere resurrection or reduplication of an individual does not seem sufficient for personal immortality: what does it matter to me if someone like me appears in the distant future (cf. IV.2.14)? Psychic continuity within our ordinary spatio-temporal frame would seem theoretically sufficient (and this is

perhaps what Plato counted on—the literal departure of a physical soul), but against the evidence. A much more plausible model, adopted by many immortalists, is provided by the experience of waking from sleep. This may be made clearer with the help of an analogy: suppose it is possible to guide men's dreams. Suppose we submit a number of men to our device: as far as we are concerned they are lying on their beds, plugged into our *oneirotokon*. As far as they are concerned (with whatever qualifications about the possibility of thinking while asleep) they are engaged in the common pursuit of a bear. They are enduring and partly inventing a shared dream which they take to be waking reality. We make it seem to them that one of their number dies: they dream-bury his dream-body and forget. But he, the identifiable being that was asleep and dreaming, merely wakes up. Waking to life eternal, by analogy, is waking from a masquerade, to find that reality of which *this* world is no more than a copy—as Plato said. In short, the best model for *post-mortem* continuity is one that requires that this world is, relatively, an illusion, that we do not see things as they are, that some other condition of things (of which we can have only interior conviction) is true reality. And we have already seen (III.1.27) that Aristotle entertained no such doubt about the world of the senses. He cannot allow survival by 'waking-to-a-new-world', for this is the only world there is. Any survival must be of some element of the psycho-physical personality (not the whole), some element which is not simply the form of the body. It must be survival of something which can be found in the world of the four elements, the spheres, the whole complex of the natural universe. Plato argued for the immortality of the divine element in a man, and apparently accepted the immortality of the whole man: Aristotle could accept no more than the former. Plato made a division between this world and reality: Aristotle denied it (see V.3.28, VI.12f.).

13. Death, in Aristotelian terms, is the falling apart of the organism, and if anything of us but our material is to survive it must be some formal element which is more than the organized unity of our organism. Could such a thing provide any resolution of Aristotle's shifting attitude to death? In an early work he repeated the story of Midas and a captive Silenus, who sardonically told the king, in the best Greek tradition, that non-existence was man's best hope. From this Aristotle concluded that the godlet meant to say that 'the

state of death is better than living' (*Eudemos* fr. 6 Ross). If we had had the choice, non-existence would have been preferable (*E.E.* 1215ᵇ20f.), though dying is clearly unpleasant (otherwise the akolastic would be dying all the time (*E.E.* 1229ᵇ34)), and even those with nothing left to live for cling to life for its natural sweetness (*Pol.* III, 1278ᵇ27f.). Non-existence may be better than life, but 'death is most fearful, for it is a limit and it is thought that there is nothing either good or bad for one who's dead' (*N.E.* III, 1115ᵃ26). This may not be Aristotle's own opinion, but only a report on common belief: he gives no evidence that he disagrees (the discussion in *N.E.* I, 10, embodying the dictum that 'there is thought to be some good and bad for the dead, as also for one who is alive but unaware' (*N.E.* I, 1100ᵃ18), is to an entirely different point (see V.1.22)). The discussion of death, in relation to courage, in *N.E.* III 6 is clear that death is an end. We should perhaps remember that Aristotle is capable of declaring that there is nothing beyond the heavens and then placing the most high in that nothingness (*De Caelo* 279ᵃ12f.), but it is unlikely that he has any such esoteric codicil in mind here. 'The more of every virtue that a man has and the more *eudaimon* that he is, the more will he be displeased at death' (*N.E.* III, 1117ᵇ10f.). In old age 'the soul's release is unnoticed' (*De Resp.* 479ᵃ22), but while we are aware we must resist the approach of death. Aristotle follows Plato in resisting Pindar's orthodoxy, that 'mortal things suit mortals' (*Isth.* V.20; cf. *Pyth.* III.61), but it is Pindar's information which is correct.

14. One reaction to this fate is to find the eternal in glorious endeavour. But whereas Pindar admired the noble athlete or the poetic eagle, Aristotle's ideal is apparently that *meteorolesches* whom the spokesmen for orthodoxy and scientific empiricism alike disdained. Despite the differences between gods and men 'yet we can in greatness of mind and body be like the immortals' (Pindar.*Nem.* VI.4f.). Hardly for Aristotle in greatness of body (though cf. *Pol.* I, 1254ᵇ34f.), but he is working within the same tradition (cf. II.1.30). In the only extant Aristotelian use of '*to athanatizein*' other than *N.E.* X, 1177ᵇ31f. it seems to refer directly to an immortality via honour: 'I would never have deliberately sacrificed to Hermeias as to an immortal, but as for a mortal I prepared a memorial and wanting to immortalize his nature I adorned it with funeral honours' (fr. 645 Rose). To immortalize oneself is not to treat oneself as an

immortal but to make oneself as like such as possible, by doing something fine. In so doing it may be necessary to discount one's personal survival (cf. *E.E.* 1215ᵇ27f.): 'death is more to be chosen than life on such terms' (*N.E.* III, 1116ᵇ20). The *megalopsuchos* in particular is on suitable occasions careless of his life, as it is not worthy of him to survive on just any terms (*N.E.* IV, 1124ᵇ8f.). Treachery and an eye to the main chance may sometimes produce our physical or economic survival, but they cannot buy our survival as good men either at the civil or the theoretic level. To live in accord with the best that is in us is sometimes to reckon our own deaths the better course. Longevity is not all-important, nor is a good necessarily better for being long-lasting (*N.E.* I, 1096ᵇ3f.).

15. Simultaneously it is this very mode of life which makes death particularly hard to bear. The good man is grieved at death for he loses what he knows to be a good. Death is terrible because after it there is no awareness of either good or ill, and it is awareness, knowledge, which marks the best in us. We would prefer a life with only touch and taste left to us to the sheer unawareness of death (*De Gen. An.* 731ᵇ3f.), and the loss of sense-awareness is itself equivalent to death (*Protrepticus* fr. 7 Ross; *E.E.* 1244ᵇ26f.). Death is the greatest of evils, particularly for the Aristotelian saint, but he none the less may choose physical death when the choice is between that and the separation from the best in him which is its emotional equivalent (cf. II.1.14): particularly where such physical death may result in some fine thing's being done. We are in the world, and the world survives us; it is that world with whose perfection we should be concerned, for ourselves if possible, but also and more especially in itself. It is because we can be aware of the world in itself that we can be virtuous and maybe self-sacrificing (cf. N. Hartmann: SPIEGEL-BERG p. 366). Our awareness of the world is a value, but it is the world itself which enshrines the highest value (V.1.23, V.3.8). It is with the nature of this awareness that my next chapter must be mainly concerned.

16. I have said that to immortalize oneself is not to treat oneself as an immortal, but in a sense it is. A motion that has no end is no motion, or else one motion after another (cf. V.1.6). No motion, because *energeia*. To devote oneself to the production of any one thing is foolish in the face of death: rather engage in a pursuit that is endless and therefore contains its end within itself (cf. V.1.28f.).

Waking, perceiving, and thinking are *energeiai*, and therefore pleasant (*Met.* XII, 1072^{b}16f.). The model for a life that is complete at every moment and can therefore cheat death is that of walking: not to any place, for that would be *kinesis*, but only walking. Or to put the point differently: we should place our heart not in immediate personal concerns, though they matter, but in that which is the Unborn in each of us (see V.3.20). Nor should we follow the advice of those who urge us to accept the rhythms of the world and play the part of old men to the hilt (C. G. JUNG p. 7). We must live according to the best in us, and that best does not age (*De An.* 408^{b}23). As sublunary things we fade, and must take that inevitable fact into account in planning our lives: but this decay is not of our essence, and we should not surrender to it. Equally, though we cling to life we should not cling to the life of sensual pleasure at all costs, for to live in accord with the best in us is to live for more than our immediate selves. 'It is not altogether possible for men to get the best of all things nor share in the nature of the best' (*Eudemos* fr. 6 Ross). In his beginning Aristotle explained the words away, but though he came more or less to believe them, he did not therefore cease to believe in that best of all things and its influence on human life. It is because we are aware of the world as more than our own world, that we are aware of our impending death: it is because we are aware of the world as more than our own world, that we can conceive the extinction of our worlds as the possibly better alternative. And this awareness of the world is at once 'most especially the self' (see III.3.29f.) and the world itself. This last point will be the topic of my next chapter.

V.3. Nous

1. That which is most basic to a man, or a philosophy (which is only a man in abstract), is least open to explication or justification. All instruction given or received by way of argument proceeds from pre-existent knowledge (*Post. An.* 71ᵃ1), and we cannot learn the fundamental principles (*Met.* I, 992ᵇ24f.: I doubt if this is a purely *ad hominem* argument, even though it is one 'contra Academicos')— though presumably our attention can be drawn to them (cf. *N.E.* I, 1098ᵇ3f.). How could we know the objects of sense without having the sense in question (*Met.* I, 993ᵃ7f.)? Whatever a man blind from birth means by 'red' it is not what we experience (*Phys.* II, 193ᵃ7). Whatever is most basic, most inarguable, is also most nearly ineffable, 'for knowledge of the first principle is of another sort than demonstrative' (*De Gen. An.* 742ᵇ32f.). It is for this reason that the concept of *nous*, the most basic element in the Aristotelian identity, is at once so pervasive (see above, *passim*) and so difficult to understand. Aristotle gives us no clear guidance in this, so that any interpretation is more than usually debatable. The doctrine that I impute to him is, with some important qualifications that I shall discuss below, that plausibly attributed to Albinus (ARMSTRONG), who combined the Alexandrine reading of *nous*'s becoming *ta noeta* with the view that the Ideas are the thoughts of God: so that 'for God to think himself is to think the Ideas, that is the whole of intelligible reality'. In expounding this doctrine I shall make use of Buddhist and Neo-Confucian parallels: 'there is a universal mind in which all sages participate, be they from east, south, west or north, past or future' (Lu Hsiang-shan: DAY p. 214). I hope that what follows will make this view seem plausible, in both its literal and metaphorical sense. For I shall also follow Alexander of Aphrodisias in identifying poetic *nous* with the Prime Mover.

2. Plotinus castigated Aristotle for retreating from his earlier suspicion that there was some yet more perfect thing than *nous*. In the *Peri Euches* (fr.1 Ross) we are told that 'the god is either *nous* or something beyond *nous*'. Similarly in the *Eudemian Ethics*, '*logos* is not the source of *logos*, but something greater is; and what would be

greater than knowledge or *nous* except God? (*E.E.* 1248ª27f.). For
the most part *nous* and the god are identical (cf. *N.E.* I, 1096ª24f.),
but this divine *nous* is not the same as *dianoia*, and is likely to be as
far removed from ordinary thinking as Plotinus' One.

3. Consider first the Unmoved Mover of the Whole, as presented
in *Metaphysics* XII, 'On Entity'. In attempting to outline the conditions under which we find the world intelligible Aristotle arrives
at the concept of a self-referential thinking which keeps the world
in being and in motion solely by its attractiveness. This conclusion
is odd enough to license indefinitely many interpretations, and his
arguments for it are hardly less obscure.

4. Entities, substances, *ousiai* are ontologically prior to other phenomenal features of the world, whether or not the world itself is a
whole and therefore a substance (*Met.* XII, 1069ª18f.). Unless there
is always at least one substance, therefore, all things are destructible
(*Met.* XII, 1071ᵇ4f.). But it is impossible that there should be a
period when nothing existed, for if there is a before and after there
is time, and time is a number of motion: for there to be a period there
must be motion and therefore some moving entity (*Met.* XII,
1071ᵇ6f.). There can be no gaps in chronology, for if there were the
beginning and ending moments would simply be the same moment.
Nor can we imagine that the world is a privileged oasis in acres of
dusty eternity: if there was ever a first event it was never future;
if there is ever a last it will never be past (cf. PRIOR (4) p. 40).

5. Suppose the temporal span of all things is finite, without this
implying any periods of empty time: still, we cannot suppose that
non-being is prior to being, for this is to invent the question 'why is
there anything?' and to find no intelligible answer (cf. *Phys.* VIII,
250ᵇ11f.). To paraphrase the mystical question 'why is there anything?' as 'why are things the way they are?' is to admit this conclusion, that some being cannot but be. Similarly, since the dynamic
moment of time contains pastward and futureward categories, we
cannot conceive a world which just starts or just stops (cf. IV.1.13f.).
Rather than face a world which is mere brute contingency, flagrant
incomprehensibility, we must conclude that everything cannot be
destroyed or have not-existed. Things decay thanks to their material
elements (V.2.7)—which must always leave those elements, and the
laws of the world in which they exist, still surviving. Can we suppose

that something always exists, but not the same thing? A sort of relay race. But such a series cannot guard against failure—there is no reason why the next runner should not be late. Nor does such a series provide any stable framework for its own existence. In this case it does follow that as there must always be something, there is something that must always be. There must be, or must be taken to be if we are to have an intelligible world, something whose essence is actuality (*Met.* XII, 1071^{b}20) and which is without matter: necessarily without matter, for matter is precisely the potential for being otherwise (cf. II.3.20). This something cannot simply be, though it may be in part, the set of things that do in fact exist: for if x could not-be and y could not-be, the combination of x and y is clearly yet more unstable.

6. Some one thing must be supposed eternal, and in the phenomenal world existence is motion. The only sort of motion which is secure is that which secures itself, by continually generating the conditions of its own continuance (*Post. An.* 95^{b}37f.; cf. *De Gen. Corr.* 337^{a}1f.): that is to say, cyclical motion. And indeed the first heaven, the heaven of the fixed stars, does so revolve and may be presumed eternal (*Met.* XII, 1072^{a}22f.). But just in that it is in motion it is capable of being otherwise than it is (*Met.* XII, 1072^{b}4) and is to that extent non-necessary. We must therefore posit something that is necessary and that 'causes' the motion of the first heaven. In all cases of self-movement so-called there must be something that is at rest (*De Motu* 698^{a}16f.), for nothing can literally move itself (cf. V.2.9). 'But surely every part of the heaven is moved by that pressing on it from behind? Why do we need something else to explain the motion of the whole when all the parts have been explained?' But this objection merely raises the question 'why is there such a circular motion?' What is it about the heavens' activity that is credibly to be taken as necessary? Further, the motion of the heavens is not to be taken as the accidental sum of their parts (why then do they maintain a perfect circle?): rather the parts' motions are isolable aspects of the heavens' being (cf. *Phys.* IV, 219^{a}10f.).

7. What is the formal-final cause of being? Plainly the pure actuality which we are seeking in our present study (*Met.* XII, 1072^{a}23f.), and a plausible parallel to its mode of being is the way in which objects of desire and thought (*noeton*) move us, by attraction rather than action. 'Just because the axle moves not, the spokes revolve'

(Lao Tzu: SUZUKI (2) p. 354; cf. CHAN (2) p. 144.11; Parmenides 28B1DK: KOSMAN). Something which is itself unmoving is such that the heavens can approximate to its being only by that self-renewing *energeia* which has its end in itself: that is absolute Being. And Aristotle finds a credible parallel to it in those *energeiai* which are best known to us, seeing and thinking. 'On such a principle then depend the heavens and the world of nature. And it is a life such as the best that we enjoy, and enjoy for but a short time (for it is ever thus, as we could not be)' (*Met.* XII, 1072ᵇ13f.).

8. Can we pin it down more exactly? *Nous* thinks itself, for it becomes an object of *nous* in coming into contact with and thinking its objects, so that *nous* and object are one (*Met.* XII, 1072ᵇ20). The supreme example of this 'thinking' deals with and therefore becomes the supremely good (*Met.* XII, 1072ᵇ18), the sum of those features in the column of goods (*Met.* XII, 1072ᵃ31). Now what *can* receive the object and the substance is *nous*, but it is only actual when in possession of the object, 'so that possession rather than the receptivity is the divine element which *nous* seems to have' (*Met.* XII, 1072ᵇ22).[1] Divine *nous* is at the second stage of thinking described in the *De Anima*: 'when the mind has become each of its objects, as the learned man is said to do . . . it can then also think itself' (*De An.* 429ᵇ6f.). The divine *nous* does not have to acquire the idea of its objects, it already is and thinks its objects (NORMAN): it is never (as it were) merely virtuous (*hexis*), but always doing virtuous things (*energeia*: cf. *N.E.* I, 1098ᵇ33f.).

9. The supremely good state of noetically being the supreme good is that which the Prime Mover, which is the god, perpetually enjoys, and lives in so enjoying: for the actuality of *nous* is life, and the god is that actuality (*Met.* XII, 1072ᵇ26f.). 'And the god's self-dependent actuality is life most good and eternal. We say therefore that the god is a living being, eternal, most good, so that life and *aion* continuous and eternal belong to the god, for this is what the god is' (*Met.* XII, 1072ᵇ28). It does not appear during the course of evolution, for it cannot exist only as potential nor is there anything but itself from

---

[1] τὸ γὰρ δεκτικὸν τοῦ νοητοῦ καὶ τῆς οὐσίας νοῦς. ἐνεργεῖ δὲ ἔχων. ὥστ' ἐκεῖνο μᾶλλον τούτου ὃ δοκεῖ ὁ νοῦς θεῖον ἔχειν. Alexander of Aphrodisias' interpretation of the final sentence, 'so that the divine element which *nous* seems to have is rather of That, i.e. the Prime', is a trifle strained but does express something that Aristotle could well have said (cf. ROSS (3) II.380-1).

which it could come (*Met.* XII, 1072ᵇ30f.; cf. II.3.29). That something that cannot but be, which we require to make the universe intelligible, is to be found in that mode of being of which we have occasional experience. We, being doubly potential, must weary (*Met.* IX, 1050ᵇ22f.; cf. V.1.33): that-which-is is unwearying. 'Absolute sincerity (ch'eng: cf. I.16) is ceaseless . . . Such being its nature, it becomes prominent without any display, produces changes without motion and accomplishes its ends without action. The Tao of Heaven and Earth may be completely described in one sentence: they are without any doubleness and so they produce things in an unfathomable way' (*Doctrine of the Mean* § 26: CHAN (2) p. 109, cf. p. 96).

10. 'The nature of the divine thought involves certain problems' (*Met.* XII, 1074ᵇ15f.). In so far as it is purely actual, it is itself that it thinks. It is *noesis noeseos*. The orthodox interpretation has usually (with some honourable exceptions) been that Aristotle's God is wholly narcissistic, though what It has to admire in Itself, being no more than the act of self-contemplation, is obscure. Are we really to be left with a divinity that is no more than a self-gnawing mouth? The author of the *Magna Moralia* contemptuously observes that 'whoever is preoccupied with himself is counted as insensible. A god like that would be absurd' (*M.M.** 1213ᵇ4f.). The argument revived by NORMAN that '*hauton noon*' is no more than a technical expression for the highest variety of thinking, equivalent to '*ta noeta noon*', admittedly reaches what is surely the correct solution of this paradox, but rather ignores the oddity of the expression. There is more to the argument than a technicality.

11. Science, perception, opinion, and discursive thought seem to be always of something else and of their respective selves only 'on the side' (*Met.* XII, 1074ᵇ35). If you see something coloured then you also know that you see it (cf. III.1.9), and so throughout. But in some cases the act of knowing and the object known are the same (*Met.* XII, 1075ᵃ1f.), except in so far as the object is material. The sense-awareness receives the form, not the matter, so that in a way the soul is everything that is (*De An.* 431ᵇ20f.). Where there is no matter, so that the object is pure form, act and object are identical. Therefore 'the thinking is one with what is thought' (*Met.* XII, 1075ᵃ4): the divine *nous* cannot be anything but *ta noeta*, for it would then be doubly potential. If it could be without thinking it could

sometimes sleep: as it cannot sleep, it cannot transcend its being a thinker (cf. II.1.17).

12. Nothing can affect itself (V.2.9), nor therefore know itself where this implies touching and being touched (as *Met.* XII, 1072^{b}21), unless it has parts. The mouth can gnaw itself only in the sense that the teeth can gnaw the lips. What has no parts cannot turn upon itself. The highest state of all can be described as 'a knowing without touching things: that is, without making things into objects in one's consciousness' (DUMOULIN p. 165: after Dogen). In this state the gap between subject and object is bridged, for when one knows everything all together in a single, perfect whole (*Met.* XII, 1075^{a}5f.) there is nothing else against which this Whole can be seen, and hence no awareness of separate selfhood (cf. EVANS p. 169f.) 'Sunyata (emptiness, the absolute) is to be experienced in a unique way. This . . . consists in sunyata's remaining in itself and yet making itself an object of experience to itself. This means dividing itself and yet holding itself together . . . Sunyata is experienced only when it is both subject and object . . . "Knowing and seeing" sunyata is sunyata knowing and seeing itself' (SUZUKI (1) pp. 261-3). The knowledge of God is the same as God's knowledge (*Met.* I, 983^{a}5).

13. Before turning from the universe to the individual, it may be helpful to consider the eighth chapter of *Metaphysics* XII, which has occasioned argument far in excess of its importance, at least to us, who cannot take its pre-Ptolemaic complexities for scientific truth (though see App. D). In order to save the astronomical appearances Aristotle finds that he must posit several distinct cyclical motions, each of which must be presumed eternal and each of which requires an unmoving cause. Having settled this he insists that there is only one heaven (*Met.* XII, 1074^{a}31): for if there were more there would have to be more than one unmoved mover, which is impossible as all things that are formally singular but numerically plural have matter. The unmoved cannot, for it cannot be anything other than it is, and there cannot therefore be more than one version of its type. I do not propose to argue Aristotle's consistency here: I agree with MERLAN (1) III, (2) and WOLFSON (cf. OWENS (3)) against JAEGER (3) and ROSS (3) that the planetary movers are of different species, whereas two Prime movers would have to be of the same species. The planetary spheres are hierarchically arranged, and there

can be no single form for the members of such a prior-posterior series (COOK WILSON; *N.E.* I, 1096^{a}17f.; *E.E.* 1218^{a}1f.; *Met.* III, 999^{a}6f., XIII, 1080^{b}11f.). Two universes could not be so arranged, but would instantiate one and the same form (cf. *De Caelo* 276^{a}18f.). To put much the same point in another way: to say that there are two worlds is to say that two worlds partake in being, are individual wholes within a more ultimate framework: their movers would not then be the Prime.

14. But how do the movers of the planetary spheres differ from the Prime? The latter is not movable either in itself or accidentally (*Met.* XII, 1073^{a}23f.); the lesser movers are described only as unmovable in themselves (*Met.* XII, 1073^{a}33f.). It therefore seems reasonable to suppose that the lesser movers are moved accidentally, particularly as Aristotle admits such a class of movers in *Physics* VIII, 259^{b}21f. How are we to make sense of this? As Aristotle has no belief in absolute space, but only in place, he concludes that the heavens are not in anything (*Phys.* IV, 212^{b}22). In a way they are, for their parts are, but the Whole is not anywhere (*Phys.* IV, 212^{b}13f.). The planetary spheres on the other hand are somewhere, and obviously change their places relatively to each other and to the first heaven. The planetary movers are, as it were, carried about with the spheres, though without prejudice to their essential immobility.

15. For the movers, both the Prime and the lesser, are at once separate from the life of their spheres and bound up with them: even the Prime cannot be clearly distinguished from the life of the first heaven—if it could might there not be two heavens each striving after one and the same Mover? Aristotle's ontology may become clearer in my chapter on Body–Mind: for the moment I wish only to emphasize that the Prime must both transcend its physical acolyte and be of the essence of that sphere's life. The movers are eternal, unchangeable, separate from all sensible things, without parts and without magnitude (*Met.* XII, 1073^{a}3f.). Similarly the most high that we encounter in the *De Caelo* (279^{a}12f.) is outside space and time, where there is neither place nor change: 'is' or 'are', for Aristotle leaves their number open. 'On the same principles the fulfilment of the whole heaven, the fulfilment which includes all life and infinity, is *aion* immortal and divine. From it derive the being and life which other things, some more or less articulately but

others feebly, enjoy' (*De Caelo* 279ᵃ25f.). GUTHRIE (3) argues that Aristotle cannot intend an Unmoved Mover in the *De Caelo* as he explicitly denies that the heavens are moved by anything exterior to them (*De Caelo* 279ᵃ34). But this is to confuse a denial of enforced motion with a denial of natural, finalistic motion. Whatever the precise status of the heavens and the divine in the *De Caelo*, it is worth taking Aristotle's words seriously: the divine exists in the Void outside the world (cf. *Phys.* VIII, 267ᵇ6f.), not in the vacuum of absolute space beyond the furthest stars (as our own ontological model might suggest), but Nowhere (*De Caelo* 279ᵃ34)—the world does not exist in anything, and the realization of this is the realization of its wholeness.

16. That it is a whole (cf. II.3.30) also answers ROSS's further objection ((3) I.cxxxvi) that in so far as there is only one Prime, only one ruler, this prime must attract the intelligences that move the spheres as ends. This is an error precisely parallel to the confusion implicit in the dominant account of *eudaimonia*. An entity may have its own individual *ergon*, and also a part to play in the universal economy. A particular activity may be a good in its own right, and also a possible means to some higher good. Organisms are precisely organic (cf. *De Gen. Corr.* 336ᵃ32f.). That which is not for anything else ever is, on the ethical level, the free man, and on the cosmological the life of the Whole itself. That one end is supreme neither disallows nor explains (though it may limit) the goodness of other ends (see V.1.11, App. D).

17. I have spoken in terms of our realization of the world's wholeness, of the sort of life we occasionally experience, as if this were Aristotle's chief ground for his cosmology: I believe that it was. To make the connection between cosmology and psychology vital to the discussion may seem to ignore the purely scientific aspect of Aristotle's thought in the *Metaphysics*. That it does not will, I hope, be made clear in what follows.

18. Every apparent self-mover contains something that is at rest (V.3.6; cf. *Phys.* VIII, 256ᵃ8f.). What this unmoved mover may be in the case of other living creatures remains uncertain: everything naturally has something of the divine in it (*N.E.* VII, 1153ᵇ32) and perhaps unconsciously pursues the same pleasure. More likely, what is unmoved in each creature is the present image of that creature's

end. For us the important question must be what the unmoved is in us. 'In a way the divine in us moves everything' (*E.E.* 1248ª26f.): I suggest that this divine thing is *nous* (though cf. V.3.2, 21).

19.   '"Immovable wisdom" is intuitively acquired after a great deal of practical training. "Immovable" does not mean to be stiff and heavy and lifeless as rock or a piece of wood. It means the highest degree of motility with a centre which remains immovable' (Takuan (1573–1645): SUZUKI (2) p. 352). What is here 'acquired' is rather recognized as having been there all along. It is the end of a journey, not the product of a process: a fulfilment, not a transformation (III.2.7).

20.   'Man has nothing divine or blessed except the one thing worthy of trouble, whatever there is in us of *nous* or reason. This alone of what we have seems immortal and divine' (*Protr.* fr. 10c). *Nous* alone enters the developing human being from outside, and alone is divine, 'as somatic activity has nothing to do with activity of *nous*' (*De Gen. An.* 736ᵇ27f.; cf. *De An.* 413ª4f.). Not all soul, but only *nous* can be said to survive the organism's death (*Met.* XII, 1070ª25f.). '*Nous* seems to be an entity engendered in us, and to be imperishable' (*De An.* 408ᵇ18f.). Aristotle's argument for this is that bodily decay does not cause the decay of *nous*: 'the power of *noein* and *theorein* decays because something else within perishes, but is itself unaffected' (*De An.* 408ᵇ24f.). Discursive thought (*dianoeisthai*), loving, hating are affections of the individual, not of *nous*, and memory and affection alike perish with the individual: *nous* is something more divine, unaffected and immovable (*De An.* 408ᵇ25f.). What it is not in any ordinary sense is mind. There is an old age of mind, *dianoia*, as well as of body (*Pol.* II, 1270ᵇ40).

21.   This is not to say that the terms '*nous*' and '*to noein*' are not sometimes used interchangeably with '*dianoia*' and '*to dianoeisthai*'. *Nous* is said to act with a purpose in view (*De An.* 415ᵇ16) and can be clouded by emotion, disease, or sleep (*De An.* 429ª8f.). *Nous* commands and *dianoia* speaks (*De An.* 433ª1f.) interchangeably. '*To noein*' comprises imagination and judgement (*De An.* 427ᵇ27f.), and even when we think speculatively we require some image (*De An.* 432ª9): 'there is no thinking without an image' (*De Mem.* 449ᵇ31f.). But these features are of *nous* as it is embedded in the psychophysical whole that is a human entity. In the biological continuum 'last and most rarely comes reasoning and thought' (*De An.* 415ª7f.): 'theo-

retic *nous* is another story' (*De An.* 415ᵃ11f.), for it seems to be a different sort of soul and to be capable of separation (*De An.* 413ᵇ25f.). It is that by which we think and know (*De An.* 429ᵃ22), but it does not think things through. '*To noein*' is like perceiving (*De An.* 429ᵃ13f.): 'so it must be unaffected and receptive of the form and potentially such as its object, though not (in most cases) identical'. As it thinks all things it must be unmixed, for the intrusion of anything foreign threatens it—it can have no quality except its sheer potentiality (*De An.* 429ᵃ21f.; see III.2.19). 'It is not save when it is not itself' (ROSEN), and therefore is not mixed with the body: if it were it would have some quality, or even some organ, as it does not (*De An.* 429ᵃ26f.)—the masukhacakra, highest of the centres of the Tantric psychology, is likewise without location. The soul, or specifically the noetic soul, is the place of forms, potentially (*De An.* 429ᵃ27f.). *Noesis* and perception are not entirely alike, for perception can be blinded by excess, whereas *nous* is *choristos*, separable, and so yet more able to 'touch' the excessively thinkable (*De An.* 429ᵇ4; cf. *Met.* II*, 993ᵇ9f.). *To noein* is the immediate and intuitive grasp of non-composite and immaterial reality. And it does not admit of error: as regards non-composites 'it is not possible to be deceived, but either to "see" (*noein*) or not' (*Met.* IX, 1051ᵇ31; cf. *De An.* 430ᵃ26f.). *Nous* is *choristos* not merely in that it may survive our deaths, but in that it is already in some sense separate (cf. *Met.* XIII, 1086ᵇ9 *et al.*, *re* the Platonic forms): it is in fact as puzzlingly disentangled from our lives as the Prime from the heavens.

22. The Prime thinks and is the principles of the things. Chu Hsi's Supreme is 'full of the normative Principles governing the Yin and Yang and the Five Elements that go to make up the multitudinous entities in the world' (BRUCE (1) pp. 16f., 269f.). Hui Neng (A.D. 638–713) takes a further step: 'The Voidness of the universe is not vacuity but filled with heavenly bodies, mountains, rivers, good and bad men, deva-planes, hells, oceans . . . Yet we are neither attracted to nor repelled by the goodness or badness of these things or other people . . . This Voidness of mind is not blankness . . . for the mind pervades the whole universe . . . This is what is meant be realizing one's own essence of mind for the attainment of Buddhahood' (Wong Mou-lam tr. pp. 27f.: DAY p. 139; YAMPOLSKY p. 146, from an earlier manuscript, is more succinct). This perfect knowledge is

the self-realization of one's nature (DUMOULIN p. 48), the realization of that spark of the ultimate which is prajna, intuitive wisdom (SUZUKI (1) p. 172). 'Self-nature is always pure, just as the sun is always shining' (Hui Neng: CHAN (2) p. 437). Similarly the theoretic *nous* says nothing of what is or is not to be pursued, but contemplates all alike without disturbance (*De An.* 432ᵇ27f.; cf. III.1.17). Nor does *nous* think intermittently (*De An.* 430ᵃ22).

23. Aristotle solves some of the problems this raises, notably why one is not always thinking (*De An.* 430ᵃ5f.), by analysing *nous-thurathen*, *nous* from outside (*De Gen. An.* 736ᵇ28), more closely in a chapter which has proved as intractable as, and certainly more important than, *Metaphysics* XII.8. Everything is analysable into the potential, i.e. matter, and the actualizer, i.e. form. *Nous* in one sense becomes and in the other makes and is all things (*De An.* 430ᵃ14f.). Poietic *nous* is like light in making potential into actual, and is *choristos*, impassive and unmixed. The actual knowledge produced in the individual *nous* is identical with the thing known (*De An.* 430ᵃ20f.) Poietic *nous*, when separate, is what it is, and this alone is deathless (*De An.* 430ᵃ23): 'we do not remember, because this is impassive (unaffected), and pathetic (potential) *nous* is perishable'. We shall not remember our earthly existence: *nous* takes no colour from the changeful. Our potential for grasping reality is realized only by *receiving* that light which eternally *is* conscious Reality.

24. 'Again it is like the sun illumining the world. Does the light suffer any change? No, it does not. How, when it does not illumine the world? There are no changes in it either. Why? Because the light is free from affections, and therefore whether it illumines or not, the unaffected sunlight is ever above change. The illuminating light is prajna' (Ta-chu Hui-hai (eight century A. D.): SUZUKI (1) p. 182). SUZUKI ((1) p. 183) goes on to say that discriminatory thinking, cutting and dividing, is based on non-discriminatory prajna. Prajna does not divide, just as *noesis* has an incomposite as its object (*Met.* XII, 1075ᵃ5). Epistemic knowledge is similarly based on noetic (*N.E.* VI, 1140ᵇ31f.; cf. II.3.22).

25. Nothing but the Prime Mover is exempt from reciprocal action (*De Gen. An.* 768ᵇ16f.), though we should perhaps not take this claim too seriously. The identification of poietic *nous* (not, of course, the actualized reason of an individual man) and the Prime Mover,

made by Alexander of Aphrodisias, is none the less convincing. The arguments against this identification to be found in ROSS (3), HAMLYN (2), and elsewhere derive from Themistius: (i) that the immortal *nous* is described as existing in the human soul: 'Aristotle would not have described the deity as alone immortal and divine' (HICKS p. lxv); and (ii) that the description of poietic *nous* as making all things cannot be meant literally as no human mind could do so. I fear that I can see no force in these arguments. Certainly poietic *nous* operates in the human soul—it is not therefore restricted to the soul; nor can I see any better candidate than the god for being uniquely immortal and divine. As to the second point, certainly poietic *nous* is not described as making material tables, chairs, and vampire bats: but neither is the god a demiurge. Poietic *nous* is essentially *energeia*, as is the Prime (*De An.* 430ᵃ18; *Met.* XII, 1071ᵇ20). The god is the activity of *nous* (*Met.* XII, 1072ᵇ27) and poietic *nous* when considered in itself is specifically and (in the absence of matter) numerically the same. There are many noetic individuals, but only one light.[2]

26. 'Material *nous* is actually nothing and potentially everything' (Alex. *De An.* 84.14–24; cf. MORAUX App. III, fr. 3e). Pathetic *nous* and matter, which is also actually nothing and potentially everything (*Met.* XI, 1060ᵃ20), may be revealingly compared. Both *hule* and *hulikos nous* (Alexander's phrase, but Aristotle's idea) become the myriad things. The soul is in a way everything (*De An.* 431ᵇ20f.), but there is a larger world in which the soul exists: so that there are other versions of those entities which appear as objects in the soul. The world itself is not in anything larger than itself—there are no other versions of things than the things in the world. I shall develop the analogy between world and soul in chapter VI. My point here is

---

[2] The planetary spheres, which cannot all be of the same form nor mirror the light of the whole, 'as the moon on water', do provide a difficulty here: it may be that the unmoved movers of these spheres are other than *noi*—the organic universe would then exactly parallel organic *eudaimonia*. The planets would be physical analogues of the compromises between ends which we must make in the light of the paramount end. Astrological philosophers would perhaps agree: I know of no Aristotelian evidence for this account. Even if, however, the identification of poietic *nous* (not of the substantial, mortal *nous* in each individual) with the Prime be rejected, it remains certain that there is not a *different* poietic *nous* for each man—there could be a plurality of such poietic *noi* only if there were many species of *noi*: and Aristotle's philosophy does not admit, as Plotinus and some Indian thinkers did, the existence of individual forms (IV.2.6). We should then have the Prime, the various movers of the planetary spheres, and 'The Mind of Man' as unrelated, specifically distinct, immaterial entities: this seems excessive (see App. D).

that in intuiting the first principles of being, which cannot be other
than they are, a human being receives and becomes their only version
—'if I can completely develop my mind I thereby become identified
with Heaven' (Lu Hsiang-shan: FUNG II.573f.). Or rather, as Ch'an
Buddhists have taught, if I leave my mind alone and permit the
disturbances to subside (*Phys.* VII, 247^{b}17f.) I will discover the light
which was always there. '*Nous*, the noetic element, would seem to
be each man most especially' (*N.E.* IX, 1166^{a}22f.): just so Plato's
heroes climb up to the sun and find it the source of the light by
which they had climbed.

27. The model I am presenting, in effect that the presence in us
of *nous thurathen* is the presence in us of the principles of the world's
being, may be misunderstood. RANDALL (2) has argued that the
theological aspect of Aristotle's thought is entirely disposable. *Nous*
is simply the set of principles that govern the world, and it is the
entry of these into the human soul, the imposition of these on the
receptive soul (cf. *Post. An.* 100^{a}13f.) in an entirely naturalistic way,
that constitutes the entry of *nous*. But Aristotle's God is not simply
the list of natural laws (cf. ORGAN): rather he contains and unifies
those laws in a single undivided whole. 'There is no other way to
investigate principle to the utmost than to pay attention to everything
in our daily reading of books and handling of affairs. Although there
may not seem to be substantial progress nevertheless after a long
period of accumulation, without knowing it one will be saturated and
achieve an extensive harmony and penetration' (Chu Hsi: CHAN (2)
p. 610; cf. Pl. *Ep.* VII, 344 b 3f.). HU SHIH (1) has argued that this
description of dhyana, leading to prajna, is an account of scientific
empiricism. Certainly there is the same dispute in Neo-Confucian
studies between the mystical and scholarly interpretation as in
Aristotelian: I venture to think that the division is unreal, and based
on a misunderstanding of the nature of the noetic vision in either case.
Let us certainly contemplate the heavens, for there order is more
clearly manifest than in ourselves (*De Part. An.* 641^{b}18f.). The being
of the Whole is divine (see II.3.22f.). To 'see' that Being is not
simply to recite Newton's laws of motion: as always, material description is not to the point (and see App. D).

28. To immortalize oneself, to practise *theoria*, is to realize the
presence in the soul of the undying which is itself the Prime. And
therefore to be aware of the world. For suppose that the god is aware

of, and so is, the forms, as Albinus would have it. He is not aware of them in separation, for Aristotle does not believe they exist in separation, except in so far as e.g. health exists as the art of medicine. Rather the god is aware of them, is them, in their place. Aristotle can think it a refutation of Empedocles that his system entails that God is ignorant of the principle of strife (*Met.* III, 1000^{b}4f., *De An.* 410^{b}5f.): it is absurd to suppose that the god could be ignorant of any principle—on the contrary he is *sophos*, has knowledge of causes (*Met.* I, 983^{a}8f.). And as such he knows, in a sense, all that falls under those principles (*Met.* I, 982^{a}23). To realize the god in oneself is to discover the world, the phenomenal world (which is the only one there is), as an intelligible and undivided whole, such that there is no room for any grasping ego. The convoluted introspection implied by '*noesis noeseos*', the impossible self-immortalization implied by Aristotle's Platonist advice, vanish in the discovery of the world. 'Living with oneself' is a logical fiction: the good man rejoices in his awareness of the world. The Prime thinks itself not because it introspects, but because it is, knowingly, the World.

29. This highest sort of knowledge is a joyful one. Aristotle does not argue that God cannot feel delight in his world, or rather cannot be that delight: that he only thinks himself proves that he and man are not wholly coincident, not that he cannot (in some sense) love (*E.E.* 1245^{b}16f.; cf. *E.E.* 1238^{b}18, *N.E.* X, 1179^{a}22f.). Wisdom and love, prajna and karuna are conjoined in it (DUMOULIN p. 26, SUZUKI (3) p. 161). Even at the naturalistic level intelligence and affection go together (*De Gen. An.* 753^{a}11f.). It is because and in so far as we are aware of a larger world than that defined by our own immediate interests that we can appreciate and assist our fellows (and vice versa). The Hindu trinity of Sat–Cit–Ananda (Being, Mind, and Joy) is also Aristotle's.

30. The god, though queerly involved in our lives, is not simply identical with our immediate egos, our ordinary self-images: even for Ch'an it is 'the never-sick one that is the true self' (WU p. 189). It is very easy to confuse the self created by our pleasure/pain responses with the Self. Thus Fichte's service of the transcendent ego ends in German nationalism, accepting a merely contingent feature of Fichte as a necessary feature of Sunyata. Aristotle is perhaps similarly inclined occasionally to assume that he is at the centre. Nothing is at the centre: or to put it another way, it is the law which

is the mean, and no personal will of men (cf. III.2.19). VERDENIUS (2) is quite right to distinguish the godlike from the god: but what *makes* us godlike is our mirroring of that God.

31. Spinoza, partly following Maimonides, advanced a system interestingly similar (apart from its strict determinism) to Aristotle's probings, which enables me to draw a further parallel between West and East. 'The mind's highest good is the knowledge of God, and the mind's highest virtue is to know God' (*Ethics* IV.28). Memory and imagination die with the body (*Ethics* V.21) but something eternal remains—the essence of man. We do not remember our eternity, nor will it remember us (*Ethics* V.23n). Our love of God is identical with God's love of himself (*Ethics* V.36). Our salvation, blessedness, and freedom consist in this eternal love, this eternal consciousness (*Ethics* V.36n). The more perfect, the more real, the more active (*Ethics* V.40). Immortality cannot be bought for the self, but only at the price of the self, yet the essence of any composite being is its impulse to self-preservation (*Ethics* III.7; cf. III.3.4 above). Further, Spinoza's metaphysics decree that it is only possible to be God if one's body is infinitely extended. How could that be?

32. 'Only one entirely liberated from concepts can possess a body of infinite extent' (HUANG PO p. 74). For only such a one, freed from the categories of self, can follow Chang Tsai (1020–77) (CHAN (1) II.89): 'That which fills the universe I regard as my body and that which directs the universe I consider as my nature.' It is very easy to take this in a sense which amounts to a regression to the felt omnipotence and omnipresence of infantile solipsism. I am my world, but I am not the world[3], nor are all men myself—despite Sokei-an Sasaki: 'one day I wiped out all the notions from my mind. I gave up all desire. . . . I lost the boundary of my body. I had my skin, of course, but I felt I was standing in the middle of the cosmos . . . I saw people coming toward me, but all were the same man. All were myself! I was the cosmos! No individual Mr. Sasaki existed' (WATTS p. 141). On the one hand *nous*, which is the being of the world, is in me and is me most especially: on the other it is the light

---

[3] In distinguishing the immortal and timeless light which is the Self from the individual human being who only occasionally finds himself illuminated, Aristotle can also distinguish the light from the changeful and doubly potential world which it illumines. The Prime is not 'in time', does not change and is bounded by nothing: this does not imply that the world, which is intelligible only in the light of the timeless, is not truly indeterminate (see IV.1.18f., IV.2.21).

from outside. My ordinary self is not divine, but that by which I can
be a self is the god. What Sasaki seems to forget is that in intuiting
the spectacle of being one finds oneself part of the spectacle (cf.
II.3.30). To intuit the undivided wholeness of the world, so that
'the Real Nature and your perception of it are one' (HUANG PO p. 116),
is to behold the sheer suchness of event, Tathata, the supreme
individual This which cannot in the end be exhaustively described
or scientifically known (cf. II.3.32, IV.2.7). To be aware of this is to
be illuminated by a self whose body is co-extensive with the universe, and also to be aware that one's own, personal self is not so
co-extensive.

33. I shall try to describe how we intuit this unlearnable fact, that
there is a world which is more than our immediate experience of it,
in my final chapter. That we do intuit it, with complete conviction,
is obvious enough: without such an intuition we would be unable
even to conceive of living in a social or scientific manner. We *can*
thus intuit Being, and the Being which we intuit is the crown of our
metaphysical and our ethical system alike: of the former, because it
is in terms of the principles of Being that we account for everything
else; of the latter, because in intuiting it we experience it as the object
of love and desire. The problem of fanaticism (V.1.14, 26) dissolves
finally with the realization that it is *not* my knowledge of the world
which is to be the end of all my action, but the World itself: it is
the *being* rather than the receptivity which is the divine aspect of
nous (V.3.8)—poietic *nous*, which is the same in all men and in the
world, not my pathetic *nous*, my capacity thus to be illumined. One
who has realized the being of the world needs no further incentive
to be 'moral'—both because he has brought his soul to rest already
in order to find that something wise and knowledgeable which was
hidden there (III.2.7), and because to serve the 'Mind of Heaven' is
to do what comes naturally: and 'the wicked man is contrary to
nature' (*E.E.* 1240ᵇ21f.). The Buddhist and the Aristotelian saint
alike are not pressed by self-control to do what is right, nor do they
accompany their actions with verbal conclusions about what they
ought to be doing—the conclusion of the practical syllogism is
for them, as for animals, an action (*De Motu* 701ᵃ10f.), not as it is
for most of us a murmured encouragement to virtue. To introspect
is 'as if the mouth were to gnaw the mouth, or the eye to gaze at itself'
(HOCKING p. 118, after Chu Hsi): just so the Buddha nature of Ch'an

is 'like a sword that cuts but cannot cut itself, like an eye that sees but cannot see itself' (Zenrin Kushu: WATTS p. 154). There are more interesting things to contemplate than one's own personality (II.1.1). The Fa-yen school of Ch'an earned Chu Hsi's particular commendation for opening its eyes to the world (WU; see also HU SHIH (2)).

34. Because we are aware of the World, as a whole of wholes and an expression of great beauty and form (II.3.30f.), we can investigate it. 'Another name for satori is ken-sho, meaning to see essence or nature' (SUZUKI (1) p. 272). The universe is such that we can see what is going on in it (III.1.24, cf. IV.2.23): human sense-awareness is impressionable vis-à-vis the forms of being, and an inquiry (*historia*) into those forms as matter struggles to conform to the eternal Being of the whole is pre-eminently a worthy task for one who has occasionally intuited, or who hopes occasionally so to do, the Being of the Whole. 'We must not recoil with childish aversion from the examination of the humbler animals. Every realm of nature is marvellous: and as Heraclitus, when the strangers who came to visit him found him warming himself at the furnace in the kitchen and hesitated to go in, is reported to have bidden them not to be afraid to enter, as even in that kitchen divinities were present, so we should venture on the study of every kind of animal without distaste; for each and all will reveal to us something natural and something beautiful' (*De Part. An.* 645ᵃ15f.; cf. CHAN (2) pp. 203, 445). We should do so in our pursuit of the intuition of the whole (V.3.27), to fill in the details of that intuition, and to be able to act in the world with due awareness of the way it works.

35. 'Asked what the Buddha-nature is, the Zen Buddhist would probably answer: "It is unmoved"' (HERRIGEL p. 117). Their answers have in fact often been somewhat cruder and deliberately less to the point, but Herrigel's intuition is still sound. *Theoria* is the practise of enlightenment, and its culmination is the discovery of the divine world. It cannot be proved, but only prepared for, and once seen it is recognized as our natural being. 'Those being brought to their completion (the initiates) need not to learn but to receive something' (τοὺς τελουμένους οὐ μαθεῖν τι δεῖ, ἀλλὰ παθεῖν; fr. 45 Rose). We, to be completed as men, do not have to learn (cf. *Met.* I, 992ᵇ24: IV.2.7), but to receive (V.3.24f.).[4]

---

[4] This from Synesius. That Aristotle himself drew this analogy between enlightenment and the mysteries is further attested by Michael Psellus (*Peri Philosophias* fr. 15 Ross). See CROISSANT.

VI. Body–Mind

1. My concluding remarks are intended to suggest the sort of ontological model which best makes sense of the views I have been imputing to Aristotle. The key to it is the realization that what we
believe about the world is part of what we are: our cosmological
models are expressions of our personal concerns. I make no apology
for the 'unreasonableness' of what follows from the point of view
commonly called realistic, for it is the latter which seems to me more
truly absurd.

2. I have already remarked on the concept of the primeval giant
from whom the world was made (II.2.28, App. A.9; cf. II.3, V.3),
whether he be called Spihr, Ymir, P'an-ku, Aglaophamus, or Purusa
(CONGER, cf. RADHAKRISHNAN/MOORE p. 77).[1] Whether or not Aristotle was right to see all folklore as the remnant of past philosophy
(cf. IV.2.13), the concept fades naturally into a more sophisticated
doctrine of reality. If Needham's claim that Leibniz's monadology
is based on that of the Sung and Hua-yen Buddhism (App. C.5) is
even partly true, Leibniz bears much the same relation to Chu Hsi
as Plotinus to Aristotle. For Plotinus 'each being is all . . . Yonder,
the sun is all the stars, and each of them is the sun . . . A different
characteristic stands out in each being; but all the characteristics
are manifested too' (*Enneads* V.8.4). Each being is a thought, a
universe. For Plotinus each individual has its own distinctive form
which is eternal: the Real Socrates remains forever (*Enneads* V.7).
Aristotle could not thus suppose a form for each individual (IV.2.6;
cf. LLOYD, A.C. (2)), accepting that the real Socrates was the indefinitely determinable individual emergent from the confluence of
forms, able both to receive and to reject the light from beyond. The
only eternal part of man is the Real Man, which is the god. But each
soul is in a way everything (*De An.* 431^{b}21): is in a way one of the
jewels of Indra's net. I am a world but not one in which everything
is essential, nor an eternal one.

---

[1] Compare Zoroastrian doctrine: 'for the likeness of man is as the revolving firmament
of the sky' (*Zatspram* 30.1: cited by ZAEHNER p. 112).

3. What is it like to be a world? Where are these images of the world that my perceiving soul receives? Those in my mind's eye are somewhat hazy, no more than echoes. In perceiving tables and stars and my fellow men I am not aware of mirror images simultaneously appearing in my mind's eye: I am aware of a world. And that is my answer—the forms that I am, that I receive are precisely what I perceive. Phenomenally at any rate the world is in me, not I in the world—which is why I and my typewriter are not 'in this room' in the same sense. I cannot compare my trees with some further tree-in-itself, though I can compare my memories with the present reality. A given reality becomes red in so far as I see it as red: its actual reddening does not exist apart from my perception of it. What is it like in itself? It is, amongst other things, of a nature such as to be actualized, realized as red by a perceiving creature. We can discover, by experiment and comparison, what the nature of individuals of a certain type may be: we can understand what it is, we have knowledge of its form. We can acquire knowledge of the principles of things and these principles are beyond our own self-worlds—inevitably, for reality is what confronts us unavoidably. How does this process operate?

4. First of all, what is my self-world like? What would one expect it to be like if it is truly only mine? 'Nothing is more difficult than to know precisely what we see' (MERLEAU-PONTY p. 58). Divesting myself of certain common assumptions and contemplating the phenomena as they impress a pure solipsist, I discover that I am a headless and (by comparison with my images) a mis-shapen giant with hands considerably, though variably, larger than my feet. I am confronted by objects that shrink as they draw further from my immediate presence, by a world that spins about me as I turn my head. Objects change their colour, their shape, and everything else in somewhat puzzling ways: sometimes they have mutually incompatible properties, or split in two and join again. These features of my solipsistic world are visual, but other lists could be constructed for other aspects of my sense-awareness. This is the basic world of sense-awareness upon which some philosophers have attempted to build my knowledge of the more ordinary world. If it is basic, it is rather oddly so: for it is quite clear that my ordinary world is not like that at all, and that it is rather difficult than otherwise to acquire the sort of mental squint necessary for the undifferentiated and

non-interpretative awareness posited as my norm (note that it is superficially similar to the world of satori). In short I do not live in a purely egocentric world. I do not in general see things shrink as they retreat from me (GREGORY (1) p. 151). Unlike a camera I do not 'see' the world spinning about me (save when drunk or at a fun fair). As a child I may make errors about other people's left and right, for I lack the ability to 'put myself in their place' (see PIAGET p. 135), but I doubt if even those who are more or less blind to the left/right distinction are blind to the other perspective when adult. We do not just 'see' the images cast on our retinas without more ado: we see objects—consider the difference between seeing a tree and seeing it after being told that it is a cardboard silhouette . . .

5. These thoughts lead to a broad distinction between the ego-centric and exocentric. The former is doubtfully and in some degree the first condition of any sentient individual, the occasional condition of almost all of us (at least in its emotional aspect), the pathological condition of the insane and the philosophical condition of some philosophers. It is not our normal condition, nor is our normal condition generally a reinterpretation on the basis of general rules of inference from the immediately given egocentric experience. There are no rules given solipsistically by which we can convince ourselves of the world's stability, of other people's existence and importance. We do not justify or argue to or infer an objective world, or a morality, on the basis of egocentricity, and attempts to do so are automatically failures: instead we contemplate a variously exocentric world. We are not aware of the world as it is from one point of view only, but of the world as it is for something at once in and beyond us.

6. This is in essence a familiar enough point: 'There can be one person only where there is the possibility of every person: where there is a shared world . . . (it is) communion as such that constitutes the person' (GRENE (2) p. 107, after Plessner). In fact it seems to be the basic idea of twentieth-century man, corresponding to such earlier ruling dogmas as Nature and Spirit, and professed in various forms by Buber, Sartre, and Strawson: we realize ourselves as persons in so far as we greet others as persons. I here attach it to the sort of world we see (cf. BERGER/LUCKMANN). Normally we see exocentrically, but the degree of our exocentricity may vary, and so may its manner. We may be sociocentric, living in a world, living a world

that is determined by the good of our group, and blind to any perspective which might infringe that. Escaping this trap we may pretend to see a world determined by the minimum consensus, the scientific world of weights and measures—discounting, or even being completely unaware of the subjective miasma of our emotional responses. In following this route we claim to be discovering the objective reality, the world just as it is. I say 'pretend', because I doubt if any man's world is really like that—in fact it could not be, for his world is inevitably sensual and sensory. If this vision of the world is accepted on its own terms and human beings revealed as the mechanical products of atoms clashing in the void 'we shall go mad no doubt and die that way'. It is arguable indeed that this minimum consensus world is much more a retreat to the egocentric than to a higher exocentricity: a world in which individuals compete for space (as atoms) and for sustinence (as egoistic animals). It is the world of a man who dare not trust his softer emotions and wishes always to reduce things to rule. It is Blake's Ulro.

7. Alternatively we may seek rather a lowest common denominator than a highest common factor, a world into which all self-worlds may fit rather than one which reveals all self-worlds as illusions—save that of a man turned machine. We would not in ordinary life accept such a man's judgement on any problem above the level of scale and ruler: why should we accept it as definitive on the question of the world's nature? On the other hand, having abandoned such a minimum reality we must ask ourselves if there is any possibility of discovering the 'correct' world-view. The techniques of measurement alluded to may be inadequate to specify a human world, being no more than abstractions from the wealth of our experience (cf. *De An.* 431^{b}15f.), but they do at least offer an easily specifiable mode of discovery. Length, weight, speed are abstractly definable so as to provide an easy resolution of opinion-difference (though cf. IV.1.17): colour, beauty, moral significance seem to admit no standards other than personal taste or majority consensus. If my self-world is one of richly perceived colour, beauty and love and yours of drab colours, aggregates rather than wholes, and quarrelsomeness, then mine may well be more enjoyable than yours, but is there even any sense in asking which is right?

8. So long as we equate 'being right' with 'matching an objective

reality that contains nothing more than is available to measurement', there is indeed no sense in asking the question—for we have already replied that both are wrong. We are surely at liberty to refuse the equation. We directly see objects and people as objects and people, and no amount of measurement either can prove or is needed to prove this to us. Opinions that are generally taken to demonstrate the speaker's lunacy, that he is a machine or that there 'is nobody behind anyone else's behaviour', do not suddenly become reputable, though they become respectable, when uttered by a philosopher in philosophical (i.e. insincere) tones. In practice we take as the test of correct opinion not that it corresponds with ruler and scales as operated by a prepubertal philistine with a block against tenderness and a gift for mathematics,[2] but that it is thus that a reasonably experienced and well-balanced man in good health lives his world while awake.

9. We take this as the test, even though the exemplar we pick or the opinions we expect of such a man are not in fact plausible candidates for the post. From the unanswerable question 'Does this match abstract reality?' we have in fact reached the equally baffling question 'Who is the sane man?' Protagoras professed to have abandoned the question, retreating to the view that any man was right, about himself at least, that any man was sane to himself (or that no man was), but in fact offered the expert as the standard—the expert being he who could change his patient's world for the better. Plato (if I may thus sum up his philosophy) objected to the doctrine of *force majeure* that this seemed to imply—the psychiatrist forcibly normalizing his patient, making him happy, transforming him out of himself—and demanded that the expert invoked be the real

[2] Compare DEVEREUX p. 151: 'Such a sterile paring down of data to inessentials is not methodology, but a defense against anxiety. It does not solve the problem of objectivity; it only smuggles it out of sight.' Devereux's own account of right thinking, if allowance be made for the psychoanalytic tradition in which he writes, is thoroughly Aristotelian. 'The correct perception and interpretation of reality is both facilitated and hampered by man's tendency to consider his self, his body, his behavior and his manner of experiencing as archetypal or at least prototypal and to refer to it—and model upon it—his image of the outer world' (p. 162). Aristotle is certainly 'guilty' of this, but in progressively narrowing down the relevant aspect of man's form, progressively drawing closer to that idealized subjectivity which is indistinguishable from proper objectivity (being compound of love and knowledge), he shows the way out of egoistic interpretations of the world more safely and clearly than those who rely on quantifiable aspects of reality to save them.

expert, one who knows from his own experience the principles of reality, who understands men and seeks not to normalize but to draw upward to the world of light that will then be recognized as man's home. By the time of the *Laws* he had defined his position in explicit opposition to Protagoras' Man by naming the god as measure of all things (*Laws* 716 c 4). In so far as the god is *nous*, Aristotle does not disagree (*N.E.* III, 1113^{a}33; cf. *Met.* X, 1053^{a}35f.), but does not share Plato's implicit and explicit disdain for the mass of mankind. Everyone has something to contribute to the truth (*E.E.* 1216^{b}30f.; *Met.* II*, 993^{b}11f.). It is impossible that all common opinion should be wholly mistaken (*N.E.* I, 1098^{b}27f.; cf. *Pol.* II, 1264^{a}1f.), and the most probable view is that which best harmonizes the various views of men (cf. Owen: MORAVCSIK; I.13, III.2.25). The good man, the well-balanced man in whom all human potentials are present and correct, can best understand the various views of men. Thus Aristotle's canonical man arises within a given social setting and therefore perhaps has some features that he would not have had or is without some that he would have had if Aristotle had taken a wider view. But there also enters another factor in becoming canonical, which I shall try to isolate in the category of theo-centricity.

10.   For the very fact of exocentricity impels us to believe in a common world; the very certainty of death impels me to believe in a world wider than my own in which I die. And this world cannot just be the set of self-worlds, for this set is strictly a fiction (cf. *Phys.* VIII, 258^{b}20f.): until the self-worlds are united there is no more than a mathematical aggregate, a potential, and this is no actual field within which to achieve unity. What is needed is a world that does already embrace all lesser self-worlds, from which all other worlds derive: 'there is something that comprehends them' (*Phys.* VIII, 259^{a}3). In attempting to comprehend and sympathize with other self-worlds we dimly intuit the god's world, begin to approximate to an awareness of intelligible reality, of things as they are in them-selves. It may be that the god is but an expression of our group's world-view, so that Zeus, Yahweh, and Thor stare at each other from within their respective camps—but nothing human is alien, and in so far as we can converse we realize an increasingly universal god. Not more universal in being more abstract, in having fewer and fewer distinct characteristics, but in being more comprehensive.

This intuition, this audience with the god, this increasing seeing from the god as centre, that 'circle whose centre is everywhere and whose circumference nowhere', and therefore with both compassion and comprehension, defines the sort of world and thereby the sort of man who may justly be taken as standard. There is no inference from egocentricity to the exocentric: neither is there from the exocentric to the theocentric. Theocentricity, like egocentricity, is perhaps a limiting case, but the exocentric must always hover between these poles, of self and the god. In seeing with the god, we see with our own eyes but in a certain way, and in seeing thus, momentarily, we meet *not* a self-world ordered by our pleasures and pains, but the World. Not as an object over against us, but enthusiastically—for *enthousiasmos* is in origin inspiration and possession by the god. Reality is not the dead world of myth (II.3.29) but the realized, actualized world of human living, and its core is the realization of the divine.

11.   This model handles a great deal of what many theists would wish to say, specifically those like Aristotle and Plotinus. The latter indeed seems to offer a rather similar one (*Enneads* V.8.9). What sort of action does this god's view lead to? Plainly, if we are to serve the god, and that is the intelligible or intellectual world, we are to serve the beautiful: 'this is the end of virtue' (*N.E.* III, 1115^b13, IV, 1122^b6f.). If we are virtuous we do what is right for its own sake, because the deed is 'beautiful', and seek no further end by the individual act. We practise virtue, we concern ourselves with what is thus worth while, in order to clear the way to the knowledge of the god, and having reached that end we act correctly in the world. We act as the knowledgeable man would in order to become knowledgeable.

12.   Plato despised the bodily, for he distrusted sensory experience and held that reality was other than it appeared. He is the ancestor of all later 'objective realists' in supposing that true reality is other than our experience of it—both unlike our present experience and separate from our possible knowledge (see POPPER pp. 122f., 153f.). Aristotle, in denying both these in favour of a reality which is, in the end, self-explanatory and which cannot be separated, even in thought, at least from *God's* experience of it, also finds a more congenial place for the bodily. 'The body is no-body without its use, and the body is the use' (SUZUKI (1) p. 174). My body is a living body,

not a trap or tomb for my real self, nor a material object with which consciousness can be identified only by a *tour de force*. It may be more or less healthy, more or less balanced and integrated with my central purposes, but it is not essentially at odds with the soul. VAN DEN BERG's (1) patient complains of a pounding heart and other physical symptoms for which no somatic correlate can be found by medical technique. It is tempting to observe, on the basis of a belief in the abstract objective as the only truth, that the patient is imagining things, that he is 'really' quite well, and at last embroil ourselves in the horrors of Cartesian duality or body–mind identity theory. Van den Berg prefers to admit that there is something wrong with the patient's heart, his self-heart. Medical research, for certain purposes, adopts the minimum consensus heart as its object, but it is not this heart which is actually lived by anyone. The self-heart of the patient is indeed disturbed.

13. Similarly, I suggest, when Aristotle blandly declares that anger is both an appetite for revenge and a boiling of the blood about the heart (*De An.* 403^{a}29), and that there is only one event here—as soul and body are one as the stamp and the wax are one (*De An.* 412^{b}6f.). The minimum consensus heart does not boil, but even so our self-heart does. In the early days of medical research, where much evidence is necessarily personal, lived experience rather than dissective, radiological, and the like, the barriers between abstract and self-heart are not so clear.[3] Anger as desire and anger as blood boiling are a single experience. Moving outward from what we, not Aristotle, regard as the contingently associated phenomena of the pathologist's object-body, we enter the domain of action. Emotion involves act: thus Aristotle advises the would-be poet to enter his character's emotions by acting out the gestures (*Poet.* 1455^{a}30). It is not the Cartesian soul that is angry, any more than it weaves webs (*De An.* 408^{b}11f.), but rather the individual-in-society, the shared society that is Reality. Our expressions, our gestures, our feelings of nausea or rage are not merely contingently associated with our emotional responses. We do not see a particular twist of mouth and eyes and infer from past experience that the man is most probably amused:

---

[3] We might also note that the Greeks made no distinction between natural and artificial measures (see DEVEREUX pp. 162f.). This is not unconnected with Aristotle's conception of the unit of measure as a norm (cf. III.2.7). The construction of non-natural units does not seriously affect his doctrines, however.

we see his smiling. In fact we are so disposed to see expressions, rather than merely physical features, that we commonly see them even in the inanimate. Similarly we do not observe in ourselves a particular pounding of the heart and associate it, after puzzled introspection, with our feeling of dread or excitement. The pounding is the feeling: not that a certain medically observable phenomenon is the feeling (cf. *N.E.* IV, 1128^{b}10f., VII, 1147^{a}14f., X, 1178^{a}14), though some feelings are evinced also in the acts of our parts (e.g. shame, lust). Nor are all events associated with the stream of my life directly part of my life-world: some are aspects of the lesser worlds of my cells. My world, my life, comprehends and sympathizes with the lesser. In short, Aristotle's entelechy does not rivet the internal-mental and external-physical together by philosophical fiat, for the whole notion of the abstract-external, the world constructed for special purposes by technicians and since hypostatized as ultimate reality, is alien to his thought (compare IV.2.17: the laws of money and the laws of matter alike are abstractions from lived experience (see DOUGLAS (2)). The heart's central importance is an obvious truth of the self-world experience; so are most of his claims about *pneuma* products of self-experience (cf. App. A.7, A.9). I have already argued that time, the set of dating systems, is no more than an abstraction from experienced change; space, similarly, is the set of spatial relations and not their transcendent ground; so is the *purely* physical body also an abstraction. The world of sense is not an effect of material motion in the abstract void; it is the actualization of potential (III.1.13) in accordance with the intelligible principles which exist eternally as *nous*. At all levels Aristotle seeks to answer the question 'what is?' as if it were the same as 'what can we reasonably experience as being?' There is, indeed, no other way to attempt the question: to believe in a world beyond all possible experience is to condemn oneself to permanent uncertainty. Semi-permanent uncertainty is indeed our fate, but sometimes at least 'God sheds a brightness' (V.1.31) and we may see the world of sense in the light of the intelligible.

14. 'What the expression is to the body, the whole of intelligible reality is to the whole of the sensible world ... To think, for Plotinus, is then to comprehend the unity of a composition of which sensations acquaint us only with the dispersed elements—the intention of the dancer in the multiplicity of movements in a dance

figure, the living unity of the circular course of a star across the infinity of positions it occupies successively' (BREHIER pp. 10–11) (cf. V.3.6). Seeing the principles of being is no more a matter of measuring and counting than is seeing the intent of a painting or the mood of a man (cf. M. POLANYI pp. 29f.). In catching glimpses of this wholeness of things we hear the voice of the god within, which is our true self. As UEXKUELL saw, an animal's form, its way of living, provides for it a particular life-world, the routes through which, the important features of which are dictated by the animal's interests and abilities. The life-world of the fully developed man, the Aristotelian saint, who best shows what it is to be human, is the absolute reality from which all other ways of experiencing reality are diminutions or abstractions (cf. II.2.28). It is in terms of the principles of intelligible being intuited (occasionally) by the saint that all other principles, beliefs, and habits are to be explained—just as a modern anthropologist explains 'savage' customs in terms of the principles he accepts from his own society. The difference between saint and ordinary anthropologist is that the former has a direct intuition of being, realized after prolonged attempts to see the truth in all human claims (cf. III.2.25, V.1.33).

15. The Supreme that manages all things without action (wu-wei: CHAN (2) p. 140) is the centre of the world and of the good man's life (cf. III.2.26): for Zen Buddhism the world is already enlightened (cf. *Met.* XII, 1072^{b}30f. *et al.*)—only man is seemingly at odds and insecure. The life of the world, 'the god and nature' (II.3.21), is the unforced operation of the Tao, working itself out despite the intransigence of matter (cf. IV.2.7), and our efforts to do what is beautiful are themselves an expression of that Tao—a wicked man is contrary to nature (III.3.27). The good man and the man who sees the world as it is are the same, for to see the world as it is is to see the form within the material, expressing itself over time. Aristotle's mysticism, his reliance on the intuition of the divine, differs from some accounts of more overtly mystical thinkers in that he recognizes the reality of change and development (and therefore of failure). The principles of being are evidenced over time, although the god who thinks and is them is not 'in time' (see IV.1.13,19): his everlasting present is not the static '*totum simul*' of Boethius. In seeing things as they are the saint sees also what they might be, 'what they were to be', and seeks to reveal in matter the form which eter-

nally is, whether or not matter or the material *nous* (see V.3.26) receive it.

16. Brahman and Atman, the Absolute and the real self of man, are one. The solipsistic and antinomian excesses which this belief produced in other traditions are avoided in Aristotle's account. Maimonides (I.18) was perhaps correct.

Appendix A: *Pneuma*

1. The theory of *pneuma* has rarely been accorded any philosophical significance by modern commentators and perhaps has none. The concept of *pneuma* is none the less an integral part of Aristotle's philosophy and is therefore worth sketching (for bibliography see REICHE; JAEGER (1); PREUS). From my point of view it may also serve as an example of the sort of position I impute to Aristotle, between the archaic and the sophisticated.

2. At *De Sensu* 438ᵇ16f. Aristotle outlines (rather mockingly, for he has already rejected the physical association of touch and the element earth (*De An.* 435ª20f.)) the only possible way of linking the senses and the elements: sight and water, hearing and air, smell and fire, touch (and taste) and earth. As he says, earlier theorists had difficulty linking five senses and four elements (*De Sensu* 437ª20f.), but Aristotle himself has five elements to play with, and *aither* is conspicuous by its absence. This is to be linked to the primary sense itself: it is not omitted in this passage as being only superlunary.

3. The early dialogue *Peri Philosophias* apparently suggested (fr. 27 Ross) that the human *nous* was aitherial. The late *De Generatione Animalium* suggests that the generative principle of the semen, the *pneuma*, is analogous to the substance of the stars and is 'the so-called heat' (736ᵇ33f.). This threefold association of the heat, *pneuma* and *aither* is unique in Aristotle's extant works, and is discussed to admittedly small effect by SOLMSEN (2) (cf. (3)), rather more illuminatingly by REICHE.

4. The analogy of the generative element to the aitherial could perhaps be cashed as a rather roundabout way of mentioning or an obscure way of explaining the analogy of procreation to the cyclic eternity of the heavens (*Pol.* I, 1252ª28f.; *De An.* 415ª26f.; *De Gen. An.* 731ᵇ31f.). Certainly it does not seem that Aristotle has any very novel point in mind: *pneuma* seems only to be air, whose presence in the liquid semen turns it to white foam (*De Gen. An.* 735ᵇ10f.), and which is also present in the froth of spontaneous generation (*De Gen. An.* 762ª20f.). Foam has celestial overtones simply because the goddess Aphrodite sprang from such a froth (*De Gen. An.* 736ª18f.), but in this context Aristotle seems to be offering a crudely mechanical picture. *Pneuma* is also the air responsible for the penis's expansion (*De Part. An.* 689ª23f.). None the less if it is air it is air of a peculiar sort.

5. Consider the heat first of all. Parmenides (Diels 28A26^{ab}; cf. Heraclitus 22B36) was apparently the first philosopher to make the connection between life and warmth. He was followed by Empedocles (31A85). For Aristotle 'everything living has soul, and this does not exist without natural warmth' (*De Vita* 470^{a}19). The destruction of this heat is death (*De Vita* 469^{b}19 *et al.*), its slackening is age (*De Gen. An.* 783^{b}6f. *et al.*; see V.2.6), its subsiding to the lower and inner parts of the body is sleep (*De Somno* 457^{b}1; cf. Hakuin: DUMOULIN p. 262). Its presence 'about that place with which we think and hope makes us of good courage' (*Probl.** XXX, 954^{b}33f.). The hierarchy of living beings is marked by the degree of this natural heat (*De Resp.* 474^{b}25f.; *De Gen. An.* 732^{b}31f., 733^{a}33f.). The very notion, introduced by Plato (*Tim.* 78^{b}f.), that heat is responsible for digestion (*De Part. An.* 650^{a}3f., *et al.*) is an aspect of this: for digestion is a function of the nutritive soul, that psychic activity common to all sublunary life. Hippocrates (*De Carne* 2^{b}6, *De Nat. Hom.* 12) makes this heat divine.

6. *Pneuma* has many uses (*De An.* 420^{b}16f.; *De. Gen. An.* 789^{b}8f.). Considered simply as a sort of air, it is needed to cool the body to a reasonable temperature (*De Part. An.* 668^{b}33f.; *De An.* 420^{b}16f.; *De Resp.* 472^{b}34f.). In this aspect it is commonly introduced from outside the body, but there is also the native *pneuma* (*De Part. An.* 669^{a}1f.; *De Somno* 456^{a}12), innate breath, which all animals possess (*De Motu* 703^{a}15; *De Part. An.* 659^{b}17f.) and which is centred on the heart or its equivalent (*De Motu* 703^{a}15; *De Somno* 456^{a}6f.). Bloodless animals are adequately cooled by their own inborn breath (*De Part. An.* 669^{a}1; *De Somno* 456^{a}11f.), but the reference of 'inborn breath' is the same as that of 'natural fire' (*De Resp.* 474^{b}12, 478^{a}7). *Pneuma* is the stabilizing element in the heat/cold balance of animal life: if the creature lives at a more intense level it must incorporate outer air to aid its own resources.

7. *Pneuma* is also the origin of movement (*De Part. An.* 659^{b}17f.; *De Motu* 703^{a}9f.; cf. PECK appendix B1), and the source of differentiation (*De Gen. An.* 741^{b}37). The heart is formed first, in the embryo, then veins from the heart for blood and the 'innate pneuma'. The pulse is the pneumatization of the blood in the heart's furnace (*De Resp.* 480^{a}13f.). But this is more than a blank physiological fact—it has practical implications. Strength is produced by holding one's breath (*Pol.* VII, 1336^{a}37f.; *De Somno* 456^{a}16; *De Gen. An.* 737^{a}36f.). Women should hold their breath in childbirth (*De Gen. An.* 775^{b}1f.; *Hist. An.* 587^{a}4f.). Men hold their breath to release sperm (*De Gen. An.* 718^{a}2f.; *Hist. An.* 586^{a}15f.). All these facts are explicable by our need to utilize a limited supply of *pneuma* to the best advantage. Similarly we must hold our breath in

order to speak (*De An.* 421^{a}1f.). This action marks determination, tensing for the effort. Dolphins 'catch their breath as if they had just remembered something' (*Hist. An.* 631^{a}26f.) (or 'as if calculating'—but this seems implausible), and then leap over boats. The same phrase is used by a Hippocratic author to describe the Cheyne–Stokes breathing of a terminal case (see *Epidemics*: Philesios' case), and the phenomenon in this context doubtless helped to create the picture of the soul hovering on the lips of the dying. Theophrastus observes that birds use up their *pneuma* in digestion and levitation, and are therefore not intelligent (*De Sensu* 44). The Yogic concept of holding one's breath to produce strength here meets the modern suggestion that e.g. marine life, which exists on the brink of suffocation (there being a limited amount of oxygen dissolved in the water) could never develop intelligence.

8.   The higher animals need extra *pneuma* from outside to regulate their more intense inner heat. That is, they and the world together form a working system: they live more and more of the world. The same is true in the case of perception. *Poroi*, channels, connect the eyes to the veins in the brain, the ears to the back of the head (*De Part. An.* 656^{b}16f.; probably Alcmaeon's discovery: LONGRIGG). The *poroi* of smell and hearing are full of the innate *pneuma* and terminate at the veins in the brain (*De Gen. An.* 744^{a}2f.). From the brain the veins carry the sensory data to the heart (*De Part. An.* 656^{a}29; *De Sensu* 439^{a}1). Air and water, including the water in the eye, are transparent because they have a quasi-aitherial nature in them (*De An.* 418^{b}8f.). This can only be *pneuma*, both as air and as the essence of transparency: that foam is white, and that pneumatized water is light are subsumed under a single doctrine.

9.   The doctrines of pneumatism have had a partial success in influencing others, particularly via the Stoics (cf. SAMBURSKY). Harvey accepted *pneuma* as the source of movement (ALLBUTT pp. 224f.) and Newton concludes his *Principia* with some remarks on that aetherial nature which is responsible for gravitational, and electro-magnetic attraction, light and heat, sensation and animal motion. Aristotle himself contains the seeds of a theory which would bridge the moon's orbit (and cf. App. D). It is none the less a metaphysical view, that the wind in the world is the same as the breath in our bodies (*Meteor.* 366^{b}15f.), that the light in our minds is the same as the light before our eyes. 'As the soul which is our air rules us, so *pneuma* and air envelops the whole world' (Anaximenes 13B2D–K). The similarity of this doctrine to that of the Upanishads, where *prana* is similarly universal, need not (pace WEST pp. 104f.) lead us to think that the Greeks borrowed from the Hindus. The background of either doctrine is that body of mythological thought which treats the

universe as a single giant man, and the ordinary judgements of mankind. Folklore from all over the world testifies to the importance of *five* elements—four and a central fifth (REES/REES p. 148). Nor is it a mere coincidence that in the Tantric system *bodhicitta* is both semen and the ultimate (TUCCI p. 124). In particular consider the role played by the sun in generation: Rees and Rees are not wholly wrong to relate this to the superhuman element supposed essential to reproduction by many people (REES/REES pp. 226–7; cf. II.3.21). The production of inner heat, a concept at once physiological and mystical, and closely connected with that of inner light, by holding one's breath is standard shamanistic practice, which was taken up and modified in the techniques of yoga (ELIADE (1) pp. 330f.). The Greeks inherited much primitive pharmacy which they share with other cultures (SINGER (2) pp. 82f.); they were certainly acquainted with shamans (cf. HUMPHREYS (1); DODDS). We need not be surprised if Aristotle shows such 'archaic' traits: so, I suggest, does his whole system.

10. There is also a possible descendant. To equate pneumatization with oxygenation is to ignore too much. But it is perhaps not impossible to treat *pneuma* as energy. That all manifestations of energy are to be brought under one rule, and that there is a limited supply of such energy in a given system, are basic scientific dogmas: Aristotle chose a semibiological, semi-mystical model and has left us hardly more than a set of puzzles and the startlingly evocative picture that stellar energies are involved in human coition, but the attempt was none the less real.

Appendix B: The Sexes

1. The best society is one that provides for freedom, equality under the law, and love. 'The collapse of such social entities [as do not] is caused by the incapacity of the 'we' in question to guarantee natural ways of existence for individuals' (GOLDSTEIN (2) p. 212). Any group of people wholly disposed to assess each other solely in terms of the roles assigned by the group so far frustrate the development of the individuals' self-images as free and responsible beings as to ensure the collapse of the group. But on the other hand any society concerned for the welfare of its members must provide some standard of development, ideally in terms of love: it is therefore very likely, particularly as different kinds of individual are needed for the various jobs of society (*Pol.* II, 1261ª24f.), to adopt some sort of role-determination on the basis of immediately given facts. For example, if it were generally true that red-headed people were good with their hands, a general expectation would be set up, and the phenomenon familiar to educationalists as self-fulfilling prophecy would ensure quite a high proportion of at least reasonably good hand-craftsmen among the red-headed. In a Sartrean utopia we might all begin from scratch in the construction of our identities, though the results would probably be far from utopian: in the world as it is we begin in part from the expectations that others have of us, and our self-images are mingled with the societal.

2. The threefold division of the free classes of society seems common to many cultures: in India the brahman (priest), the ksatriya (warrior, king), the vaisya (farmer); in Ireland the drui or fili (druid or poet), the flaith (lord), the bo-aire (freeman) (REES/REES pp. 111f.; DUMEZIL). Similarly in Plato's *Republic*. Aristotle does not follow the symbolic stringencies of his inheritance—even pointedly substituting the number 5,000 as the optimum citizen population for Plato's *Laws* (*Pol.* II, 1265ª10) as against 5,040 (Pl. *Laws* 737 e). Such things had little hold on his mind. That man is a microcosm of the universe he does believe, but declines to take the details of this correspondence unduly seriously (cf. App. A.2).

3. On one point however, he appears to have a strong preference for a societal image dictated by almost metaphysical considerations. His attitude to slaves and barbarians, as I have already suggested, is not as illiberal as it is sometimes made to sound. But his attitude to women

may seem a prime example of the dominance of the societal over self-image, and therefore a counter-example to the interpretation of Aristotle's social theory which I have been giving. Whereas the unmarried and spiritually pederastic Plato at least suggests that women may be the equals of men (Pl. *Symp.* 201 d f., *Rpb.* 451 d f.), the married Aristotle's consistent description of the female state is as a sort of weakness (*De Gen. An.* 775ᵃ15). Women are like eunuchs (*De Gen. An.* 766ᵃ16f., 788ᵃ6f.; cf. II.2.24) or young boys (*De Gen. An.* 728ᵃ17); similarly bulls fall into a class contrasted with 'cows and calves' (*De Gen. An.* 787ᵇ9f.). It is one of the signs of degeneracy in non-mammalian creatures that the female is larger and longer-lived than the male (*Hist. An.* 538ᵃ22; cf. II.2.3). The Pythagorean list of contraries accepted by Alcmaeon of Croton (*Met.* I, 986ᵃ23f.) classes the female along with the unlimited, the even (where man is one, women is two; cf. REES/REES pp. 201f.), plurality, the left-hand side (cf. *De Gen. An.* 765ᵇ1f.), the mobile, the crooked, darkness, evil, and the oblong (i.e. the two-faced): Aristotle shows signs of agreeing, and adds various yin concepts—cold, passivity (*De Gen. An.* 729ᵃ28f.), matter (*Phys.* I, 192ᵃ22f.), back and bottom (*De Inc.* 706ᵃ24f.). In so far as he has a tendency to reduce polar opposites to the presence or absence of some one form (*Met.* IV, 1004ᵇ27f.; *De Gen. Corr.* 318ᵇ14f.; *Pol.* IV, 1290ᵃ13f.), Aristotle is disposed to regard femaleness as a privative rather than a positive attribute (cf. treatment of plants: II.2.21).

4. As to the sort of character to be expected of women 'it is not appropriate in a female Character to be manly or clever' (*Poet.* 1454ᵃ23) (this does not mean that *women* should not be manly etc, but that female Characters in a *play* should not be). 'Woman is more compassionate than man, more easily moved to tears, at the same time is more jealous, more querulous, more apt to scold and strike. She is more prone to despondency and less hopeful than the man, more void of shame or self-respect, more false of speech, more deceptive and of more retentive memory. She is also more wakeful, more shrinking, more difficult to rouse to action and needs less food' (*Hist. An.* 608ᵇ11f.). This differentiation between male and female is most obvious in the case of humanity (*Hist. An.* 608ᵇ5 *et al.*). But though it is very tempting to conclude that Aristotle had a low opinion of women's worth, his critique of the usual character of young and of old men (*Rhet.* 1389ᵃ3f.) is similarly detached. A virtuous woman, a female individual who does as she ought, is not one who exemplifies the general characteristics of women, but one who acts well in her particular situation (which does not include fighting in the ranks): temperance and courage are not the same in a man as in a woman (*Pol.* I, 1260ᵃ20f.), but both man and woman can be virtuous.

5. In fact the view that women are inferior men is a relic of Plato (cf. Pl. *Tim.* 91). Whereas Plato allows that women, if they renounce the things which women generally want, may do well enough in a basically male-oriented society, Aristotle argues for a multiplicity of virtue which permits the female variety of human being to achieve virtue in her biological and social situation. Male and female are one species (*Met.* X, 1058ᵃ29f.), and both sides of the complete man are necessary to humanity. 'The community needs both male and female excellences or it can only be half-*eudaimon*' (*Rhet.* 1361ᵃ8f.). 'The friendship of male and female is natural, for man is naturally a creature of couples even more than of cities' (*N.E.* VIII, 1162ᵃ16f.; cf. III.3.9). In fact the nature of this coupling is an important clue to the nature of humanity (cf. II.1.28). The female is not *per se* a citizen, but the male is so primarily as a householder: the male is perhaps more important, more essential, for he is the soul of the couple (cf. *Pol.* IV, 1291ᵃ24), but both are necessary. Whereas a slave merely enlarges his master (*E.E.* 1241ᵇ17f.) a wife creates a new creature. To add water to wine only results in an increase of wine (*De Gen. Corr.* 321ᵃ34f., *Poet.* 1461ᵃ27f.; N.B. the Greeks watered their wine), but in a mixture the components act on each other (*De Gen. Corr.* 328ᵃ32f.). 'Mixing is the coming to be one of what is mixed as they are changed' (*De Gen. Corr.* 328ᵇ22; cf. *De Sensu* 447ᵃ12f.; cf. III.3.11). The metaphysics of form and matter perverts, but does not quite obliterate the theory of mixture, which is employed both in Aristotle's account of generation (*De Gen. An.* 767ᵃ13f.) and in his social theory. He is not far from the doctrine he imputes to Empedocles (*De Gen. An.* 722ᵇ8f.; cf. Pl. *Symp.* 191 d 4). Opposites love each other from a desire to reach the mean (*E.E.* 1239ᵇ30f.; cf.*N.E.* VIII, 1159ᵇ19): it is the complete human being which we sundered parts of humanity wish to be, and cannot be except in marriage.

6. This model of union in diversity is on a par with the general theory of organic differentiation (cf. II.2.26), and (on a more trivial level) the theory of handedness: man is more disposed to the right as against the left than any other animal (*Hist. An.* 493ᵇ17f. *et al.*; cf. *De Caelo* 284ᵇ6f.). But only man can become ambidextrous (*Hist. An.* 497ᵇ31; *N.E.* V, 1134ᵇ33f.; cf. *Pol.* II, 1274ᵇ13; Pl. *Laws* 794 d).

7. Two entities do not make a third simply by their conjunction, any more than do two points make a line (*Met.* XIII, 1082ᵇ30f.; cf. II.3.5). Nor is the syllable *AB* simply *A* and *B* or vice versa, or flesh simply fire and water (*Met.* VII, 1041ᵇ11f.). When elements are conjoined appropriately, serving as the material for the ensuing form, another thing is produced (obedient to the laws of a higher level: Grene: GRENE (5)): 1 + 1 = 1 (always remembering that we must ask 'one what?' (*Met.*

X, 1053ᵇ24f.). A married couple is one by virtue of its single purposes, which are primarily those of the man (*N.E.* VIII, 1160ᵇ32; *Pol.* I, 1260ᵃ9f.) save in the case of unnatural unions (*Pol.* I, 1259ᵇ1f.; cf. *N.E.* VIII, 1161ᵃ1f.)—these not necessarily being bad, but merely likely to be unsatisfactory and therefore unsuitable for the general rule. But the two are thus homonoetic because they are friends. 'In organic unities there is something identical in both parts' (*Met.* V, 1014ᵇ23f.; III.3.11). What is this something?

8. 'If every lover, in virtue of his love, would prefer that the beloved should be inclined to favour him (*A*) but not do so (not *B*), than that the beloved should grant him her favours (*B*) but be disinclined to do so (not *A*), clearly *A* is preferable to *B*. To be loved is preferable in love to sexual intercourse. Love then is more dependent on friendship than on intercourse, and if it is more dependent on being loved, then this is its end. Intercourse then is either no end at all or one relative to being loved' (*Prior An.* 68ᵃ39f.; III.3.24; V.1.5). Love is more than desire, for hatred is opposite to 'mental friendship' while bodily desire has no opposite (*Top.* 106ᵇ1f.: perhaps a doubtful claim). Love is other than desire, for one who loves does not (necessarily?) therefore desire intercourse more than one who does not (*Top.* 146ᵃ10f.). Human couples are linked by the human passion for *sunousia* at something more than the animal level. Marriage is for mutual help and comfort, and in this Aristotle is its champion against Plato's naïvely reductionist account (*Pol.* II, 1261ᵃ6f.) and the laxity of Sparta (*Pol.* II, 1269ᵇ12f.). 'In a state having women and children in common, love will be watery' (*Pol.* II, 1262ᵇ15): everyone will be cared for less, because everyone cares for him (*Pol.* II, 1261ᵇ33f.; cf. III.3.26). In a state where women are left free of social demands, and their war-oriented menfolk fall under their irresponsible influence, 'half the state is without laws' (*Pol.* II, 1269ᵇ18; see App. B.5). In both cases the ordering of the state so overrules the proper ordering of the family, that personal affection and care are dulled or exaggerated (thereby ceasing to be love—care for another's *well-being*) beyond the bounds of right living. 'Everyone wants companionship in whatever end he can achieve' (*E.E.* 1254ᵇ7): so that families are at once essential and to be subordinated to the higher companionship of the state.

9. Male and female help each other by throwing their peculiar gifts into the common stock (*N.E.* VIII, 1162ᵃ22f.), but it is the male who must in general control the marriage: 'the man rules as is his due, and in the matters which a man ought to decide, but leaves whatever fits the woman to her' (*N.E.* VIII, 1160ᵇ33). The point of this may be understood by noting particularly the relation of conservation to expenditure (Aristotle

goes on to speak of heiresses, who control the money): the *oikonomos*, the head of the household exercising his good sense in its management, is a model for the *phronomos* no less than the statesman. But his virtues are not those of economic man: 'It is time to remember that, at least in Homer, the verb *nemo* is used mostly of generous hosts dispensing meat and drink, not in order to allocate scarce resources according to marginal utilities, but in order to do honour to guests and justice to their own greatmindedness' (K. SINGER pp. 39f.). Thrift is a feminine virtue (*Pol.* III, 1277^{b}24f.), as it still is in many areas that do not pretend to be societies of autonomous and unconditioned individuals. Women, whether in their virtue or their vice, should not be taken as exemplars for one who lives well, not even for women. Because 'political' *sunousia* matters more than sexual, the preservation of the *polis*, which is commonly in the hands of men, is more important than the preservation of a family, which is commonly in the hands of women. These concepts, of 'housewife' and 'citizen', can be generalized beyond their original application even to fit such societies (if such there be) who commission men as housewives and women as citizens: where there are things that ought to be done, and one cannot do them, there is a prima facie obligation to do whatever will make it possible for someone *else* to perform the initial obligation. In so far as the aims of the state are broader, the 'housewife' must so act so as to facilitate the 'citizen's' action. Equally the state (and its citizens) must so act as to help and preserve the family. It may even be that one individual unites both functions (*Pol.* IV, 1291^{a}28f.).

10. In applying these general rules about social ordering (Aristotle is of course aware that all general rules may bear hardly on particular cases, and must sometimes be bent: *N.E.* V, 1137^{b}26f.), Aristotle does select males and females for their contemporary Greek roles. The female is incomplete at a social level: so also at a biological. In coition the male is attempting to impose his form upon maternal matter (which must be of a sort to receive it)—where he fails to impose it wholly, the offspring remains female (*De Gen. An.* 766^{b}27f.; compare sex chromosomes—*XX* (female) and *XY* (male) (a relationship reversed in 'degenerate' insects (II.2.3)). The transfer of heat (*De Gen. An.* 728^{a}29f.; 783^{b}29f.; see App. A) involved in this is the corporeal aspect of the female's becoming momentarily male, which is what is wanted—as matter desires to be filled with form (*Phys.* I, 192^{a}22). In coition two animals become one (*De Gen. An.* 731^{a}9f.) and the female is completed. For whereas the male is complete, and all his bodily parts are active without coition, the female's parts are not in use nor therefore actualized. No female can be expected to resist the male's seductive powers (*N.E.* VII, 1148^{b}32, 1150^{b}15f.) for precisely this reason. The similarity of this to modern Freudian doctrine at a psychological level, and to certain Tantric doctrines on a mystical, lies beyond my pres-

ent purposes. It is enough to note that Aristotle's doctrines are not the product of unthinking prejudice, but a serious attempt to come to terms with the fact of male/female differences and dependence.

11. These arguments may seem unconvincing either as demonstrations of Aristotle's good sense or of female inferiority. Perhaps the ideal society would order things differently, but it must preserve those aspects of life which Aristotle labels male and female, even if it does not commission men and women respectively to perform them. Not to do so is to be only half-*eudaimon*. Equally the female must not predominate over the male. Aristotle himself would commission men and women for the male and female roles. He does not therefore advocate the oppression of women: indeed he distinguishes woman and slave most carefully, and against the tenor of his biological theories (*Pol.* I, 1252ᵇ1; cf. *De An.* 420ᵇ16f., *De Part. An.* 688ᵃ22, 690ᵃ2f.). We should not identify human beings solely according to their sex, but equally we should not (generally) expect the same from all human beings whatever their bodily nature. Aristotle's will makes it clear that he lived on excellent terms with both wife and mistress (Diog. *Vit.* V.1.11): it is to be expected of one who saw the human need for loving couples aiding each other in the pursuit of right-doing. Plato did eventually see the worth of marriage (Pl. *Laws* 773 b): it was Aristotle, whatever his faults, who was the author of a more truly humane effort to understand the ordering of human life on this sphere.

Appendix C: Aristotle and the Sung Neo-Confucians

1. The Neo-Confucian movement of the Sung dynasty is typified in the person of Chu Hsi (A.D. 1130–1200). During his lifetime he suffered the usual fate of the righteous (and perhaps somewhat incompetent) philosopher, being employed by turns as teacher, civil servant, and scapegoat. He was early attracted to Buddhism, but after studying the work of Ch'eng Yi (1033–1107) he became ardent in his support of the new Confucianism and his criticism of Buddhism, always retaining many of the concepts particularly of Hua-yen Buddhism. Once dead he became the main channel and interpreter of orthodoxy, opposed by the idealists of the Mind School deriving from Lu Hsiang-shan (1139–93) after Ch'eng Hao (1032–85: Yi's brother) and culminating in Wang Yang-ming (1472–1529). The philosophers of the Ch'ing dynasty rejected him as impractical, in their discomfort at the collapse of the Ming (cf. Nivison: WRIGHT p. 123), but his influence remained. Neo-Confucianism entered Japan in close association with Ch'an Buddhism (DUMOULIN pp. 124, 177), though Wang Yang-ming was perhaps more prominent. The early Jesuit missionaries conveyed his thought to Europe, where it intrigued Leibniz, more as confirmation than as inspiration (MUNGELLO; cf. BERNARD, NEEDHAM II.496f.). Needham argues that Leibniz's monadology is derived from Chu Hsi, who in turn (FUNG II.541f.) derived it from the Hua-yen metaphor of Indra's net, in which each jewel reflects all others (VI.2; CHAN (2) p. 412). Further studies of the Sung may be found, ignoring certain displeasingly contemptuous work in the nineteenth century, in BRUCE (2), FUNG, CHANG, WRIGHT (De Bary, Nivison) and CHAN (4). Chu Hsi himself may be studied in BRUCE (1) and CHAN (2), together with the Four Books which he made the basis of the new Confucianism (*Analects, Great Learning, Doctrine of the Mean,* and *Book of Mencius*). CHAN (1) is a compendium of earlier Neo-Confucian thought edited by Chu Hsi.

2. The inescapable parallel between Aristotle and the Sung is made most forcibly by CHANG (pp. 253f.). His thirteen points of resemblance are not always clearly distinguishable from each other, nor am I quite sure of the validity of some of them. They are none the less impressive. Thus: (i) no separate formal principles; (ii) the One is the li, the principle, of the Many, not something apart from the Many; (iii) no separate universals—the separation of ch'i (matter?) and li (form?) is a Buddhist fallacy; (iv)

ch'i, matter, is capacity and (v) does not exist without li; (vi) matter is the source of imperfection and plurality; (vii) li is prior to ch'i; (viii) li is the final, formal, and efficient cause; (ix) there is an Unmoved Mover; (x) the essence of this latter is *energeia*; (xi) man is distinguished from the animals by his use of reason; (xii) the doctrine of the mean.

3. Such a superficial comparison may not be really significant—comparing philosophies is always a difficult game, nor is it one which I wish to play at any length. Some idea of the worth of the parallel between Aristotle and Chu Hsi may be gained, however, by considering the differences alleged by Orientalists.

4. Firstly by Chang himself: (a) Chu Hsi believed there to be an eternal, unchanging truth in the field of morals—did not Aristotle? (b) Chu Hsi did not write a treatise on logic—certainly, for he did not live in a society that put a premium on rhetorical expertise (HU SHIH (2)); (c) the Chinese are uniquely focused on man and morals rather than logical abstractions —there is nothing abstract or 'academic' about Aristotelian concepts; (d) they have a rationalistic and monistic turn of mind—so did Aristotle; (e) they insist on mind-control and character reform rather than exterior techniques of investigation (see *N.E.* I, 1095^{a}2f.); (f) they insist that 'a man of noble character should prefer to be killed in a noble cause rather than to seek his life at the cost of his virtue' (*Analects* 15.9; see *N.E.* III, 1116^{b}20).

5. NEEDHAM II.475f. criticizes the Aristotelian interpretation of ch'i and li, and also what he takes to be the suggestion of a god. He objects (a) that the form of a living being is a soul, whereas the Chinese tradition has no use for souls (but the Aristotelian soul is the life of the body, not an extra); (b) that form confers substantiality on things, whereas ch'i is not brought into being by li (neither, in the sense intended, is matter by form); (c) that form is essence, primary substance, while li is not substantial, nor a type of ch'i (neither is form a type of matter); (d) that li are not metaphysical but organizing fields at every level of reality (I cannot conceive what he supposes forms to be); and (f) that pure form is God, whereas Chu Hsi allows for no Chu-tsai, no Governor. On this fifth point Chu has suffered as much from his interpreters as Aristotle: FUNG reckons Li, the li of the whole, more like Aristotle's God than Needham allows, though also more mystical, as being immanent in every individual (cf. *N.E.* VII, 1153^{b}32). It is not surprising that Chu Hsi differs from the stereotypic Aristotle of Orientalist myth—what is surprising is that Needham should reveal such ignorance of the real Aristotle. It is hardly too much to say that every time he applauds Chu Hsi for a distinctively modern notion he is praising Aristotle unawares. In attributing Leibniz's organicism to the Sung he wholly ignores a more immediate ancestry—even when admitting

the influence of the Cambridge Platonists he declares 'for Cudworth all events in the universe depend not on forces operating from without, but on formative principles acting from within (how strangely Chinese the doctrine sounds [!])' (II.503). There is a difference between the occasionally animistic principles of Cudworth and true forms, *endelecheia* and *entelecheia*, but Aristotle saw it long ago. The only overt difference that I can see between the two metaphysical systems is that ch'i is less purely passive—and even this can be exaggerated (see *Phys.* I, 192ª16f.). Needham claims, perhaps correctly, that Chu Hsi was a believer in evolutionary transformism, but the passages cited to prove this seem to me to imagine the devolutionary transformism I attribute to Aristotle (cf. II.2.28).

6. Other scholars confirm the parallel. P.E. CALLAHAN declares that li is a broader concept than that of *eidos*, as it 'makes a thing what it ought to be': it is a guiding and directing principle. Like most Orientalists he seems to suppose that '*eidos*' means shape. Tung-sun CHANG makes the familiar point that the west has been seduced by Greek grammar into a belief in substance, whereas China has operated with a notion of relationship in which there is no exact identity nor static being. 'Chu Hsi's doctrine of opened the door to "substance"': being is dynamic, process rather than fixity, but there are certain types of orderly and cohesive process which constitute things. Plato and Aristotle would have been glad to hear it, for the door from 'Heracleitean' chaos was opened for them in exactly the same way (cf. V.1.10).

7. HOCKING's discussion of Chu Hsi's theory of knowledge suggests parallels particularly with Plato. 'When one has exerted oneself for a long time finally one morning a complete understanding will open before one. Thereupon there will be a thorough comprehension of all the multitude of things, external or internal, fine or coarse, and every exercise of the mind will be marked by complete enlightenment' (quoted by FUNG II, p. 561). Wisdom and *nous* blaze up at long last after the prolonged friction of words and arguments that cannot of themselves convey the truth (Pl. *Ep.* VII, 344 b 3f., 341 c 4). Scholarship, science, and the mystical are not clearly distinguishable. Hocking further emphasizes Chu's recognition of the biological continuum and man's unique place in it: 'Man is born endowed with the mean, the attribute of Heaven and Earth'—because he has that mean, because he has balance he can deliberate (cf. II.2.28, III.2.26).

8. DAY, following FUNG in particular, summarizes Chu's philosophy conveniently under six heads. Firstly, Principle or the Supreme Ultimate (Li or T'ai chi). This Supreme is above shapes, beyond space and time, existing from the beginning: it is full of the normative principles that

govern phenomena. Each object contains the Principle of all, not identically but specifically, as the moon in water. 'As the heart of the Tathagata
(the Buddha-nature) is not born and does not perish it mirrors itself in
all things, as the moon on water' (Ghanavyuha Sutra (Hua-yen): HOCKING
p. 120; cf, Chu Hsi *Conversations* 4). To apprehend this Supreme is to
be able to recognize the lesser laws.

9. Secondly, ch'i and cosmogony. Ch'i is creative as li is not. A house
visibly reveals its plan, materials take shape according to plan. Li and ch'i
are mutually dependent. Chu's view is organismic. Ch'i generates Yin and
Yang, the basic polarity, which are differentiated into the five elements
(water, fire, earth, wood, metal) and so produce the myriad things, each
with its own li. The earth settles at the centre, while the sun and other
celestial bodies revolve forever at the perimeter. The universe goes through
periodic dissolutions. There is at it were a person, the Ruler, but this
Ruler is none other than Law.

10. Thirdly, human nature. Man's endowments are determined by the
degree to which ch'i is controlled and purified by li. His nature has five
constants: love (wood), righteousness (metal), propriety (fire), wisdom
(water), and sincerity (earth). These should be in harmony: 'tender-
hearted men are lacking in the judicial faculty, while men in whom the
critical faculty is prominent tend to be tyrannical; for the more love is
developed, the more is righteousness obscured, and the more righteousness
is developed the more love is obscured' (BRUCE (1) p. 59; TU): ants and
bees show a gleam of righteousness, wolves and tigers a gleam of love
(cf. NEEDHAM II.488; cf. III.3.1). 'By chung is meant what is not one-
sided' (Chu Hsi: CHAN (2) p. 97; cf. III.2.26).

11. Fourthly, spiritual cultivation and ethics. Man is born with the
mean, but bad habits engendered by ch'i obscure the mean. Concentrate
therefore on expanding the mind until complete understanding opens
before you. Love is the fulfilling of the law. 'To be sincere, empty of self,
courteous and calm is the foundation of the practice of love . . . To love
others as we love ourselves is to perfect love' (DAY, p. 209, after BRUCE (1)
ch. 6,7). The Confucian chun tzu and the Greek *kaloskagathos* are upon
the same model (MORTON): both are raised to higher levels in the respective philosophers (cf. Hwa Yol JUNG).

12. Fifthly, political philosophy. Chu Hsi's ideals are the six sage-kings
of Chinese tradition. The natural order is in some way connected with
the moral: 'in time man will lose all moral principles and everything will
be thrown together in chaos. Man and things will all die out, and then
there will be a new beginning' (CHAN (2) p. 642). It is not a doctrine

entirely alien to Aristotle (cf. II.2.15; III.2.26; IV.2.13), or to the Greeks (cf. Thuc. I.23, Hdt. I.174.5).

13. Sixthly, the weakness of Buddhism. Apart from some doctrinal and sometimes misplaced criticisms (particularly his denial of any immortality save that of the Law, hsing (BODDE)), Chu Hsi's attack is particularly on those who disregard the five familial relationships of human life. Here he effectively joins with Aristotle's attack on Plato, and it is this crucial point which chiefly divides both Aristotle and Chu Hsi from the iconoclasm of Ch'an Buddhism.

14. 'According to the principle of the world, a thing will begin again when it ends and can therefore last forever without limit . . . The way to be constant is to change according to circumstances' (CHAN (1) I. §13: Ch'eng Yi). As Philoponus (*De An.* p. 75, 11f. Hayduck) remarks on *Phys.* I, 192^{b}13, persistent motion is the same as rest. 'Resting in one's resting point is resting in one's proper place. Most people are unable to rest. For all things are complete in man' (CHAN (1) IV, §53: Ch'eng Yi). 'All things are complete in man. If he is impartial and responds to things as they come and does so properly he will be resting in his proper place' (CHAN (1) IV, §53: Mao Hsing-lai). Man is in his proper place, is fulfilled (cf. III.3.3), when he is a whole man living energetically rather than kinetically. Such a man can judge correctly. 'Only the superior man or sage can conform to the three conditions of emptiness, concentration (unity), and unperturbedness and can judge by an inner standard' (Hsun Tzu 320–*c*.238/5 B.C. DUBS p. 173).

15. I conclude that Aristotle may profitably be considered in a Chinese setting: Aristotle can be understood and passages which have hitherto been emended or ignored given a coherent sense if we treat him as something like a Mahayana Buddhist. For him as for Neo-Confucianism and Zen the end of enlightenment is the opening of the world. It is not wholly impossible that there should have been some cross-cultural contact between the Mediterranean and Chinese milieux: the Mahayana entered China via Iran and the Hellenistic kingdoms, and was contemporary with Nestorianism (REICHELT pp. 106f.). An early Chinese Madhyamika Buddhist, Chi-tsang (A.D. 549–623), had a Parthian father (CHAN (2) p. 358). Islamic traders visited China. I think it more likely that both philosophies are sophisticated attempts to codify elements of archaic tradition and experience of science, society, and the god. What is eternally true may be discovered independently: only falsehood need diffuse.

Appendix D: *Ta Noeta* and the Unmoved Movers

1. I have suggested (V.3.10f.) that the Prime's thinking Itself should not be taken as narcissism but as the contemplation of the principles of being —a contemplation which, being perfect and eternally actual, is (i) indistinguishable from the Prime's own being and (ii) leaves nothing uncontemplated in its objects. The human soul in 'becoming all things' necessarily leaves the things themselves external to its own activity—for they exist as thinkable etc. (see III.1.13) before they are thought by us, and may be realized by other thinkers in ways other than ours. In wakefully confronting the world we experience its being as making demands on us which may conflict with our immediate tastes (see VI). The Divine, on the other hand, does not have to 'become all things', nor do the objects of its thought exist as potentially thinkable before it thinks them, nor are there any other versions of those objects than the ones it eternally is. The Divine is not confronted by something to which it must conform— rather is it itself the light to which we conform. This account of divine self-awareness, not as an empty consciousness that it is conscious, but as a 'finding' of its being in its eternal activity of contemplating the principles of being, is at one with my account of self-love (III.3.29), and with KRAMER's analysis of the topic.

2. Of the secondary movers I have said little, insisting only that the relationship between them and the Prime is the typically Aristotelian one of whole (chief part) to other parts (V.3.16), and suggesting in passing that they may not be *nooi*, as is commonly assumed (what, after all, do *they* intuit? V.3.25n.). It is perhaps possible to say rather more, and to connect the topic with the Prime's contemplation. Both JACKSON and Kramer have attempted this, though for different reasons. Jackson found a contradiction between Aristotle's rejection of an 'episodic' universe in favour of a 'monarchy' (*Met*. XII, 1075^{b}37f.), and his admission of a plurality of unmoved movers (*Met*. XII, 1073^{a}14f.; see *De Caelo* 279^{a}18f.). He resolved this by supposing that the secondary movers were the thoughts of the Prime, so that no other *arche* was in question (cf. III.3.25 on kings). Kramer, working from the other end, seeks to find some object of thought for the Prime that is not external to it (see *Pol*. VII, 1325^{b}28f.). Because he holds that the forms of the *kosmos* must be thus external, the only plausible objects for the Prime's 'interior contemplation' are those 'forms

in separation', the secondary movers. The hierarchy of movers is therefore offered as an account of the structure of the Divine, which both knows nothing that is not itself and equally is not empty awareness of awareness. If this interpretation, as it stands, is correct, it seems that God need not know the world (against V.3.28), and that our reception of the Divine involves a turn away from the world of sense into Platonism (against V.2.12 *et al.*).

3.   Jackson's problem is, I think, unreal. In the *Peri Philosophias* (fr.17 Ross) Aristotle inquires: are the *archai* one or many? If many, are they *tetagmenoi* or *ataktoi*, ordered or disorderly? If ordered (as they surely are), by something else or by themselves? If by themselves, then they have *koinon ti sunapton autas*, something in common that unites them (see App.B.7). In any event but that of an episodic and disordered universe (which is absurd), there is some one supreme *arche*. τὰ δὲ ὄντα οὐ βούλεται πολιτεύεσθαι κακῶς: things are unwilling to be badly co-ordinated (*Met.* XII, 1076ᵃ3f.). That there is one such *arche* does not exclude the existence of other *archai*, any more than there being one supreme end excludes, *or includes*, the goodness of other ends (V.1.11 *et al.*). It is the Divine which introduces law and order into the otherwise disorderly (*Pol.* VII, 1326ᵃ30; see III.2.19). REICHE (p. 98) has emphasized the parallel between astral and biological psycho-physics (as at *De Caelo* 292ᵃ18f.; see also App.A): I would emphasize, as before, the parallel between astronomy and ethics. We may explain, or govern, our desires by reference to higher or more distant ends (see II.2.27, II.3.30, V.1.13), but this does not mean that the objects of those desires are merely means. Similarly the First Heaven's pursuit of the Prime provides a setting, and an ordering, for the planetary spheres, without the *Prime*'s therefore having to comprise the movers of those spheres. Order does not necessitate tyranny. Nor is an ordering principle wholly defined by the order it induces.

4.   This is, in effect, to reiterate my suspicion that the lesser movers are no more *nooi* than the lesser gods of the Greek Pantheon are Zeuses. Reiche's new fragment of the *Peri Philosophias*, continuing fr.18 Ross (coaxed from Philo *De Aeternitate* 4.13), shows Aristotle speaking with approval of Plato's astral gods as a *theoprepes ekklesia*. The gods of Olympus may all be gods—they are far from indistinguishable (see OTTO). D. J. Allan has suggested to me that Aristotle truly intended only *seven* secondary movers, one per planet. This would give a clear hierarchy of movers (*Met.* XII, 1073ᵇ1f.) and accords with my suggestion—for the association of the planets with principles of being less than the supreme is familiar, e.g. from Dante. This might be what Aristotle would have

preferred, but his insistence that each planet has several motions (*Met.* XII, 1073ᵇ8f., *De Caelo* 292ᵇ31f.) seems to require that there be many more than seven movers. This in fact provides that the planets may represent our own involvement in decision-making and occasional preference of one end to another (see *De Caelo* 292ᵇ2f.). The movers' hierarchy is fixed by the hierarchy of planets (*De Caelo* 292ᵃ1f.) and also because the spheres of each planet are contained and conditioned one by another (*De Caelo* 293ᵃ4f.). How exactly Aristotle would have paired the values of astronomical movers and human goods is a matter on which we can have no opinion. The detail of such correspondences, in any case, seems to have been of little concern to him (see App.B.2). It remains plausible that some such correspondence is intended. The Prime is functionally identical with Zeus, as Aristotle recognizes (*De Motu* 699ᵇ38f.), and there are other, although lesser, gods. The rule of the *kosmos* is not tyranny, in which all ends but one are barred, but Law. This Law is God and Nous (*Pol.* III, 1287ᵃ28f.). As in a household the freeman's choice of action is most constrained by principle, while slaves, animals (and children?) may live more at random, so also in Nature the higher entities are most principled: further down much more occurs that is non-systematic (*Met.* XII, 1075ᵃ19f.). Order is most visible in the heavens, and the contemplation of that order is a great good (see *Protrepticus* fr.11 Ross).

5.   Though Jackson's problem is unreal, his conclusions may well be partly true: namely that the Prime *does* contemplate the secondary movers. Kramer has argued that this is all It can contemplate without passing to externals. Certainly the Prime's objects of thought must be 'without matter'—for it is matter which disallows the pure identity of thought and thinking. So that only the separate forms, it seems, are suitable objects for the Prime. All the Prime knows, and orders, is that hierarchy of being which incidentally to its own essence attracts the *kosmos* at various levels. The *kosmos* is therefore a copy of an immaterial and eternal world which knows nothing of the *kosmos*. This is a strangely super-Platonic doctrine for Aristotle to espouse. If that is what goodness is, let us seek something other than goodness which has some relevance for men (see *N.E.* I, 1096ᵇ32f. against separate, universal, unattainable goodness). Do we need this step? I have suggested (V.3.26) that as the *kosmos* itself is not in anything, as there is not more than one *kosmos*, the *kosmos* itself as a whole is *in a sense* without matter (cf. II.3.20, 32): for the form of the *kosmos* is not one which can be instantiated more than once. To contemplate and be the forms of the *kosmos*, then, is not to leave anything contemplatable outside that contemplation. It is not to be associated with any externals. The *kosmos*'s material indeterminacy at its lower levels is not thus known, by anyone. The *kosmos* is not therefore external to the Prime.

6. To elaborate: the *kosmos* is one, but there is no more than one *kosmos*. How shall this be? One swallow does not make a species (IV.2.6). If the *kosmos* is a unique individual it is unknowable. There is no such thing as the *kosmos*, for there cannot be one of a kind unless there could be many (see II.3.29). In such rarefied heights of speculation there are no final solutions: my suggestion has been that our occasional intuition of the world as a hierarchic order of great beauty is to be interpreted, in Aristotelian vein, as our noetic capacity's actualization by the One, the preexistent and Comprehensive Divinity which both the World's components and ourselves desire and seek to imitate. By its actualization of our capacity it engenders many human, incarnate *nooi* and many orderly and beautiful life-worlds (see VI). The supreme Nous, and the Supreme *kosmos* are, in a sense, of *kinds*. They are in fact the same kind. As Kramer observes, it is significant that the *Politics* passage he cites (*Pol.* VII, 1325^{b}28f.) links God and the *kosmos* as alike having no external relationships. If God is the order of the *kosmos*, or conversely the *kosmos* embodies over time the forms of life which are eternally intuitable by human beings and eternally intuited by the Supreme, this is hardly surprising. The Prime can contemplate the forms of the *kosmos* without thereby contemplating what is external to Itself, or what involves matter in the opprobrious sense. Whatever *our* intuited world may be, the World Itself continues unabashed by our insight or our error. Things exist before we see them. They do not exist before or independently of the Divine. God-and-*Nous* eternally contemplates and is God-and-Nature: the principles at work in the *kosmos* are the eternal objects of Divine apprehension.

7. This said, that there *need* be no exclusion of the Prime from knowledge of the principles of cosmic being, it remains true that the secondary movers are plausible candidates for the Prime's chief contemplation. It is they after all that are responsible for the clear order of the heavens. The moral, particularly if my suggestion about their general nature is accepted, is that the sublunary world also seeks to embody (though imperfectly) those same ordered principles that the spheres successfully embody over time. These principles are *separate* in that they are not exclusively embodied even in the heavens: they are available for sublunary encouragement. This suggestion was to be taken by later thinkers as an excuse for discovering the nature of the good life from a contemplation of the sky. I do not suggest that Aristotle would have gone so far. The sublunary world, none the less, is not wholly random, and its cycles and changes are largely dependent on the heavens (IV.2.11f.). But our own internalization of cosmic Law and Order is dependent in the end upon a direct enlightenment by Divine Nous, rather than a pedantic appreciation of astrological correspondences. We do not *need* to inspect

the heavens to discover the principles of being. Even if we restrict the Prime's knowledge to the hierarchy of secondary movers we may still suppose that in our capacity to be guided by *Nous* and its lieutenants (see *Pol.* III, 1287ᵇ8f.) we demonstrate that this Good (both as the ordered life and as the supreme form of life: V.1.19) is after all available to man without his turning wholly from the world of sense.

8. Nothing that is intelligible is outside the Prime. Of nothing can it be said that it is intelligible (by us) but not understood by the Prime. Certainly, It has no knowledge of the accidental—there is no such knowledge. (IV.2.6f.). Certainly, It has no perception of the world of our senses. But we in turn only have such perception in so far as we make use of, or receive the sense of, the entity and entities of the *kosmos* (see III.1.25). The heavens, for Plato, were a mirror of the Divine. So also, despite necessary qualifications, were they for Aristotle. Neither philosopher imagined the dead universe of our present cosmologies, nor were they satisfied by merely mathematical accounts (cf. *Met.* XII, 1075ᵇ37f.), but rather inhabited the 'human' *kosmos* of archaic thought (II.3, VI). The backwards and forwards dance of the planets under the arch of the first heaven was for them an exposition of the divine-human life which it was our responsibility to enact and understand below the moon (see *Peri Phil.* fr.12b Ross; CHROUST (2) I ch. 16). If we failed in this, yet could we still be sure that the whole company of Heaven eternally succeeds. The forms of the secondary movers are not separate (as are Plato's forms) because never wholly instantiated. Rather are they separate because they are not equivalent even to the most exhaustive description of the sphere's movements—they are the sense of those motions. They are separate also in that they may be known (*are* known by the Prime) in an undivided moment (see IV.2.23), but can be approached by the spheres only over a period, and are never wholly instantiated by the spheres at a single moment. We do not need to look away from the world to find them, but to examine the world in honesty, and wait upon the God. What that God may be expected to announce is beyond my brief.

Bibliography

Abbreviations used for journals:

AGP	Archiv für Geschichte der Philosophie
AJP	American Journal of Philology
Ant. Cl.	L'Antiquité Classique
APQ	American Philosophical Quarterly
BJPS	British Journal of the Philosophy of Science
CQ	Classical Quarterly
CR	Classical Review
HJAS	Harvard Journal of Asiatic Studies
HSCP	Harvard Studies in Classical Philology
IPQ	International Philosophical Quarterly
JHB	Journal of the History of Biology
JHI	Journal of the History of Ideas
JHS	Journal of Hellenic Studies
JP	Journal of Philology
M	Mind
PAS	Proceedings of the Aristotelian Society
PASS	Proceedings of the Aristotelian Society, Supplementary Volume
PBA	Proceedings of the British Academy
PEW	Philosophy East and West
PPR	Philosophy and Phenomenological Research
PQ	Philosophical Quarterly
PR	Philosophical Review
RM	Review of Metaphysics
UCPP	University of California Publications in Philosophy

ABELSON, R. 'Cause and Reason in History': *Philosophy and History* (ed. S. Hook), New York 1963, pp. 167f.

ACKRILL, J. L.
(1) 'In Defence of Platonic Division': *Ryle* (ed. O. P. Wood and G. Pitcher), New York 1970, pp. 373f.
(2) *Categories and De Interpretatione*, Oxford 1963.

ADKINS, A. W. H.
(1) *From the Many to the One*, Oxford 1970.
(2) *Merit and Responsibility*, Oxford 1960.
(3) '"Friendship" and "Self-sufficiency" in Homer and Aristotle', *CQ* 13 N.S., 1963, pp. 30f.

AGAR, W. E. *A contribution to the theory of the living organism*, 2nd ed., Melbourne 1951.

ALLAN, D. J.
(1) 'Causality, ancient and modern', *PASS* 39, 1965, pp. 1f.
(2) *The Philosophy of Aristotle*, Oxford 1952.
(3) 'Individual and State in the Ethics and Politics', *Entretiens Hardt* 11, 1964, pp. 53f.

ALLBUT, T. C. *Greek Medicine in Rome*, London 1921.

ANSCOMBE, G. E. M. 'The Intentionality of Sensation', *Analytical Philosophy II* (ed. R. J. Butler), Oxford 1965, pp. 158f.

ANDO, T. *Aristotle's Theory of Practical Cognition*, Kyoto 1958.

ARBER, A. 'Interpretation of leaf and root in the angiosperms', *Biological Reviews* 16, 1941, pp. 81f.

ARMSTRONG, A. 'The background of the Doctrine "That the Intelligibles are not outside the intellect"', *Entretiens Hardt* 5, 1957, pp. 391f.

AUSTIN, J. L. 'A Plea for Excuses', *PAS* 57, 1956–7, pp. 1f.

AYER, A. J. *The Problem of Knowledge*, Harmondsworth 1956.

BALME, D. M.
(1) 'Genos and Eidos in Aristotle's Biology', *CQ* 12 N.S., 1962, pp. 81f.
(2) 'Theory of Spontaneous Generation', *Phronesis* 7, 1962, pp. 91f.
(3) 'Aristotle on Nature and Chance', *CQ* 33, 1939, pp. 129f.
(4) *De Partibus Animalium I and De Generatione Animalium I*, Oxford 1972.

BAMBROUGH, R. (ed.) *New Essays on Plato and Aristotle*, London 1965: R. Bambrough, 'Aristotle on Justice', pp. 159f.

BECKNER, M.
(1) *The Biological Way of Thought*, New York 1959.
(2) 'Function and Teleology', *JHB* 2, 1969, pp. 151f.

BERGER, P. L. and LUCKMANN, T. *The Social Construction of Reality*, New York 1966.

BERGER, P. L. *Invitation to Sociology*, New York 1963.

BERNARD, 'Chu Hsi and Leibniz', *T'ien-hsia Monthly* 5, 1937.

BERTALANFFY, L. von
(1) *Problems of Life*, London 1952.
(2) *Modern Theories of Development*, Oxford 1933.
(3) *Robots, Men and Minds*, New York 1967.

BEVAN, E. *Symbolism and Belief,* London 1938.

BLACK, E. 'Aristotle's Essentialism and Quine's Cycling Mathematician', *Monist* 52, 1968, pp. 288f.

BLAKE, W. *Complete Writings* (ed. G. Keynes), Oxford 1966.

BLOCK, I.
(1) 'The Order of Aristotle's Psychological Writings', *AJP* 82, 1961, pp. 50f.
(2) 'Aristotle and the Physical Object', *PPR* 21, 1960–1, pp. 93f.
(3) 'Truth and Error in Aristotle's Theory of Sense Perception', *PQ* 11, 1961, pp. 1f.

BLUM, H. F. *Time's Arrow and Evolution,* 2nd ed., Princeton 1955.

BODDE, D. 'Chinese View of Immortality', *Review of Religion* 6, 1942, pp. 350f.

BONITZ, H. *Index Aristotelicus,* Berlin 1870.

BORGES, J. L.
(1) *Labyrinths,* Harmondsworth, 1970.
(2) *Other Inquisitions, 1937-52,* Texas 1964.

BRÉHIER, E. *The Philosophy of Plotinus* (tr. J. Thomas), Chicago 1958.

BRUCE, J. P.
(1) *The Philosophy of Human Nature,* London 1922.
(2) *Chu Hsi and His Masters,* London 1923.

BURNET, J.
(1) 'Aristotle', *PBA* 11, 1924, pp. 109f.
(2) *Nicomachean Ethics,* London 1900.

BURY, J. *The Idea of Progress,* London 1920.

BUTLER, R. J. 'Aristotle's Sea-fight and Three-valued Logic', *PR* 64, 1955, pp. 264f.

CALLAHAN, J. F. *Four Views of Time in Ancient Philosophy,* Cambridge, Mass. 1948.

CALLAHAN, P. E. 'Chu Hsi and Thomas Aquinas', *Harvard Papers on China* 4, 1950, pp. 1f.

CAMPBELL, J.
(1) (ed.) *Spirit and Nature* (Eranos Papers I), London 1955.
(2) *The Masks of God,* London 1960–8.
(3) (ed.) *Man and Time* (Eranos Papers III), London 1958:
  H. C. Puech, 'Gnosis and Time', pp. 38f.
  H. Plessner, 'On the Relation of Time to Death', pp. 233f.
  M. Knoll, 'Transformations of Science in our age', pp. 264f.
  G. van der Leeuw, 'Primordial Time and Final Time', pp. 324f.

CANFIELD, J. V. (ed.) *Purpose in Nature,* New Jersey 1966.

CANNON, W. B. *The Wisdom of the Body*, London 1932.

CAPEK, M. *The Philosophical Impact of Contemporary Physics*, New York 1961.

CARR, E. H. *What is History?*, London 1961.

CHAN, Wing-tsit
(1) (ed.) *Reflections on Things at Hand*, New York 1967.
(2) (ed.) *Sourcebook in Chinese Philosophy*, Princeton 1963.
(3) 'Evolution of the Confucian Concept of "Jen"', *PEW* 4, 1954–5, pp. 295f.
(4) 'Neo-Confucianism: New Ideas in Old Terminology', *PEW* 17, 1967, pp. 15f.

CHANG, C. *The Development of Neo-Confucian Thought*, New York 1957.

CHANG, Tung-sun 'A Chinese Philosopher's Theory of Knowledge', *Yenching Journal of Social Studies* 1, 1938, pp. 155f.

CHARDIN, T. de *Man's Place in Nature* (tr. R. Hague), London 1966.

CHARLTON, W. *Physics I and II*, Oxford 1970.

CHORON, J. *Modern Man and Mortality*, New York 1963.

CHROUST, A. H.
(1) 'Aristotle and the Philosophies of the East', *RM* 18, 1964–5, pp. 572f.
(2) *Aristotle*, London 1973.

CLARK, S. R. L. 'The Use of "Man's Function" in Aristotle', *Ethics* 82, 1972, pp. 269f.

CONEN, P. F. 'Aristotle's Definition of Time', *New Scholasticism* 26, 1952, pp. 441f.

CONGER, G. P. 'Did India Influence Early Greek Philosophies?', *PEW* 2, 1952–3, pp. 102f.

COOK WILSON, J. 'On the Platonist Doctrine of the *Asumbletoi Arithmoi*', *CR* 18, 1904, pp. 247f.

CROSSON, F. J. 'Psyche and Persona: the Problem of Personal Immortality', *IPQ* 8, 1968, pp. 161f.

CROISSANT, J. *Aristote et les Mystères*, Liège 1932.

DARWIN, C. *The Origin of Species*, London 1859; Everyman edition, London 1965.

DAY, C. B. *The Philosophers of China*, London 1962.

DAY, J. and CHAMBERS, M. 'Aristotle's History of Athenian Democracy', *UCPP* 73, 1962.

DEVEREUX, G. *From Anxiety to Method in the Behavioural Sciences*, The Hague 1967.

DODDS, E. R. *The Greeks and the Irrational*, California 1963.

DOUGLAS, M.
(1) *Purity and Danger*, London 1966.
(2) *Natural Symbols*, 2nd ed., Harmondsworth 1973.

DUBOS, R. *Mirages of Health*, London, 1960.

DUBS, H. H. *Hsuntze, Moulder of Ancient Confucianism*, London 1927.

DUMOULIN, H. *History of Zen Buddhism*, New York 1963.

DUMEZIL, *Jupiter Mars Quirinus*, Paris 1941.

DURKHEIM, D. E. *Sociology and Philosophy*, London 1953.

ELIADE, M.
(1) *Yoga: Immortality and Freedom*, 2nd ed., Princeton 1969.
(2) *Cosmos and History*, New York 1954.

EVANS, C. O. *The Subject of Consciousness*, London 1970.

FEUERBACH, L. A. *Foundations of a Philosophy of the Future.*

FINLEY, M. I. 'Myth, Memory and History', *History and Theory* 4, 1964–5, pp. 281f.

FLEW, A. G. W. (ed) *Body, Mind and Death*, London 1964.

FORTENBAUGH, W. W.
(1) 'Aristotle's Rhetoric on Emotions', *AGP* 52, 1970 pp. 40f.
(2) 'Emotion and Moral Virtue', *Arethusa* 2, 1969 pp. 163f.

FOX, D. A. 'Zen and Ethics: Dogen's Synthesis', *PEW* 21, 1971, pp. 33f.

FOX, R. 'Comparative Family Patterns': *The Family and its Future* (ed. K. Elliott) London 1970, pp. 1f.

FRAISSE, *The Psychology of Time*, New York 1963.

FRASER, J. T. (ed.) *The Voices of Time*, London 1968:
J. Piaget, 'Time Perception in Children', pp. 202f.
K. C. Hamner, 'Experimental Evidence for the Biological Clock', pp. 281f.
O. Costa de Beauregard, 'Time in Relativity Theory', pp. 417f.
M. Capek, 'Time in Relativity Theory', pp. 434f.
S. Watanabe, 'Time and the Probabilistic View of the World', pp. 527f.

FREUD, S. 'Thoughts for the Times on War and Death': *Collected Works* 14 (tr. J. Strachey), London 1957.

FRITZ, K. von 'Aristotle's influence on the Practice and Theory of Historiography', *UCPP* 28, 1958.

FUNG, Yu-lan *History of Chinese Philosophy*, 2nd ed., Vol. 1, Princeton 1952, Vol. 2, London 1953. See also *HJAS* 7, 1942–3, pp. 1f., 84f.

GALE, R. M. (ed.) *The Philosophy of Time*, London 1968:
D. C. Williams 'The Myth of Passage', pp. 98f.
N. Rescher, 'Time and Necessity in Temporal Perspective', pp. 183f.

GILDIN, H. 'Aristotle and the Moral Square of Opposition', *Monist* 54, 1970, pp. 100f.

GILLIARD, F. D. 'Teleological Development in the *Athenaion Politeia*', *Historia* 20, 1971, pp. 430f.

GOLDSTEIN, K.
(1) *The Organism*, New York 1939.
(2) *Human Nature in the Light of Psychopathology*, Cambridge, Mass. 1940.

GOSSE, P. *Omphalos*, London 1857.

GOUDGE, T. *The Ascent of Life*, Toronto 1961.

GREENE, J. C. 'Biology and Social Theory in the Nineteenth Century': *Critical Problems in the History of Science*, (ed. M. Clagett) Madison 1959, pp. 419f.

GREGORY, R. L.
(1) *Eye and Brain*, London 1966.
(2) *The Intelligent Eye*, London 1970.

GRENE, M.
(1) 'Two Evolutionary Theories', *BJPS* 9, 1958–9, pp. 110f., 185f.
(2) *Approaches to a Philosophical Biology*, New York 1968.
(3) *A Portrait of Aristotle*, London 1963.
(4) 'The Logic of Biology': *The Logic of Personal Knowledge* (presented to M. Polanyi), London 1961, pp. 191f.
(5) (ed.) *Interpretations of Life and Mind*, London 1971:
   M. Grene, 'Reducibility: Another Side Issue?', pp. 14f.
   H. Dreyfus, 'The Critique of Artificial Reason', pp. 99f.
   W. T. Scott, 'Tacit Knowledge and the Concept of Mind', pp. 117f.

GRONINGEN, B. A. van *In the Grip of the Past*, Leiden 1953.

GUNNELL, J. G. *Political Philosophy and Time*, Middletown, Conn. 1968.

GUTHRIE, W. K. C.
(1) *In the Beginning*, London 1957.
(2) 'Aristotle as a Historian of Philosophy', *JHS* 77, 1957, pp. 35f.
(3) 'The Development of Aristotle's Theology', *CQ* 27, 1933, pp. 162f. 28, 1934, pp. 90f.

HAMLYN, D. W.
(1) 'Aristotle's Account of *Aisthesis* in the *De Anima*', *CQ* 9 N.S., 1959, pp. 6f.
(2) *De Anima II and III* Oxford 1968.
(3) '*Koine Aisthesis*', *Monist* 52, 1968, pp. 195f.

HANTZ, H. D. *The Biological Motivation in Aristotle*, New York 1939.

HARDIE, W. F. R. *Aristotle's Ethical Theory*, Oxford 1968.

HARRIS, E. E. *Foundations of Metaphysics in Modern Science*, London 1965.

HART, H. 'The Ascription of Responsibility and Rights', *PAS* 49, 1948–9, p. 171f.

HARTSHORNE, C. *Man's Vision of God*, New York 1941.

HEATH, T. *Aristarchus of Samos*, Oxford 1913.

HENDERSON, L. J. *The Fitness of the Environment*, New York 1913.

HERRIGEL, E. *The Method of Zen*, New York 1960.

HICKS, R. D. *De Anima*, Cambridge 1907.

HINTIKKA, K. J. J.
(1) 'The Once and Future Sea-fight', *PR* 73, 1964, pp. 461f.
(2) 'Necessity, Universality and Time', *Ajatus* 20, 1957, pp. 65f.

HOCKING, W. E. 'Chu Hsi's Theory of Knowledge', *HJAS* 1, 1936, pp. 109f.

HOLLIS, M. 'Monadologue', *Analysis* 30, 1969–70, pp. 145–7.

HOME, R. W. 'Electricity and the Nervous Fluid', *JHB* 3, 1970, pp. 235f.

HUANG PO *The Zen Teaching of Huang Po* (tr. J. Blofeld), New York 1958.

HULL, D. 'What Philosophy of Biology is not', *JHB* 2, 1969, pp. 241f. Also in *Synthèse* 20, 1969, pp. 157f.

HUMPHREYS, S. C.
(1) 'The Work of Louis Gernet', *History and Theory* 10, 1971, pp. 172f.
(2) 'Karl Polanyi', *History and Theory* 8, 1969, pp. 165f.

HU SHIH
(1) 'Religion and Philosophy in Chinese History': *Symposium on Chinese Culture* (ed. S. C. Zen), Institute of Pacific Relations, Shanghai 1931.
(2) *The Development of Logical Method in Ancient China*, Shanghai 1922.
(3) 'Ch'an Buddhism in China: its History and Method', *PEW* 3, 1953, pp. 3f.

JACKSON, H. 'Some Notes on Aristotle's *Metaphysics*', *JP* 29, 1904, pp. 139f.

JAEGER, W.
(1) 'Das Pneuma in Lykeion', *Hermes* 48, 1913, pp. 29f.
(2) 'Aristotle's use of Medicine as Model of Method in his Ethics', *JHS* 77, 1957, pp. 54f.
(3) *Aristotle*, 2nd ed., Oxford 1948.

JOACHIM, H. H.
(1) 'Aristotle's Conception of Chemical Combination', *JP* 29, 1904, pp. 72f.
(2) *De Generatione et Corruptione*, Oxford 1922.

JONES, J. W. *Law and Legal Theory of the Greeks*, Oxford 1956.

JUNG, C. G. 'The Soul and Death': *The Meaning of Death* (ed. H. Feifel), New York 1959, pp. 3f.

JUNG, HWA Yol 'Confucianism and Existentialism: Intersubjectivity as the Way of Man', *PPR* 30, 1969–70, pp. 186f.

KAHN, C. H. 'Sensation and Consciousness in Aristotle's Psychology', *AGP* 48, 1966, pp. 43f.

KATZ, D. and KAHN, R. L. 'Common Characteristics of Open Systems': *Systems Thinking* (ed. F. E. Emery), Harmondsworth 1969, pp. 86f.

KEANEY, J. J. 'The Structure of Aristotle's *Athenaion Politeia*', *HSCP* 67, 1963, pp. 115f.

KENNY. A. J. P. 'Happiness', *PAS* 66, 1965–6, pp. 93f.

KETTLEWELL, H. B. D. 'Darwin's Missing Evidence': *Readings in Physical Anthropology*, (ed. N. Korn and F. Thompson) New York 1967, pp. 52f.

KING, H. R. 'Aristotle without Materia Prima', *JHI* 17, 1956, pp. 370f.

KNAPP, R. H. and GARBUTT, J. T. 'Time Imagery and the Achievement Motive', *Journal of Personality* 26, 1958, pp. 426f.

KOSMAN, L. A. 'Aristotle's Definition of Motion', *Phronesis* 14, 1969, pp. 40f.

KRÄMER, H. J. 'Zur Geschichtlichen Stellung der Aristotelische Metaphysik', *Kantstudien* 58, 1967, pp. 318f.

LAMEERE, W. 'Au temps où F. Cumont s'interrogeait sur Aristote', *Ant. Cl.* 18, 1949, pp. 279f.

LANDSBERG, P. L. *The Experience of Death* (tr. C. Rowland), London 1953.

LEACH, E. *Genesis as Myth*, London 1969.

LLOYD, A. C.
(1) 'Genus, Species and Ordered Series in Aristotle', *Phronesis* 7, 1962, pp. 67f.
(2) 'Aristotle's Principle of Individuation', *M* 79, 1970, pp. 519f.

LLOYD, G. E. R.
(1) 'Right and Left in Greek Philosophy', *JHS* 82, 1962, pp. 56f.
(2) 'The role of Medical and Biological Analogies in Aristotelian Ethics', *Phronesis* 13, 1968, pp. 68f.
(3) 'The Development of Aristotle's Theory of Classification of Animals', *Phronesis* 6, 1961, pp. 59f.

LONES, T. E. *Aristotle's Researches in Natural Science*, London 1912.

LONGRIGG, J. 'Philosophy and Medicine: some Early Interactions', *HSCP* 67, 1963, pp. 147f.

LOUX, M. J. (ed.) *Universals and Particulars*, New York 1970:
M. J. Loux, 'Particulars and their Individuation', pp. 189f.
D. C. Long, 'Particulars and their Qualities', pp. 264f.
I. Copi, 'Essence and Accident', pp. 285f. (also in MORAVCSIK).

LYCOS, K. 'Aristotle and Plato on "Appearing"', *M* 73, 1964, pp. 496f.

MALCOLM, N. *Dreaming*, London 1964.

MANSION, S. (ed.) *Symposium Aristotelicum 2*, Louvain 1961:
G. E. L. Owen, 'Tithenai ta Phainomena', pp. 83f. (also in MORAVCSIK).
D. M. Balme, 'Aristotle's Use of Differentiae in Zoology', pp. 195f.

MARAIS, E. N. *The Soul of the White Ant* (tr. W. De Kok), London 1937.

MARCEL, G. *Being and Having*, London 1949.

MAYR, E. 'The New Systematics': *Taxonomic Biochemistry and Serology* (ed. C. A. Leone), New York 1964, pp. 13f.

MCMULLIN, E. (ed.) *The Concept of Matter in Greek and Mediaeval Philosophy*, Notre Dame 1963.

MEAD, M. (ed.) *Cooperation and Competition*, New York 1937.

MEDAWAR, P. T. de 'Chardin's *Phenomenon of Man*', *M* 70, 1961, pp. 99f.

MERLAN, P.
(1) *Studies in Epicurus and Aristotle*, Wiesbaden 1960.
(2) 'Aristotle's Unmoved Movers', *Traditio* 4, 1946, pp. 1f.
(3) *From Platonism to Neoplatonism*, 2nd ed., Hague 1960.

MERLEAU-PONTY, M. *The Phenomenology of Perception* (tr. C. Smith), London 1962.

MIURA, I. and SASAKI, R. F. *The Zen Koan*, New York 1965.

MOMIGLIANO, A. D. 'Time in Ancient Historiography', *History and Theory*, Beiheft 6, 1966, pp. 1f.

MORAUX, P. *Alexandre d'Aphrodise*, Liège 1942.

MORAVCSIK, J. M. E. (ed.) *Aristotle*, New York 1967:
G. E. M. Anscombe, 'Aristotle and the Sea-Battle', pp. 15f.
M. Thompson, 'On Aristotle's Square of Opposition', pp. 51f.
I. M. Copi, 'Essence and Accident', pp. 149f. (also in LOUX).
G. E. L. Owen, 'Tithenai ta phainomena', pp. 167f. (also in MANSION).
J. Owens, 'Matter and Predication in Aristotle', pp. 191f. (also in MCMULLIN).
M. J. Woods, 'Problems in *Metaphysics* Z. 13', pp. 215f.
J. L. Austin, '*Agathon* and *Eudaimonia* in the *Ethics* of Aristotle', pp. 261f.

MORROW, G. R., 'Qualitative Change in Aristotle's Physics': *Symposium Aristotelicum 4* (ed. I. Düring), Heidelberg 1969, pp. 154f.

MORTON, W. S. 'The Confucian Concept of Man', *PEW* 21, 1971, pp. 69f.

MOULYN, A. C. *Structure Function and Purpose*, Indianapolis, 1957.

MUMFORD, L. *The Transformation of Man*, New York 1956.

MUNDLE, C. W. K. 'The Space-Time world', *M* 76, 1967, pp. 264f.

MUNGELLO, D. E. 'Leibniz's Interpretation of Neo-Confucianism', *PEW* 21, 1971, pp. 3f.

NAGEL, E. *The Structure of Science*, London 1961.

NEEDHAM, J. *Science and Civilization in China*, Cambridge 1956–

NEIL, R. A. *Aristophanes' Knights*, Cambridge 1901.

NORMAN, R. 'Aristotle's Philosopher-God', *Phronesis* 14, 1969, pp. 63f.

OEHLER, K. 'Die Lehre vom Noetischen und Dianoetischen Denken bei Platon und Aristoteles', *Zetemata* 29, 1962.

OLMSTEAD, E. H. 'The Moral Sense Aspect of Aristotle's Ethical Theory', *AJP* 69, 1948, pp. 42f.

ORGAN, T. 'Randall's Interpretation of Aristotle's Unmoved Mover', *PQ* 12, 1962, pp. 297f.

OTTO, W. F. *The Homeric Gods* (tr. M. Hadas), London 1954.

OWENS, J.
(1) *The Doctrine of Being in Aristotle's Metaphysics*, Toronto 1951.
(2) 'The Aristotelian Argument for the Material Principle of Bodies': *Symposium Aristotelicum 4* (ed. I. During), Heidelberg 1969, pp. 000f.
(3) 'The Reality of the Aristotelian Separate Movers', *RM* 3, 1949–50, pp. 319f.

PANTIN, C. F. A. *Relations between the Sciences*, Cambridge 1968.

PARFIT, D. 'Personal Identity', *PR* 80, 1971, pp. 3f.

PEARS, D. F. 'Time, Truth and Inference', *PAS* 51, 1950–1, pp. 1f.

PECK, A. L. *Aristotle's Generation of Animals*, Cambridge, Mass. 1943.

PEIRCE, C. S. *Collected Works*, Boston 1931–60.

PIAGET, J. *The Psychology of Intelligence* (tr. M. Piercy and D. E. Berlyne), London 1950.

PIPPIDI, D. M. 'Aristote et Thucydide': *Mélanges à J. Marouzeau*, Paris 1948, pp. 483f.

PLATT A. 'On the Indian Dog', *CQ* 3, 1909, pp. 241f.

PLATT, J. R. 'The Two Faces of Perception': *Changing Perspectives on Man* (ed. B. Rothblatt), Chicago 1968, pp. 61f.

PLOCHMANN, G. K. 'Nature and the Living Thing in Aristotle's Biology', *JHI* 14, 1953, pp. 167f.

POLANYI, K.
(1) *The Great Transformation*, 2nd ed., London 1945.
(2) (ed.) *Trade and Market in the Early Empires*, Glencoe, Illinois 1957.

POLANYI, M. *The Tacit Dimension*, London 1967.

POPPER, K. R. *Objective Knowledge*, Oxford 1972.

PREUS, A. 'Science and Philosophy in Aristotle's *Generation of Animals*', *JHB* 3, 1970, pp. 1f.

PRIOR, A.
(1) *Papers on Time and Tense*, Oxford 1968.
(2) 'Gale's *Language of Time*', M 78, 1969, pp. 453f.
(3) *Formal Logic*, 2nd ed., Oxford 1962.
(4) *Past, Present and Future*, Oxford 1967.

RADHAKRISHNAN, S. and MOORE, C. A. (eds.) *A Sourcebook in Indian Philosophy*, Princeton 1957.

RAMSEY, I. T. (ed.) *Biology and Personality*, Oxford 1965:
A. R. Peacocke, 'The Molecular Organisation of Life', pp. 17f.
C. F. A. Pantin, 'Life and the Conditions of Existence', pp. 83f.

RANDALL, J. H.
(1) *Nature and Historical Experience*, New York 1958.
(2) *Aristotle*, New York 1960.

REES, A. and REES, B. *Celtic Heritage*, London 1961.

REICHE, H. A. T. *Empedocles' Mixture, Eudoxan Astronomy and Aristotle's Connate Pneuma*, Amsterdam 1960.

REICHELT, K. L. *Religion in Chinese Garment*, London 1951.

RIFKIN, L. H. 'Aristotle on Equality: a Criticism of A. J. Carlyle's Theory', *JHI* 14, 1953, pp. 276f.

ROBINSON, R. *Politics II and III*, Oxford 1962.

ROSEN, S. H. 'Thought and touch: a Note on Aristotle's *De Anima*', *Phronesis* 6, 1961, pp. 127f.

ROSS, W. D. (1) *Aristotle*, Oxford 1923.
(2) *Aristotle's Physics*, Oxford 1936.
(3) *Aristotle's Metaphysics*, Oxford 1924.

RUSSELL, B. *Our Knowledge of the External World*, Chicago 1914.

RUSSELL, E. S.
(1) *The Interpretation of Development and Heredity*, Oxford 1930.
(2) *The Directiveness of Organic Activities*, Cambridge 1945.

SAMBURSKY, S. *Physics of the Stoics*, London 1959.

SCHLAIFER, R. 'Greek Theories of Slavery from Homer to Aristotle', *HSCP* 47, 1936, pp. 165f.

SHERRINGTON, C. S. *Man on his nature*, 2nd ed., Cambridge 1951.

SIMPSON, G. G.
(1) *Major Features of Evolution*, New York 1953.
(2) *Horses*, New York 1951.

SINGER, C.
(1) 'Greek Biology and its Relation to the Rise of Modern Biology': *Studies in the History and Methods of Science* II. 1f., Oxford 1921.
(2) *Greek Biology and Greek Medicine*, Oxford 1922.

SINGER, K. 'Oikonomia: an Enquiry into the Beginnings of Economic Thought and Language', *Kyklos* 11, 1958, pp. 29f.

SKEMP, J. B. 'Plants in Plato's *Timaeus*', *CQ* 41, 1947, pp. 53f.

SMART, J. J. C. (ed.) *Problems of Space and Time*, London 1964.

SOLMSEN, F.
(1) 'Antecedents of Aristotle's Psychology and Scale of Beings', *AJP* 76, 1955, pp. 148f.
(2) 'The Vital Heat, the Inborn Pneuma and the Aether', *JHS* 77, 1957, pp. 119f.
(3) 'Greek Philosophy and the Discovery of the Nerves', *Museum Helveticum* 18, 1961, pp. 150ff., 169ff.

SORABJI, R. 'Aristotle on Demarcating the Five Senses', *PR* 80, 1971, pp. 55f.

SPIEGELBERG, H. *The Phenomenological Movement*, The Hague 1971.

STACK, G. J. 'Aristotle and Kierkegaard's Concept of Choice', *Modern Schoolman* 46, 1968–9, pp. 11f.

STE. CROIX, G. E. M. 'The Character of the Athenian Empire', *Historia* 3, 1954–5, pp. 1f.

STRAUS, E. *Phenomenological Psychiatry*, London 1966.

STRAWSON, P. F. (ed.) *Studies in the Philosophy of Thought and Action*, Oxford 1968:

G. E. L. Owen, 'The Platonism of Aristotle', pp. 147f.
P. T. Geach, 'Some Problems about Time', pp. 175f.

SUTTIE, I. *The Origins of Love and Hate*, London 1935.

SUZUKI, D. T.
(1) *Zen Buddhism*, New York 1956.
(2) *Essays in Zen Buddhism 3rd Series*, London 1953.
(3) (ed.) *Manual of Zen Buddhism*, New York 1960.

TAYLOR, G. and WOLFRAM, S. 'Self-regarding and Other-regarding Virtues', *PQ* 18, 1968, pp. 238f.

THOMPSON, D'ARCY W. *On Aristotle as a Biologist*, Oxford 1913.

THOMPSON, W. R. Introduction to DARWIN, Everyman edition, London 1956.

TOULMIN, S. E. 'Contemporary Scientific Mythology': *Metaphysical Beliefs* (ed. A. McIntyre), London 1957, pp. 3f.

TU, Wei-ming 'The Creative Tension between *Jen* and *Li*', *PEW* 18, 1968, pp. 29f.

TUCCI, G. *The Theory and Practice of the Mandala* (tr. A. H. Brodrick), London 1969.

UEXKUELL, J. von *Theoretical Biology* (tr. D. L. Mackinnon), New York 1926.

UNAMUNO Y JUGO, M. di *The Tragic Sense of Life* (tr. J. E. C. Flitch), London 1921.

URMSON, J. O. 'Aristotle's Doctrine of the Mean', *APQ* 10, 1973, pp. 223f.

VAN DEN BERG, J. H.
(1) *The Phenomenological Approach to Psychiatry*, Springfield, Illinois, 1955.
(2) *Things*, Pittsburgh 1970.

VERDENIUS, W. J.
(1) 'Traditional and Personal Elements in Aristotle's Religion', *Phronesis* 5, 1960, pp. 56f.
(2) 'Human Reason and God in the Eudemian Ethics': *Symposium Aristotelicum* 5, (ed. P. Moraux), 1971, pp. 285f.

VLASTOS, G. 'A note on the Unmoved Mover', *PQ* 13, 1963, pp. 246f.

VOEGELIN, E. *Order and History*, Baton Rouge, 1956.

WADDINGTON, C. H. (ed.) *Towards a Theoretical Biology* 1–4, Edinburgh 1968–72.

WALSH, J. J. and SHAPIRO, H. L. (ed.) *Aristotle's Ethics*, Belmont 1967: F. Siegler 'Reason, Happiness and Goodness', pp. 30f.

WARNOCK, G. M. *Berkeley*, Harmondsworth 1953.

WATTS, A. *The Way of Zen*, London 1957.

WEIL, R.
(1) 'Philosophie et histoire: a vision de l'histoire chez Aristote', *Entretiens Hardt*, 11, 1964, pp. 159f.
(2) *Aristote et l'histoire*, Paris 1960.

WEST, M. L. *Early Greek Philosophy and the Orient*, Oxford 1971.

WHORF, B. L. *Language, Thought and Reality*, Cambridge, Mass. 1956.

WIGGINS, D. *Identity and Spatio-Temporal Continuity*, Oxford 1967.

WILSON, E. B. *The Cell in Development and Heredity*, New York 1925.

WITTGENSTEIN, L. von
(1) *Notebooks 1914–10* (ed. G. H. von Wright and G. E. M. Anscombe), Oxford 1961.
(2) *Lectures on Aesthetics* (ed. C. Barrett), Oxford 1966.
(3) *Tractatus Logico- Philosophicus* (tr. D. F. Pears and B. F. McGuinness), London 1961.

WOLFSON, H. A. 'The Plurality of Unmovable Movers in Aristotle and Averroes', *HSCP* 63, 1958, pp. 233f.

WOODGER, J. H.
(1) 'Biology and Physics' *BJPS* 11, 1960–1, pp. 89f.

(2) *Axiomatic Method in Biology*, Cambridge 1937.

(3) *Biology and Language*, Cambridge 1952.

WOODS, J. H. 'Integration of Consciousness in Buddhism': *Indian Studies in Honour of C. R. Lanman*, Cambridge, Mass. 1929, pp. 137–9f.

WRIGHT, A. F. (ed.) *Studies in Chinese Thought*, Chicago 1953:
W. Theodore de Bary, 'A Reappraissal of Neo-Confucianism', pp. 81f.
D. S. Nivison, 'The Problem of "Knowledge" and "Action" in Chinese Thought since Wang Yang-ming', pp. 112f.

WU, J. C. H. *The Golden Age of Zen*, Taiwan 1967.

YAMPOLSKY, P. B. *The Platform Scripture of the Sixth Patriarch*, New York 1967.

ZAEHNER, R. C. *Zurvan: a Zoroastrian Dilemma*, Oxford 1955.

ZIMMER, H.

(1) *Myths and Symbols in Indian Art and Civilisation*, New York 1946.

(2) *Philosophies of India*, London 1952.

INDEX

'making sense' 16, 27, 33, 42, 53f., 142f.,
199f.
man: as measure 14, 28f., 38f., 46, 79,
97, 114f., 196, 206, see 215, 219
complex 21, 148
condemned to choose 20, 98
divine 13, 26, 159, 160, 182
not best 14, 130, 142, 190
political, rational and upright 24
slavish 26, 162
social and individualist 24, 98ff.
material causation (inadequate) 50, 58,
see 91, 134, 140, 166, 194, 199, 208
mathematics 124, 133, 160
matter 58f., 166, 168, 176, 178, 184,
185, 212f., 219
mean, the mean 4, 18, 21, 35, 44, 46,
69, 78ff., 83, 84ff., 98, 104f., 106, 133,
141, 145, 188, 208, 213, 214
meaning (*see also* interpretation) 1ff., 85,
118f., 142
means to end 108, 146f., 152f., 156f., 181
medicine 18, 33, 74, 84, 85, 198, 203
memory (*see also* past) 22f., 36, 53, 81,
99, 125, 167, 184, 188, 192
middle classes 105
mixis 86, 88, 208
money 92, 107, 139, 152, 199, 209f.
moral sense 82, 84f., 106, 134, 142, 194
motion (*see also* change) 50, 57, 127
147, 172f., 176, 203, 216
myth 39, 137, 168f., 197

naturalism 17f., 82f., 97, 99, 169, 189, 221
Nature 48f., 57, 58, 59, 86, 121, 134,
138f., 141, 164f., 189, 200, 220
necessity 60f., 64, 118ff., 130, 175ff.
non-being 64, 121, 123, 124, 136, 170f.,
175f., 181
nous (*see also* vision of world, God) *see*
65, 68, 69, see 78, 82, 94, 111, 144,
145, 146, 159, 161, 162, 163, 167f.,
174ff., 182, 188f., 199, 217f., 219, 220
now 115, 116, 129, 144, 221
numbers *see* counting

old age 36, 96, 164, 166, 182, 203, 207
organisms *see* entities, *and* wholes
ousia (*see also* entities) 48ff., 61, 67, 90,
175ff.

particulars (*see also* entities, individuals,
universals) 56, 131

parts (*see also* wholes) 22, 25, 32, 44,
50, 52, 63, 66, 72, 83, 102, 104, 139f.,
153, 154ff., 166, 176, 180, 217ff.
past 7, 23, 117ff., 122, 125f., 130ff., 135,
141, 175
perception 69ff., 85, 94, 123, 158, 172,
183, 191ff., 204, 221
philosophy, as disposition 11f., 114f.,
174, 191
phronimos (*see also* man as measure,
sound man) 97, 112, 133f., 143,
149, 194f., 216
Pindar 8, 11, 84, 162, 164, 171
Plato 5, 11, 12, 15, 18, 26, 29, 34, 60, 69,
72, 84, 87, 89, 90, 92, 103, 110, 135,
149, 153, 161, 167ff., 183, 195f.,
197, 203, 206ff., 214, 216, 219
pleasure 24, see 46, 71, 77, 79, 88, 90f.,
151f., 154, 157f., 162, 170f., 172
Plotinus 138, 174, 191, 197, 199f.
pneuma 199, 202ff.
poetry 131ff.
polarities 28, 59, 86, 203, 208, 215
polis (*see also* society) 24, 103, 210
politeia (*see also* society) 87, 102, 104f.,
112, 131, 141, 160
politics 110, 135, 145, 147
possibility (*see also* actualization) 64f.,
120f., 125f., 166f., 177f.
practical syllogism *see* 151, 152f., 189
praxis 21f., 89, 91f., 128, 186f., 192,
212, 214f., 217ff.
preference, logic of 108, 147, 150, 152f.,
see 219
presuppositions 1f., 33, 76, 133f., 174
primary sense 69f., 76, 80f., 84, see 186
Prime Mover (*see also* God, nature,
nous, and world) *see* 56, 174ff., 217ff.
principles 20, 67, 91, 128, 186f., 192,
212, 214f., 217ff.
proairesis 21ff., 98, 100, 118, 140, 146f.,
151

reasonable (*see also phronimos*) 2f., 6, 11,
97, 101, 111, 121, 141, 145, 146ff.,
148, 159f., 194
reasons 21, 22, 60, 97, 162
receptivity (*see also nous*) 27, 162, 177,
183, 189, 190, 192, 200f.
reflexive activity 111, 167, 178f.
right action (*see also eudaimonia, and
praxis*) 21f., 25f., 88f., see 91, 97,
145, 150f., 158f., 162